Moshe Arens

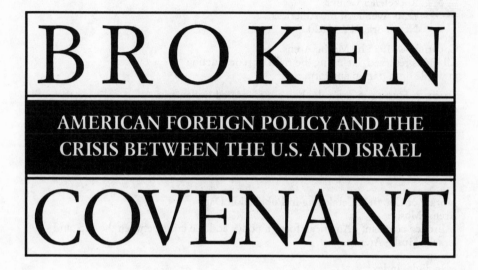

BROKEN

**AMERICAN FOREIGN POLICY AND THE
CRISIS BETWEEN THE U.S. AND ISRAEL**

COVENANT

Simon & Schuster
New York London Toronto Sydney Tokyo Singapore

This book is dedicated to the memory of my parents,
Theodore and Rose Arens

 SIMON & SCHUSTER
Rockefeller Center
1230 Avenue of the Americas
New York, NY 10020

SIMON & SCHUSTER and colophon are registered trademarks
of Simon & Schuster Inc.

Designed by Levavi & Levavi

Manufactured in the United States of America

10 9 8 7 6 5 4 3 2 1

Library of Congress Cataloging-in-Publication Data
Arens, Moshe.
   Broken covenant : American foreign policy and the crisis between the U.S. and
Israel / Moshe Arens.
      p. cm.
   Includes index.
   1. United States—Foreign relations—Israel. 2. Israel—Foreign relations—
United States. I. Title.
E183.8.I7A74 1995
327.7305694—dc20   94-45241
                                                                           CIP
ISBN 0-671-86964-7

A leatherbound signed first edition of this book has been published by Easton Press.

PHOTO CREDITS

3, 4 AP/Wide World Photos
5 Reuters/Bettmann
6 Mark Cardwell/Agence France-Presse
7 Nina Berman/Sipa Press
9 Official White House Photo
1, 2, 8, 10–16 *Yediot Aharonot*

Contents

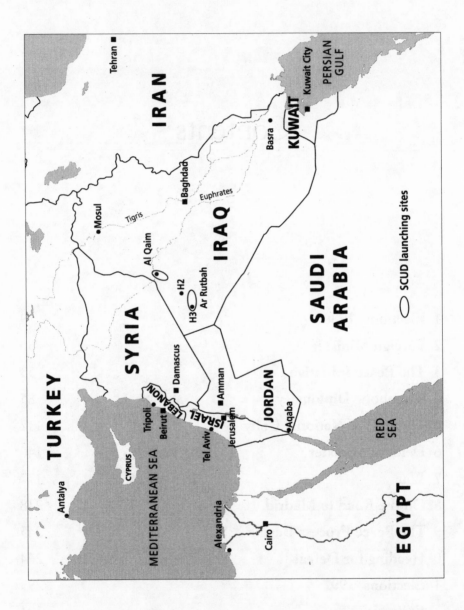

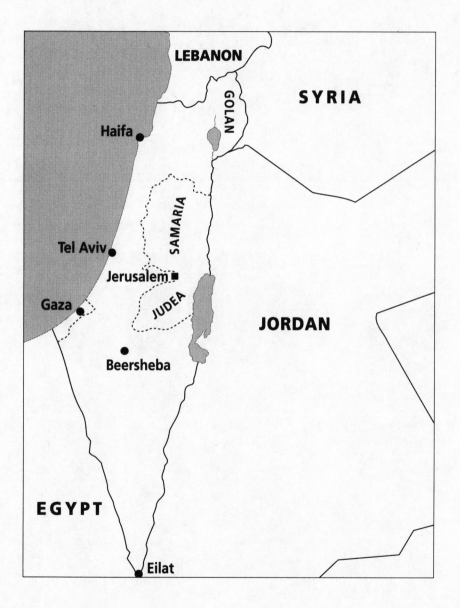

LEBANON

SYRIA

GOLAN

Haifa

SAMARIA

Tel Aviv

Jerusalem

JUDEA

JORDAN

Gaza

Beersheba

EGYPT

Eilat

Elections, 1988

During one week in November 1988, two elections were held. On November 1, Israelis—Jews and Arabs—went to the polls to vote for the 120 members of the Knesset, Israel's parliament; on November 8, the citizens of the United States chose their fortieth president. The newly elected leaders of Israel and the United States would have to work with each other during the next four years, crucial years for the Middle East, and for Israel-U.S. interests. During those four years, relations between Jerusalem and Washington would plummet to an unprecedented low, with the Bush administration interfering in the Israeli domestic political arena in an undisguised attempt to bring down the democratically elected government of Israel. Never before in its history had a government of the United States dealt in this manner with a sister democracy, bringing on a number of government crises in Israel, and eventually contributing to the downfall of the government led by Yitzhak Shamir in 1992.

But on the evening of November 1, 1988, this was still in the future. All of Israel was waiting to hear the results of the television exit polls. Israel's two major parties and historic rivals—the Likud and Labor—had squared off against each other for the twelfth time in Israel's forty-year history. Joined by over two dozen smaller parties, each hoped to obtain a sufficient number of seats in the Knesset to form and lead a coalition government. The Labor party, which had enjoyed almost total control of the Israeli political scene for the country's first twenty-nine years, had been voted out in the great upset of 1977, which had led to the formation of the first Likud government, under Menachem Begin. The elections of 1981 had been very close but left the Likud in power. While the 1984 elections had given Labor a slight edge on the Likud, neither party had been able to form a government without the other, and a bizarre practice of rotating the premiership between the leaders of these parties—then Yitzhak Shamir for the Likud and Shimon Peres for Labor—in midterm was adopted.

As chairman of the Likud's 1988 campaign committee, I had spent the long day of November 1 crisscrossing Israel, starting at Shlomi on the Lebanese border and continuing southward, visiting local Likud party headquarters to check their efforts to get out the vote and provide last-minute encouragement to our supporters and activists. I had planned my schedule so I would arrive at the Likud party headquarters in Tel Aviv only after the initial results had been broadcast, in order to be able to absorb the impact of the voters' verdict in solitude. After visiting the Negev towns of Yeruham, Dimona, Beersheba, and Netivot, I stopped at Sderot, a small immigrant township in the south, and then I drove north again to Tel Aviv.

The latest polls had indicated a Likud victory, but you never know until the votes are counted, although the Israel television exit polls had proven in recent years to be reasonably accurate. Those results would be of great importance to Israel's future but also of direct personal importance to me. I had been working night and day these past few months, directing and coordinating this electoral battle for the right to govern Israel. A great responsibility rested on my shoulders; weeks earlier I had decided that I would leave politics if we were to fail. I had told nobody of this decision and felt quite alone as the car sped north-ward and the minutes ticked away. Then the announcement came: a tie —Likud 40, Labor 40. Since I had not heard the results for the smaller parties, I could not assess whether Likud or Labor would be forming the next coalition. But before I reached Tel Aviv, the results were updated. The Likud had beaten Labor 40 to 39. The Likud, together with its potential coalition partners, would hold sixty-five seats in the Knesset; Labor and its potential partners would have only fifty-five. It was a clear mandate for the Likud; months of unbearably hard work and great tension had paid off.

It had never been my intention to take on the job of running the campaign. Although the job was considered by many to be a political plum, bringing one into direct contact with thousands of party members throughout the country, providing the authority to distribute funds to party branches, and positioning one for advancement, I had not aimed for this all-consuming responsibility. But my resignation from the government in September 1987 had created a situation that inevitably led me to the position of campaign chairman.

On August 30, 1987, after lengthy debates that stretched through a number of government meetings, the Israeli government decided by a one-vote majority to cancel the Lavi fighter project. I led the fight, supported by most of the Likud ministers, against the cancellation. But the eventual defection of one Likud minister and the pressure applied by Shimon Peres on the sole Labor minister who had dared to oppose the cancellation put an end to this great aircraft project. Yitzhak Rabin, who served as defense minister in the National Unity government, had inherited the Lavi project from me after the elections of 1984. The decision to design and manufacture, in Israel, the Israel Air Force's next-generation fighter aircraft had been taken back in 1980, in Begin's first government. Since then the program had made giant strides, despite the disbelief of the skeptics who felt, and said, that we had taken on much more than we could chew. How could Israel's fledgling aircraft industry compete with the great aerospace giants of the United States or the USSR? But the results spoke for themselves. Two prototypes were already being flight-tested, and were doing everything their designers had promised they would be able to do. The Lavi would be the most advanced fighter aircraft of its kind.

I was personally identified with the project, having been chief engineer of Israel Aircraft Industries, and having trained many of the engineers engaged in the program when they were my students at the Faculty of Aeronautical Engineering at Haifa's Technion—Israel Institute of Technology, where I had taught before moving to Israel Aircraft Industries in 1962. It was with them that I had succeeded in developing the first Israeli-manufactured fighter, the Kfir, after de Gaulle imposed an arms embargo on Israel and we feared we might not be able to acquire fighter aircraft abroad for our air force. As Israel's ambassador in Washington in 1982, I had succeeded in convincing the administra-

11

tion and Congress to permit us to use a quarter of a billion dollars annually of U.S. foreign military assistance for the Lavi project rather than for the purchase of equipment in the United States. And after returning from Washington to become defense minister in 1983, I obtained Washington's approval for the participation of U.S. industry and technology in the project.

The incredible decision to cancel the project came after a year-long campaign by a coalition—headed by U.S. Secretary of Defense Caspar Weinberger—of American aerospace companies not involved in the program, and of certain Israel Defense Forces generals who, doubting our ability to complete the program successfully, felt it was preferable for Israel to purchase major weapons systems abroad. Rabin had continued to promote the project during his first year in the Defense Ministry, but finally gave in to the pressures of these generals, demanding and receiving the support of the Labor ministers to cancel what was Israel's single most ambitious and important technological program.

I found it impossible to remain in the government; under Israeli law, all ministers bear responsibility for government decisions regardless of how they voted. I wanted to be free to criticize this decision, which I could do only if I resigned. This left me unburdened by ministerial duties, an obvious candidate to run the Likud's campaign in the 1988 elections. Several Likud ministers, seeing in me a rival in the Likud leadership race, were less than enthusiastic when Shamir nominated me for the job, but found no grounds for challenging the nomination.

It was clear from the start that the outcome would hinge on finding our way to the hearts and minds of the voters who floated between the Likud and Labor, and my job was to determine what was on the mind of the Israeli public. As it had been throughout its short history, Israel was beset by a host of problems. High on the list were the social problems that inevitably accompanied the "Ingathering of the Exiles," the immigration of millions of Jews from the four corners of the world, many of whom settled in the barren hills of the Galilee or the Negev Desert to farm soil that had been abandoned two thousand years ago or to build new "development towns." The integration into Israeli society, although advancing rapidly, was still far from complete; Israelis still spoke of the "second Israel," namely, the immigrants from the Arabic-speaking countries, most of whom still belonged to the poorer, less-educated half of Israeli society. Erasing the dividing line between the "second Israel" and the "first" required resources; but Israel's economy was severely strained. After years of runaway inflation that prevented any significant economic progress, prices had finally been stabilized during the tenure of the National Unity government, but Israel had yet to utilize its full economic potential. In terms of human resources, the talents and skills of our population, we probably ranked second to none; but in terms of GDP per capita—as good an index as any to measure the productivity and living standard of the population—we ranked far behind the industrial nations of the world. One major cause of this disparity between potential and performance was the result of a "Bolshevik" economic system imposed on the country over the years by the Labor party and the Histadrut—its all-powerful Labor Federation. Government intervention and control in all aspects of the economy as well as direct government and Histadrut ownership of more than 50 percent of Israel's business enterprises had throttled economic activity and discouraged private investment, thus severely limiting the Israelis' standard of living and the resources available to the government.

Above all, almost ten years after signing the peace treaty with Egypt, Israel still faced life-threatening security problems from its other Arab neighbors and from a multitude of Arab terrorist groups. The Middle East arms race was being fueled by Arab oil revenues, generous Soviet supplies, and the greed of Western weapons industries. Israel could not afford to be left behind in this race, even though it placed a gigantic burden on the economy.

But it was not these issues that concerned voters as the elections of November 1988 neared. What preoccupied Israelis was the Intifada, the mass violence by the Palestinian population of Judea, Samaria, and Gaza which had raged since December 1987.

Daily clashes between Palestinians and the army, daily rock throwing against cars on the roads, and mounting casualties, many of them women and children, raised the tenor and the intensity of the arguments. The problems of the Palestinian population in Judea, Samaria, and Gaza were literally hitting Israelis in the face day by day. Unlike previous acts of aggression by Arab armies or acts of terror by terrorist groups, Israel now found itself in constant and continuous confrontation with the Palestinian population in the territories. And whereas Israel had in the past enjoyed the sympathy of much of world public opinion in resisting acts of violence, daily television coverage showing seemingly unarmed Palestinian civilians facing Israeli soldiers in full battle dress, and daily casualty tolls were beginning to erode support for Israel even among its friends. In the international arena Israel was becoming increasingly isolated, while within the country itself the split was widening between those calling for more drastic measures to put down the Intifada and those who wanted a "political solution" based on Israeli concessions to the Palestinians.

I was deeply concerned that a continuation of this situation would lead to a weakening of the spirit in Israel, as well as pressure—possibly sanctions—against Israel by the international community. Although I saw the Intifada as part and parcel of the long-standing Arab-Israeli conflict, I realized that massive civilian disturbances might in the long run be more effective in weakening Israel than previous Arab attempts to destroy Israel on the battlefield. It seemed clear to me that the status quo could not be maintained indefinitely without causing lasting damage to Israel.

As the tense, hot summer of 1988 wore on, negative reports in the international media and attacks from political allies and foes alike mounted. Israel was becoming increasingly isolated. The Intifada seemed to be succeeding where Arab armies and PLO (Palestine Liberation Organization) terrorists had failed in the past. To paraphrase Clausewitz, it was war by other means. For most Israelis, the Intifada had to be seen in the wider context of the Jewish-Arab conflict raging ever since the modern-day return of the Jewish people to their homeland over a hundred years ago. But how to move to a resolution of the wider conflict with Israel's Arab neighbors? Could one be dealt with without simultaneously dealing with the other? These were the questions that the Israelis asked themselves as the casualty lists grew. Rabin began to call for a "political solution," meaning concessions to the Palestinians and to Israel's Arab neighbors, a call echoed by his Labor party colleagues and by parties to the left of Labor. The right called for immediate suppression of the Intifada, insisting that this had not been achieved solely because of Rabin's ineptitude. And somewhere in the middle were many of Israel's voters, the majority of whom apparently tended to support Labor's politics but wanted the Likud to handle Israel's negotiations with the Arabs.

It was not easy to forgo the temptation of trumpeting familiar messages, reaching out to those on the right flank and abandoning the middle ground. But many elections have been lost when this, the path of least resistance, was taken. In Israel in particular, where the main challenge is not so much coming in first as having coalition partners with whom a Knesset majority can be commanded, winning the middle ground—even at the cost of some of the traditional constituency at the fringes—is what counts. Under the Israeli system of elections—proportional representation in which the whole country is a single constituency—voters choose a party rather than an individual candidate, and so are influenced first and foremost by a party's message. Additionally, Israeli politics are pervaded by a very strong ideological climate, with much of the Israeli electorate deeply concerned about the state of the nation and profoundly committed to its future. Going for the middle ground means fuzzying your traditional message to some extent. But it was gains at the center, at the expense of our major rival, that would determine the winning coalition. So I had set out to picture the Likud as a center party, and Labor as considerably left of center.

In this task I was assisted by the man who had been chosen to head Labor's campaign, Ezer Weizman, who is a nephew of Israel's first president, Chaim Weizmann, a former air force commander and deputy chief of staff during the Six-Day War, and, as I write, Israel's president. He had been an extreme hawk, opposed to any Israeli concessions or compromise. In Begin's Likud-led government, he became minister of defense in 1977. At the 1978 Camp David summit called by President Jimmy Carter, Weizman joined Foreign Minister Moshe Dayan in pressuring Begin to accept Egyptian President Anwar Sadat's conditions: total Israeli withdrawal from the Sinai peninsula and removal of all Israeli settlements there. Within less than two years, Weizman resigned from Begin's government, ostensibly because of cuts in the defense budget. In fact, he had hoped to bring about Begin's fall, expecting to return as prime minister. He reentered politics in the elections of 1984, at the head of Yahad, a new party he founded. Although Yahad barely obtained three Knesset seats, when the votes were counted it became clear that this faction held the key to who would be able to form the next coalition. Weizman threw his support to Labor, blocking a Likud-led coalition, and bringing about the National Unity government with the "rotating" premiership. Like myself, he served as "minister without portfolio" in that government. By then, he and his faction had joined the Labor party, and he had positioned himself at the left end of its spectrum.

The Labor party of David Ben-Gurion and Golda Meir had been a hawkish, militant party; left in terms of its social and economic policies, but not too different from the Likud so far as defense and foreign policy were concerned. With Weizman as Labor's campaign chairman, Labor seemed to move further left on defense and foreign policy. I decided to target Labor supporters who were taken aback by this shift. In the early stages of the campaign, the Israeli media arranged a debate between the campaign chairmen of the two major parties. Held in a packed hall for the benefit of a few hundred local and foreign newspaper, radio, and television correspondents at Tel Aviv's Sokolow House (the home of the Israel Journalists Association), it had been uneventful until the question of possible coalitions came up. Since no single party had ever won an absolute majority in Israel's elections, it was clear that neither Likud nor Labor would obtain more than 60 out of the 120 Knesset seats in the election, so this question was crucial. In accordance with an unwritten law of Israeli politics, the Communist party—its support drawn almost entirely from Israel's Arab voters—and the small Arab parties who supported the PLO had not, in the past, been taken into the coalitions of either Labor- or Likud-led governments. Knowing that Weizman was angling for the Arab vote, I turned to him and asked pointblank if Labor was ready to form a coalition that would rest on the support of the Communist party and other Arab lists. He didn't hesitate for a moment. "Yes," he said. For the majority of Israelis, it was inconceivable that these parties would join the government and participate in decisions on Israel's defense policy, on the battle against terrorism, on negotiations with the Arabs. Nobody in the Labor party had ever hinted at such a possibility, and Weizman's reply caused a sensation. After that, we didn't let up, returning repeatedly to this issue in speeches, newspaper advertisements, and in our television campaign. Our slogan, "Labor Is Moving Left," was making an impression on many of the people who had voted Labor in the past or who were considering voting Labor now; we were scoring important points in the battle for the middle ground.

The second arm of my strategy was aimed at voters who were concerned by the lack of progress in resolving the Israeli-Arab conflict and the growing feeling of exasperation about the damage being inflicted on Israel by the continuing Intifada. Unlike voters already committed to the slogans of the far right and far left, the floating voters were confused about what needed to be done, felt that something had to be done very soon, and were looking for somebody to do it. They doubted that military measures alone could put paid to the Intifada, but also were unsure that the prescription of the left—concessions and offers of compromise—would lead to anything but a weakening of Israel. The problem to be solved in terms of the campaign was how best to craft the Likud's message so as to secure the floating vote, and I thought I knew how to do it.

I had become convinced that Israel had seriously erred in its policy on the Palestinian Arab population. Since the Six-Day War it had been a non-policy, based on the argument that the future of the Palestinians and the status of the lands on which they lived would be discussed with Jordan, when and if King Hussein decided to come to the peace table. After all, Judea and Samaria had been made part of Jordan after their occupation by the Jordanian Arab Legion in 1948; their population had been given Jordanian citizenship, which it still held. (Israel's former minister of defense and foreign minister, Moshe Dayan, used to say that he was "waiting for a telephone call from King Hussein.") So the "Jordanian option," promoted by the Labor party, remained the position of successive Israeli governments, while the Palestinians living in the territories were ignored. Whatever formal justification might have existed for this policy disappeared overnight when King Hussein—under the influence of the Intifada and fearing that it would spill over across the Jordan River into his kingdom—announced on July 31, 1988, that he was abdicating all responsibility for what he called the West Bank and for the population that resided there. It was really nothing more than an affirmation of the facts. Most of the Palestinian Arabs in Judea, Samaria, and Gaza had not viewed King Hussein as their spokesman for years now. The Intifada was a dramatic, and for the king a traumatic, expression of that reality.

In the summer of 1967, there had been close to 1 million Palestinian Arabs in the territories that Jordan and Egypt lost in the Six-Day War; about 600,000 in Judea and Samaria, and about another 400,000 in the Gaza Strip. Twenty years later, when the Intifada broke out, their number had grown by 50 percent: there were now close to 900,000 Palestinians in Judea and Samaria, and nearly 600,000 in the Gaza Strip. This population had lived with Israel—and in many ways in Israel—for twenty years. A new generation had grown up under circumstances totally different from those that existed under Jordanian or Egyptian rule. The Palestinians had come to know Israel and the Israelis. They came to work daily in Israel, listened to Israeli radio and watched Israeli television; many had learned Hebrew. They had begun to adopt, even if superficially, the norms of Israeli society, and they had learned that in democratic Israel, unlike Jordan or Egypt, the government was expected to address the grievances of the country's inhabitants. But their standard of living was far lower than that of the Israeli population. This was especially true in the Gaza Strip, where Palestinians lived in terrible squalor under increasingly overcrowded conditions. Although there had been a great improvement since the areas came under Israeli control, the contact with Israel, and their work in Israel doing the manual labor that Israelis didn't want to do, reminded them constantly that things could be different, and they demanded to be heard. It was when Israel turned a deaf ear that the Intifada erupted.

Since the Israeli prohibition against political activity left that population without any recognized leadership, the PLO in Tunis had jumped into the vacuum, claiming to speak for all Palestinians. If we did not want to deal with the PLO—and in my opinion it would constitute a grave mistake to do so—then it was up to us to find interlocutors among the Palestinians in the territories. And by democratic standards, these interlocutors would have to be elected. In the heat of the election campaign in an interview with an Israeli daily, I had broached the seemingly daring idea of holding elections amongst the Palestinian population for representatives with whom we would negotiate. It was a message that the Likud, if allowed to lead the nation, would search for new ways to break the impasse. Our election slogan—"Only the Likud Can Do It"—fitted right in. After all, was it not the Likud that had made peace with Egypt?

Prime Minister Yitzhak Shamir didn't like that interview. The following day he called me to say, "Your statement is making our people nervous." It had evidently caused some waves in the Likud and probably disturbed Shamir's peace of mind as well. Although the Likud stood committed to the Camp David agreements negotiated by Menachem Begin in 1977, which provided for an autonomy regime for the Palestinian residents of Judea, Samaria, and Gaza under an elected body, there was little regret in the party that no agreement for setting up this body had been reached. Autonomy had been a dead letter for over ten years now, a period utilized by successive Israeli governments to significantly enlarge the Jewish presence in Judea, Samaria, and East Jerusalem. While I firmly believed that Israel's security required Israeli control over Judea and Samaria, and that this control could be maintained only if there were to be a significant Jewish civilian presence there, I also believed that we had to begin talking to the Palestinians. The norms

18

and standards by which Israeli society lives required that of us. And now the Palestinians, despairing of their condition, and aware that Israel's democratic society could not long sustain the double standard, were calling attention to their plight through the Intifada.

In the end, my strategy had worked. We lost some votes on our right, and to the religious parties, but we made gains in the center: at least 50,000 votes had moved from Labor to Likud, more than enough to allow the Likud to lead the next coalition government.

On analyzing the election results, many were surprised to find that support for the Likud amongst the Druze—a small Arabic-speaking sect with its own distinct religion, which had thrown in its lot with Israel during Israel's War of Independence and whose sons served in the Israeli Army—had increased, and that for the first time the Likud had received a substantial number of votes from Israel's Arab citizens. At least one out of the forty Likud Knesset seats had been obtained by the thousands of votes cast by Arab and Druze voters. In recent elections the Likud had enjoyed the support of a minority of the Druze community, Labor garnering the lion's share; but Arab voters, having perceived us as an anti-Arab party, shied away from the Likud.

The increased support amongst the Druze should have come as no surprise to anyone. The Druze were grateful for the change of policy I initiated when I became defense minister in 1983. My predecessor in this post, Ariel Sharon, had allied Israel with the Lebanese Christian community, ignoring the Druze, Shiite, and Sunni Lebanese. I wanted to forge links with all of them. The Lebanese Druze resided not far from the Israeli border and had close links to the Israeli Druze community. When the Israeli Defense Forces (IDF) withdrew from the Shouf mountain range at the end of August 1983, fighting broke out between the Christian and Druze militias. I ordered the IDF to maintain a strictly neutral position. The Druze had feared that with Israeli help, the Christians would drive them out of their villages in the Shouf; but as it turned out the Christian militias, left to themselves, were defeated by the Druze. Ever since then I had been regarded by Israel's Druze as the savior of their Lebanese brethren.

Later, during my tenure as minister without portfolio in charge of minority affairs in the Peres-Shamir National Unity government, I initiated a policy intended to close the economic and social gap that had existed between the Israeli Druze community and the rest of Israel by increasing budgetary allocations to Druze villages. It was the first time in Israel's history that the government explicitly recognized its obligation to Druze citizens.

Throughout the country, thousands of Israel's Arab citizens, in towns and villages as well as many among the Bedouin of the Negev and the Galilee, voted Likud this election. As the minister in charge of minority affairs, I had tried to establish close contact with them. My message had been very simple: as Israeli citizens they owed Israel loyalty, and Israel in turn owed them full equality. I had encouraged the Bedouin to volunteer for service in the army, and I had lobbied for increased budgetary allocations to Arab villages. The election results proved that my efforts had made an impact; although the Likud's share of the Arab vote was still small, it was that vote which gave the Likud the edge over Labor—and I was particularly encouraged by it.

The votes counted, and the Knesset seats assigned to the parties that had passed the minimum threshold—at least 1 percent of the valid votes cast—the next stage in the process of forming the new government was about to begin: creating a coalition that could command at least 61 out of the 120 Knesset seats. Since the results mandated a Likud-led government, Israel's president, Chaim Herzog, charged Shamir with forming the new coalition, and Shamir now had a dilemma on his hands. Should he form yet another National Unity government with Labor, that would command a large Knesset majority, or a narrow coalition, based on the Likud, on the parties to its right, and on the religious parties? Commanding a large majority in the Knesset is an obvious advantage, relieving the coalition's members from scrupulously attending Knesset sessions just in case the opposition initiates a surprise vote. It also avoids the cliffhanger nonconfidence motions that are the fate of all narrow-based coalitions. But much more important, a broad-based coalition could enjoy wide support not only in the Knesset but in the nation, on condition of course that this government was united in pursuit of common policies. Could a new, broadly based Likud-Labor coalition attain such a sense of unity, or would it end up as a house divided? Would the Labor party even agree to join a Likud-led coalition knowing that, this time, because of the extent of their electoral defeat, there would be no rotation of the premiership and Labor would be relegated to second fiddle?

At first Shamir decided to play it safe, entering into negotiations with the religious parties and the parties to the right (Tehiyya, Tsomet, and

Moledet) to form a government (without Labor), which, although suffering from a small margin of votes in the Knesset, would presumably find it relatively easy to arrive at a consensus on foreign and defense policy issues. Also, it would have the advantage of giving the Likud more ministries. This, to many of the Likud politicians, was the overriding consideration. If, however, the new government were to seek some kind of an accommodation with the Palestinians in Judea, Samaria, and Gaza, and to repair Israel's position in the international arena by taking diplomatic initiatives, it would probably be next to impossible to do so with right-wing partners. On the other hand, if the Likud was going to maintain its past position, ignoring the Palestinians, a coalition with Labor was equally out of the question.

After more than fifty days of seemingly endless negotiations, and after agreements on parceling out the ministries and their political plums among the parties to a narrow-based coalition had been reached and signed, Shamir reversed course and entered into negotiations with Labor. I had done whatever I could to steer him in that direction, being convinced that the extremist politics advocated by the parties to the right of the Likud, which would inevitably influence policy in any government in which they were members, would be injurious to Israel's interests. The Labor party proved only too willing to join, their leadership not relishing the thought of returning to opposition, especially in light of the financial straits of some of the Labor Federation's economic institutions. The Histadrut's business enterprises were in desperate need of government handouts, which they were not likely to receive from a government without Labor participation.

The National Unity government helped to solve the problem of the allocation of portfolios between Shimon Peres and Yitzhak Rabin, the two perennial rivals for leadership of the Labor party for the past fourteen years. Their continuous presence on the Israeli political scene through victory and defeat was characteristic of Israel's brand of parliamentary democracy. Parties may be voted out of office, but the politicians survive through thick and thin, permanent fixtures on their party lists at election time. Thus the Israeli political arena is full of "elder statesmen" who have amassed great seniority and experience. In the process many of them become very opinionated, losing all vestige of modesty, a rare commodity among politicians in any case, and developing allergies to many of the politicians they have gotten to know and dislike as they battled each other over the years.

Peres had been active on the Israeli political scene ever since the state was established. As Ben-Gurion's aide-de-camp he became, successively, director general of the Defense Ministry and deputy minister of defense, leaving the government in 1965 to join Ben-Gurion in forming the breakaway Rafi party, which did not survive for long. Returning to the Labor fold after the Six-Day War, he held a number of ministerial posts, viewing himself as the natural candidate to become prime minister when Golda Meir resigned in the wake of the Yom Kippur War, only to be bitterly disappointed when the party elders chose Rabin instead. At Ben-Gurion's side, Peres had been responsible for the implementation of some of Ben-Gurion's more far-sighted projects, such as the Israel Aircraft Industries and the Dimona nuclear reactor. It was Peres who, in 1962, asked the president of the Technion that I be given leave from my teaching and research duties so I could take over supervision of the engineering activities at Israel Aircraft Industries at a time when German scientists who had worked for Hitler's war machine were busy developing missiles for Gamal Abdel Nasser in Egypt, and Israel was looking around frantically for an appropriate response.

Peres was a doer, supremely confident in his own judgment, having little respect for the opinion of others. His blustering overconfidence had led him at times to recklessness in word and on occasion even in deed. We had gotten to know each other during that period, and I believe he respected my professional capability, in any case enough to offer me the job of chief scientist of the Defense Ministry when he became defense minister in 1974 in Rabin's government. At the time I was already a member of the Knesset, and taking the job would have meant resigning, to which Menachem Begin, then leader of the Likud in opposition, strongly objected. Over the years I had had many occasions to disagree with Peres. From one of Israel's most prominent hawks he had in recent years become one of Israel's most outspoken doves. Now that we had become political rivals, I frequently became the object of his acerbic and sarcastic comments.

During the second half of the National Unity government, after Peres had reluctantly turned over the premiership to Shamir and assumed the office of foreign minister, a visit that I undertook to Washington at Shamir's behest threw Peres into a rage against me that has colored our relationship ever since. After having a taste of heading the Israeli government—a position he had been seeking for so many years and one for which he considered himself supremely qualified—he was restless at the Foreign Ministry. In April 1987, he traveled to London to meet with Jordan's King Hussein, and without receiving the prior consent of the government or even of Shamir, negotiated and signed an agreement with Hussein for the convocation of an international conference on peace in the Middle East. Knowing that this was anathema to Shamir and all of the Likud ministers, Peres then approached U.S. Secretary of State George Shultz, suggesting that he come to Israel and present the Peres-Hussein agreement as a U.S. initiative.

On his return from London, Peres reported to Shamir in general terms about the agreement he had negotiated but refused to give him the text of the agreement. At this point, Shamir, relying on the close relationship I had established with Shultz while I was ambassador in Washington and later defense minister, asked me to go to Washington and dissuade Shultz from coming on the mission that Peres had engineered behind Shamir's back. It took no more than a few minutes to explain to Shultz that the prime minister, as well as the Likud party, was opposed to holding an international conference on the Middle East, and that were he to come to Israel to present the Peres-Hussein agreement, he would find himself embroiled in an internal Israeli political debate. Shultz decided not to come, and Peres never forgave me.

Yitzhak Rabin has also been around Israeli politics forever, for a number of years as senior officer in the IDF and finally as the IDF's chief of staff, but all along identified with Labor. When he left the IDF after the Six-Day War, his identification with the Labor party became overt when he assumed the post of ambassador in Washington. Upon his return he was made minister of labor in the short-lived government Golda Meir headed after the Yom Kippur War, and became prime minister after her resignation. His three-year tenure as prime minister was generally considered less than successful. Peres stepped in to take over the leadership of the Labor party, but led it to defeat in the elections of 1977. Ever since, Rabin and Peres have been at each other's throats like two old prizefighters. Quick to anger, Rabin is wont to castigate his real or imagined enemies in outrageous terms. He has referred to Begin as an "archeological relic," to Peres as an "inveterate schemer," and to Peres's young aide Yossi Beilin as "Peres's poodle." His long years of service to Israel as chief of staff, ambassador, minister, and prime minister have led Rabin to the conclusion that he knows all he needs to know on whatever subject is under consideration, and that any outside advice is worse than useless.

In a National Unity government now, Shamir would have to solve a set of simultaneous equations having, as coefficients, the three major portfolios, Defense, Foreign Affairs, and Finance, and, as variables, the politicians out to grab the portfolios on which their hearts were set, any one of whom, if thwarted, might scuttle the coalition Shamir was trying to form. Not only did the demands by Peres and Rabin have to be satisfied, but in his own party, Ariel Sharon, who had been minister of trade and industry in the previous government, and David Levy, who had been minister of housing, also had their eyes on the major portfolios. I made no demands of Shamir, although it was clear to me that, considering the constraints under which Shamir was operating, I would end up with one of the key jobs. Sharon had been forced to leave the Defense Ministry in February 1983 by the government-appointed Kahan Commission of Inquiry, which charged him with "personal" responsibility for not having prevented the massacre in Lebanon's Sabra and Shatila Palestinian refugee camps by Christian Phalangist forces. Sharon had a burning desire to gain rehabilitation by returning to the Defense Ministry. David Levy had been a minister since 1977, first in charge of immigrant absorption and then as minister of construction and housing. He saw himself as heir to Begin and now aimed for the Foreign Ministry as a stepping-stone to becoming prime minister.

Shamir had confided to me on more than one occasion that in his wildest dreams he would not appoint Sharon as defense minister or Levy as foreign minister. One of his considerations in preferring a National Unity coalition over a right-wing coalition was probably the realization that in a right-wing coalition, he might be forced to give Sharon or Levy what they were seeking. In the National Unity government, at least two of the key jobs would have to go to Labor, and Sharon and Levy would have to settle for less. It was not surprising to see Sharon and some other disappointed officeseekers lead a rebellion against Shamir at the Likud Central Committee and demand a coalition without Labor. As for Rabin, even though he had not distinguished himself in dealing with the Intifada, it was clear that unless he were allowed to continue at the Defense Ministry, Labor's participation in the government would be put in question. Peres obviously wanted to stay at the Foreign Ministry, but Shamir and the Likud would not agree to this. To Shamir's aid came pressure from Peres's own party that

Peres take the Finance Ministry in the hope that from there he would be able to funnel financial assistance to the ailing Histadrut enterprises, on the verge of bankruptcy. Reluctantly, Peres accepted the call of his party. A more unwilling finance minister Israel had never seen. Now the road was clear for Shamir to appoint me foreign minister.

One week after the Israeli parliamentary elections, presidential elections were held in the United States. Although most Israeli politicians are sufficiently discreet not to voice their preferences when it comes to U.S. politics, many Israelis hoped that George Bush (rather than Michael Dukakis) would be elected. Ronald Reagan's two-term presidency had been an extended honeymoon in the U.S.-Israel relationship. Although it had not lacked occasional tensions, even crises between Washington and Jerusalem, a feeling of friendship, sympathy, and understanding for Israel had emanated from Reagan's White House throughout. I hoped George Bush would continue in the same vein, although I had some concerns on that score harking back to my memories of him as vice president during the twelve months I spent as Israel's ambassador in Washington during 1982–83.

Toward the end of 1981, Shamir, then Israel's foreign minister, asked me if I was prepared to be Israel's ambassador in Washington. I was sure that Begin was the source of the request, but thought that he was wary of approaching me directly since I had turned down his offer to become defense minister after Weizman's resignation from the government in May 1980. I had opposed the Camp David agreements committing Israel to total withdrawal from the Sinai, and removal of all Israeli settlements there, and I was not prepared to be the defense minister responsible for implementing that decision. Not wanting to risk another refusal, Begin charged Shamir with the task of approaching me on this matter. I agreed. I had been surprised and dismayed when Begin, on coming to power in 1977, had not replaced Simcha Dinitz, the ambassador in Washington who had been Golda Meir's appointee. It seemed to me that the great political upheaval of the 1977 elections called for an ambassador in Washington able to articulate the Likud's foreign and defense policy out of conviction and not merely as a professional obligation. But Begin either did not trust any of the Likud people with the job, or else preferred to act the role of national rather than partisan leader. He kept Dinitz in the job for another two years. After Dinitz's return, Begin surprised everybody by appointing another Labor stalwart, Eppie Evron, to the post. But after Reagan defeated Carter and reports came in from Washington that Evron, perceived as being too close to the Democrats, might have difficulty in establishing good relationships with the new administration, Begin finally decided to appoint someone from the Likud.

I arrived in Washington at a low point in the U.S.-Israeli relationship. It was shortly after an all-out battle between the U.S. administration and Israel's supporters in the Senate over the sale of AWACS aircraft to Saudi Arabia. The administration had won. Displeased with the June 1981 bombing of the Iraqi nuclear reactor by the Israeli Air Force, and by the Knesset law incorporating the Golan Heights into the sovereign borders of Israel, Washington had suspended the shipment of F-16 aircraft to Israel, and there was even talk of further sanctions in the air. But after an hour-long private meeting with Secretary of State Alexander Haig, we established a relationship of friendship and mutual confidence that has continued to this day. Meeting President Reagan was like meeting an old friend, and he had a strong feeling of friendship and admiration for Israel that was always apparent in word as well as in deed. George Shultz, upon assuming the office of secretary of state after Haig was forced out, made it a point to invite me as the first ambassador he would meet with at the Department of State. My wife and I were asked to his home for dinner, went to the theater with him and his wife, and the two of us had many long talks. Haig and Shultz recognized that Israel was not just another Middle Eastern country, that it was unique in the area and for that matter in the history of the world. The United States, the world's greatest democracy and leader of the democratic community of nations, could not take an "even-handed" position when it came to Israel. That was also the view held by many, if not all, members of the U.S. Senate and the House of Representatives, who were reinforced in their convictions by what they heard from Reagan's White House.

I was the first Israeli ambassador in Washington to speak forthrightly of Israel's rights in Judea, Samaria, and Gaza; of Israel as the sole democracy in the Middle East; and of the unprecedented price Israel had paid for the peace treaty with Egypt. I argued that the United States, having urged Israel to sign this treaty, which in addition to everything else involved an almost unbearable economic burden for Israel, owed Israel additional economic assistance in compensation. As for Israel's northern border, I explained that the continued presence of PLO forces with their Katyusha rockets in southern Lebanon, which

were holding Israeli towns and villages hostage and sending their inhabitants to the air-raid shelters at will, was an untenable situation. By the
time I left Washington twelve crisis-packed months later, I had succeeded in establishing a new modus operandi in the U.S.-Israeli relationship; we not only were allies but also had to behave as allies.
Whatever differences of opinion we had, we discussed among ourselves
but did not voice openly. We shared common goals, and even though
we frequently differed on the way to pursue those goals, we were united
by the understanding that we had to work in concert if we were going
to achieve them.

During the year I spent in Washington as Israel's ambassador, it
became apparent to me that a number of people in the White House
did not share Reagan's enthusiasm and friendship for Israel. The senior
White House personnel at the time were James Baker, White House
chief of staff; Michael Deaver, assistant to the president; Ed Meese,
counselor to the president, on the president's staff; and Bill Clark, the
president's national security adviser. These were the men who had
played the key role in the administration's successful attempt to overcome Israel's supporters in the Senate regarding Reagan's decision to
sell AWACS aircraft to Saudi Arabia. In this unprecedented open clash
between the administration and Israel's supporters, Israel's cause was
being championed by the pro-Israel lobby in Washington, the American
Israel Public Affairs Committee (AIPAC). After a long and grueling
fight, the administration won by a very narrow margin that was too
close for comfort. For the people around Reagan who were new to
Washington at the time, it was the first taste of the power that Israel's
supporters commanded, and they did not like it.

In seeking a direct approach to the president when I came to Washington, I expended considerable effort in attempts to meet with members of this group. In time it became clear that they did not want to
meet with me. The excuse usually advanced was that they did not meet
with ambassadors. It transpired, however, that they would meet with
Prince Bandar, the Saudi ambassador.

I finally succeeded in meeting Bill Clark with the help of Senator
Paul Laxalt, a Republican from Nevada, one of Reagan's close friends
and a staunch friend of Israel, who at my request invited the two of us
to his office on Capitol Hill, where Clark, upon being upbraided by
Laxalt for his attitude toward me, launched into a tirade about the
"improper activities" of the Israeli ambassador and his staff. He was

referring to the contacts that my staff and I were maintaining in the Congress, the kinds of contacts that brought about this very meeting. I could see that Clark felt that Israel wielded too much influence in Washington, even though it was a time-honored tradition for embassies to maintain contacts not only with the administration but also with the Congress in just the way that the U.S. Embassy in Israel maintained contacts with the Knesset as well as with Israel's government.

Eventually I also managed to arrange a meeting with Ed Meese in the home of one of Meese's friends, but I never got to meet Baker or Deaver. There was no difficulty in meeting George Bush. In our meetings he seemed very reserved about Israel's positions and policies. Although as vice president Bush did not make policy, he participated in meetings where policy was discussed and was a member of the National Security Council (NSC), which he chaired if the president was not present. After the Israel Air Force destroyed the Iraqi nuclear reactor in June 1981, Bush and Baker had called for punitive measures against Israel at a meeting of the National Security Council. And when the Israeli Army entered southern Lebanon on June 6, 1982, while Reagan, accompanied by Haig, was in Europe, the NSC was called into session and chaired by Bush. The reports I received indicated that Bush had been extremely critical of Israel at this meeting, and that only Reagan's return had prevented the adoption of sanctions against Israel. When Max Fisher, doyen of the American Jewish community, Larry Weinberg, chairman of AIPAC, Al Spiegel, who subsequently became the White House adviser on Jewish affairs, and other Jewish leaders met with the vice president to discuss the troubled state of the relationship at the time, Bush told them that "the trouble is the new Israeli ambassador."

As I thought back on these events after Bush's election as president in November 1988, I was concerned about the state of U.S.-Israel relations. My concerns grew as the first reports came in on the man Bush had appointed as his secretary of state, James Addison Baker III. In a *Time* magazine profile that appeared on February 13, 1989, Baker had discussed turkey hunting and Israel in the same breath. Michael Kramer, the *Time* correspondent, quoted him as saying about Israel: "The trick is getting them where you want them, on your terms. Then you control the situation, not them. You have the options. Pull the trigger or don't. It doesn't matter once you've got them where you want them. The important thing is knowing that it's in your hands, that you can do whatever you determine is in your interest to do." At his confirmation hearings in the Senate, Baker emphasized the Intifada: "blood is flowing . . . in the areas under Israeli military administration." I could sense we were heading for stormy weather.

Foreign Minister

On December 22, 1988, in the Knesset the government ministers were sworn in: Yitzhak Shamir as prime minister, and Peres as the new finance minister; Rabin remained defense minister. Levy had been named deputy prime minister and minister of housing; Sharon was going to Trade and Industry and I to the Foreign Ministry. On the way to Jerusalem from my home in Savyon, I listened to the radio broadcast of Shimon Peres's farewell speech to the staff of the Foreign Ministry on the lawn of the ministry compound. It was clear that moving to the Finance Ministry was a bitter pill for him to swallow. Peres was convinced that only he understood the changing world scene and the implications of that change for Israel and the Middle East, and that he had initiated the peace process with the agreement he had concluded with Hussein in London for convening an international conference on peace in the Middle East—an agreement he felt had been aborted by my trip to Washington. And now he had to turn the Foreign Ministry over to me.

Peres was all for Israeli concessions to the Arabs. Although using the seemingly reasonable slogan of "territorial compromise," suggesting that both Israel and the Arabs would have to abandon some of their territorial claims, it was obvious that neither Syria nor the Palestinians were prepared to consider anything less than Israel's return to the armistice lines established in 1949 after Israel had defeated the invading Arab armies during Israel's War of Independence. The Six-Day War in June 1967 brought Israel into possession of East Jerusalem, Judea, Samaria, the Gaza Strip, and the Sinai peninsula after its victory over the combined armies of Egypt, Syria, and Jordan. The 1979 Israeli-Egyptian peace treaty which gives back Sinai is seen by those Arab leaders who are prepared to discuss a settlement with Israel as a model for their minimum territorial claims. In other words, if there is going to be a territorial compromise, in their view, it must be a unilateral compromise by Israel. In gradual accommodation to the Arab position, Peres and his supporters had begun to substitute the slogan "land for peace" for "territorial compromise," a slogan that did not imply the need for any compromise on the part of the Arabs. Long-winded explanations that Israel did not wish to rule another people made it abundantly clear that they wanted to rid Israel of what in imitation of Arab terminology they were now referring to as the "West Bank," rather than Judea, Samaria, and Gaza. Little heed was shown for the fact that three quarters of a million Arabs reside within the sovereign borders of Israel and that these Arabs are also Palestinians in every sense of the term, and that if Israel were to preclude Israeli "rule" over "another people," even the pre-1967 borders were being called into question.

During the years after conclusion of the Israeli-Egyptian treaty, and after the Israeli-Lebanese agreement of May 1983 that was torpedoed by Hafez al-Assad, the Syrian dictator, the main argument between Likud and Labor focused on which party was more likely to advance peace with Israel's Arab neighbors. In the elections of 1984 and again in 1988, Labor under Peres's leadership insisted that it was the "peace party." Peres claimed that peace was to be attained through what he called the "Jordanian option"—namely, turning most of all of Judea, Samaria, and Gaza over to the Kingdom of Jordan, within the framework of a Jordanian-Palestinian state or confederation. He was prepared to overcome King Hussein's reticence to engage in direct negotiations with Israel by agreeing to negotiate within the framework of an international conference under the auspices of the five permanent members of the United Nations Security Council—the United States, the USSR, Britain, France, and China—and with the participation of the rest of the Arab countries, as demanded by Hussein. The Likud's position was that such a forum—which in addition to the United States would be composed of Arab countries that (with the exception of Egypt) considered themselves at war with Israel, the USSR, and China; that refused to maintain diplomatic relations with Israel and that pursued an openly hostile policy toward Israel, Britain, and France which advocated Israeli return to the 1967 lines under one guise or another—was a most unsuitable one for negotiations. Israel was likely to find itself in a minority of one as its most vital interests were being negotiated. The only explanation for Peres's agreement to negotiate within the framework of such an international conference seemed to be his readiness to agree to all or most of the demands the Arabs were expected to make.

The Likud's position had its antecedents in a program formulated by Vladimir Jabotinsky over sixty years ago. Jabotinsky founded the Revisionist movement in 1925, calling for a revision of the policies followed by the Zionist establishment under Chaim Weizmann, policies that he felt were overly compliant with British efforts to whittle away at the Mandate Britain had been granted by the League of Nations for the establishment of a Jewish National Home in Palestine. First Britain declared that the territory of Trans-Jordan (today's Kingdom of Jordan), which was 78 percent of the total area mandated to Britain, would not be subject to the provisions of the League of Nations Mandate (it was subsequently closed to Jewish settlement). Then followed further British plans for minimizing the area open to Jewish settlement. To this the British added increasingly severe restrictions on Jewish immigration and purchase of land in the area west of the Jordan River. The Revisionist movement opposed these measures and rejected British proposals to curtail the Jewish presence in Palestine.

Over the years the ideological gap between the two schools of Zionism widened, developing into mutual antipathy and at times even hatred. The Revisionists felt that the established Zionist leadership had been too passive during the years of the Holocaust and that not enough had been done to save the Jews of Europe. Then followed the confrontation between the two camps on how to resist British rule in Palestine after the war. The military arm of the Revisionists, the Irgun Zvai Leumi, under Menachem Begin's command launched a no-holds-barred battle against British forces stationed in Palestine, while the Labor-controlled Haganah was kept in check by its leadership throughout most of the remaining years of British occupation. After the British departure and the establishment of Israel, the Irgun called for the ejection of the invading Arab armies from all of western Palestine, while the government under Ben-Gurion's leadership halted the victorious Israel Army at what became the 1949 armistice lines, leaving Judea, Samaria, and East Jerusalem under Jordanian control, and the Gaza Strip under Egyptian rule.

Throughout the years of Israel's existence Herut, the political party formed by the Irgun under Begin's leadership, and later the Likud, a federation of right-wing parties led by Begin, would take a more hard-line position on foreign and defense policy issues than the Labor party. Although on coming to power Begin reversed this pattern briefly by agreeing to the Israeli evacuation of the Sinai (a concession that most of Labor supported but had never advocated and would most probably not have agreed to had they been in power), the traditional pattern of Likud-Labor positions was resumed shortly thereafter. Labor called for "territorial compromise" over the remaining areas that had come under Israeli control in the Six-Day War, and the Likud maintained that Israel had the right to claim Israeli sovereignty there. At Begin's initiative, the Knesset extended Israeli sovereignty over the Golan Heights in 1980.

The offices of the Israeli Foreign Ministry are housed in a collection of prefabricated huts on the western outskirts of Jerusalem. It is one of the few Israeli ministries that after more than forty years of statehood has still not been given permanent quarters. The foreign minister's office is a large book-lined room on the second floor of one of the prefabs. On December 23, as I walked into this office—occupied at various times by Moshe Sharett, Golda Meir, Abba Eban, Yigal Allon, Moshe Dayan, Yitzhak Shamir, and during the last two years by Shimon Peres—I found Peres, the ministry's senior staff, and a crowd of newspaper, radio, and television reporters come to witness the installation of Israel's new foreign minister. Peres could not resist the temptation to make yet another speech counseling me on the opportunities to bring peace to the area and my obligation to pursue these opportunities. Although I had come prepared for no more than the traditional handshake and fruit-juice toast, I now felt compelled to respond in kind.

"You, Shimon Peres, are now moving to one of the most important jobs in Israel, that of finance minister," I began. "Israel's future depends first and foremost on the state of its economy. If we do well economically we will do well in all other areas, and conversely if Israel is in bad shape economically we shall be in trouble in all other areas, including our foreign relations.

"Israel could be one of the richest countries in the world," I went on. "In an age where population quality is all-important, we have a highly talented and skilled population. And yet Israel is one of the poorer countries because of the Bolshevik economy that was imposed on Israel by the Labor party. Wherever you look there is government interference and control. More than half the business sector is either under government or Histadrut ownership. Many of our best entrepreneurs and professionals are leaving Israel because they cannot find an outlet for their talents. Go to the Finance Ministry," I urged, "forget your Socialist doctrines and the Labor party's vested economic interests and remove the shackles that suffocate our economy. That is the necessary condition for the solution of most of Israel's problems. Good luck!"

I had no illusions that Peres was going to take my advice seriously, but I certainly did not think that during the next eighteen months he was going to spend more time trying to bring down the government than attending to Israel's economy.

I was coming to the Foreign Ministry at a crucial period in Israel's history. I felt that an awesome responsibility had been placed on my shoulders. To me the establishment of the State of Israel was a modern-day miracle, a unique event in the history of mankind. No less miraculous was its survival in the hostile environment of the Middle East. Although tiny Israel is part of the geography of the Middle East, it is in many ways an island, surrounded by a sea of Arab and Muslim states that stretches from the Atlantic Ocean to the Persian Gulf, which the Arabs nowadays refer to as the Arab Gulf. It is a society founded on Western ideals and values, surrounded by societies with a long tradition of fanaticism, violence, brutality, and intolerance to minorities. A democracy, and all around it totalitarian rule. It is this Middle East reality that makes the one-hundred-year-old Jewish-Arab conflict so intractable. It took almost thirty years for Egypt to come to the peace table with Israel; thirty years and five wars! And there probably would have been no Egyptian readiness to discuss peace with Israel in 1977 were it not for the Yom Kippur War in 1973.

In this, the fifth Arab war of aggression against Israel, Israel was caught by surprise, off balance. Struck simultaneously by the Egyptians in the south and the Syrians in the north on the holiest day of the Jewish religious calendar, Israel had to meet the Arab onslaught with its meager regular army forces stationed in the Sinai and the Golan Heights. Outnumbered ten to one, they managed to slow the Arab advance, giving

Israel the time to mobilize its reserve forces and bring them to the front. Initially the Syrians overran most of the Golan Heights, and the Egyptians crossed the Suez Canal and captured the line of Israeli outposts east of the Canal. An entire Israeli high school class was decimated during the first forty-eight hours of fighting. But once the reserves had been brought up and a reasonable force ratio established, it was a different story. The Syrians, although reinforced by Iraqi armored divisions who had come to the assistance of their Arab "brothers," were hurled back. In the south the Israeli forces crossed the Suez Canal. After three weeks of intense fighting, with the IDF 101 kilometers from Cairo and less than 40 kilometers from Damascus, the Arabs were pleading for a cease-fire. A war the Arabs had started under seemingly optimal conditions had ended in their complete defeat. Surely this lesson was not lost on Egypt's President Anwar Sadat, the architect of the war. Israel's victory had evidently turned him into an "angel of peace."

The Yom Kippur War represents a major milestone in Israel's painfully slow progress toward an accommodation with its Arab neighbors. As long as Israel was perceived as small and weak, the Arab world trusted in its ability to destroy the state by force of arms. Successive Arab defeats were explained away and only led to preparations for the next round of fighting. Now it seemed that Israel's courage, stamina, and perseverance were beginning to make their mark in at least part of the Arab world. At the end of World War I, the Jewish community in Palestine numbered 50,000 and constituted about 10 percent of the population of western Palestine. When the State of Israel was declared in May 1948, there were 600,000 Jews in western Palestine, constituting about one third of the population. By 1977, their number was approaching 5 million and they formed two thirds of the population west of the Jordan River. The Israeli Army had demonstrated again and again that even when outmanned and outgunned, it would defeat the Arab armies. All-out Soviet support for the Arabs in materiel, instructors, and sometimes combatants was insufficient to tip the scales. Nevertheless, Arab leaders in Iraq, Syria, Libya, as well as many Palestinians, still speak in terms of historical determinism, predicting for Israel the fate of the Crusader State set up in the area nine hundred years earlier. Like it, they believe, Israel is bound to crumble before the combined Arab might sooner or later.

Israel's survival in this environment and the eventual achievement of true peace with its Arab neighbors is completely dependent upon Israel being strong—and upon being perceived as strong by the Arabs. The entire history of the State of Israel is a reminder of this painful truth. If an Israeli government were to disregard it, even momentarily, it would do so to Israel's peril. Mortal danger lurks around the corner. I do not believe, however, that the Middle East will remain forever frozen in this state. As we attempt to view it from a historical perspective, we see it changing at a slow, painfully slow, pace. Israel's ability again and again to throw back Arab aggression is having an impact. Observing Israeli democracy and the Israeli value system at close range also is having its effect. And world events, the collapse of totalitarian dictatorships, viewed on television sets throughout the Arab world as well, must surely in time weaken Arab dictatorial regimes and modify the totalitarian culture that supports them.

For Israel it is therefore a question of time and of timing. If we maintain our strength and ability to resist aggression, we will live to see the day when democracy will have come to the Arab world, and when peace will prevail between Israel and all its neighbors. But should we somewhere along the way tire or let down our guard, we may suddenly find the process that we have pursued at such great cost for so many years reversed.

It has been terribly difficult for Israel as a nation and for Israelis as individuals to live in a state of siege throughout the years. There is probably no parallel in history for such sacrifice, courage, and stamina by a small people facing seemingly overwhelming odds. It is not surprising that among some Israelis there are signs of weariness and fatigue. These frequently find expression in a desire to believe that things are really better than they are, an unwillingness to face reality, a readiness to be deluded about the dangers facing Israel. Those Israeli politicians of the left who draw an idealized picture of the Middle East and the Arab world, who minimize the dangers facing Israel and suggest that Arab hostility is the result of Israeli intransigence, strike a responsive chord with them. Add to them that significant minority, present in Jewish life throughout the ages, that is guilt-ridden about presumed Jewish moral transgressions and now "violations of Arab rights," and you get the left of the Israeli political spectrum. Peres's description of the "new world order" that has presumably altered Middle East realities, "technological revolutions" that he claims have made safe borders for Israel irrelevant, provide the foundations for the illusions they are propagating.

. . .

Before I had had a chance to settle down in the Foreign Ministry and collect my thoughts, I received an invitation to attend a conference of foreign ministers on the prevention of chemical warfare, to be held in Paris on January 9, 1989. The conference was being held at the initiative of President Reagan and convened under the auspices of French President François Mitterrand. I decided to attend. I knew that I would meet a number of foreign ministers who would raise the Palestinian problem and the Intifada, and who would urge me to talk to the PLO. I knew it would not be easy.

Everyone seemed to want an immediate solution at Israel's expense, and they were looking for Israel to provide it. I would have to explain that the Middle Eastern peace process by its very nature moves at a snail's pace. That ten years after signing a peace treaty with Egypt, we were still waiting for the next Arab country to come forward. That there were many spoilers out there: Iraq, Iran, Syria, Libya, and the various terrorist groups. That giving in to violence would only encourage further violence. That the Palestinians have access to Israel's public and leadership as well as to Israel's and world media; there is no need for throwing rocks and firebombs, endangering people's lives in order to attract attention to their grievances. That Jordan refused to speak for the Palestinians and that there were good reasons for us not to speak to the PLO, and that therefore we must find interlocutors amongst the Palestinian population in the territories. And that the new Israeli government needed time to get its act together and crystallize its policy.

On Friday, January 6, I landed at Charles de Gaulle Airport. I was met by our ambassador in Paris, Ovadia Sofer. During his tenure in Paris he had valiantly defended Israel's case on French television, which is no easy task and which had not endeared him to the Socialist president, François Mitterrand, or his government, which was pursuing an outright pro-Arab policy.

We drove directly to the Quai d'Orsay for a meeting with the French foreign minister, Roland Dumas. Dumas was an attorney who made his name by defending PLO terrorists in French courts, among them Abu Daud, who had participated in planning the massacre of Israeli athletes at the Munich Olympic Games in 1972. Now he was executing Mitterrand's pro-Arab policy, supportive of the PLO and very critical of Israel. I took the initiative and explained the complexity of the problems facing Israel: unlike the rest of the Middle East, Israel is a democracy. A new government has just been elected, we are in the process of formulating our policy. Sensing that Dumas was looking for an opening for France to take a position as mediator, I told him that no doubt France could make a contribution and I appreciated their willingness to help.

The following evening Mitterrand held a reception at the Elysée Palace for the foreign ministers who came to the conference. Unlike the usual routine at diplomatic receptions, they asked the ministers to stand along the walls of the ballroom in alphabetical order and await the arrival of Mitterrand. I should have been placed after the Iranian and the Iraqi foreign ministers. The Iraqi was nowhere to be seen; I guess Saddam Hussein thought it inappropriate to send a delegate to a conference dealing with the prevention of chemical warfare. The Iranian foreign minister, Ali Akbar Velyati, wearing a black suit and white shirt buttoned at the collar but no tie, did not want to stand next to me. He inserted himself over to the right, and I found myself next to the Indonesian foreign minister. Mitterrand shook hands in alphabetical order and exchanged courtesies. Afterward I found George Shultz in conversation with the Soviet foreign minister Eduard Shevardnadze. Shultz introduced me as Israel's new foreign minister and a good friend. "If you are such good friends, why do you disagree?" asked Shevardnadze sarcastically. He and I were going to meet during the conference and this was just the opening salvo.

The next morning I met Shultz for breakfast at his hotel, the Royal Monceau. He likes to swim in the morning and had picked the only hotel in Paris with a pool. We were old friends from the time I was ambassador in Washington and defense minister and he secretary of state. Now the vagaries of politics had brought us together again. I had been a foreign minister just a little over two weeks, and Shultz was at the very end of his tenure as secretary of state. George Bush would be sworn in as president in less than two weeks. Shultz would be going back to the Stanford campus at Palo Alto and James Baker would be taking over at the State Department. The mutual trust that had developed between us could have served as a very solid foundation for U.S.-Israeli cooperation in the years ahead had Shultz remained secretary of state.

The last few weeks of the Reagan administration had brought an unpleasant surprise for Israel: the State Department had decided to begin a dialogue with the PLO. After Yasser Arafat had been carefully coached to repeat a statement renouncing terrorism that had been set as a condition for such a dialogue by the United States, and after failing a number of times, he was finally able to get it more or less right, and the State Department announced that the conditions for the dialogue had been met. Although the matter was uppermost in my mind, I did not want to raise it at this, my last official meeting with Shultz. I knew that on the eve of a change of administration I stood no chance at all of bringing about a change in their new policy. Raising the subject now might only dampen the friendly tenor of our meeting.

Instead, I appealed to Shultz that in his last few days in office he put in writing the major points of agreement between the United States and Israel on the Middle East, such as opposition to a Palestinian state, support for a united Jerusalem, no return to the '67 lines, and continuation of U.S. assistance to Israel at the present level. Shultz promised to consider the matter. On January 19, his last day in office, he wrote a long letter to Senator Bob Kasten, a Wisconsin Republican, one of Israel's great friends in the Senate, dealing with U.S. policy in the Middle East. In addition to the points I had raised, he also wrote (in connection with the administration's dialogue with the PLO): "That dialogue represents no change in our commitment to Israel or to a comprehensive settlement. We continue to believe that performance counts and we will be watching PLO activities and statements carefully. . . . Terrorism must not only be renounced; it must be stopped. . . ." The Secretary had done his best.

Straight from breakfast with Shultz I was off for a meeting with Eduard Shevardnadze. For over twenty years the Soviet Union had not only refused to maintain diplomatic relations with Israel, but had consistently pursued a Middle East policy that was unreservedly supportive of any and all Arab positions and blatantly hostile to Israel. Even after Mikhail Gorbachev rose to power and the direction of Soviet policy to the West altered markedly, the change toward Israel was almost imperceptible. It seemed as if the Middle East section of the Soviet Foreign Ministry had remained a bastion of old-line Stalinists, and Gorbachev, beset by problems all around him, had neither the time nor the energy to call them into line. If the new Soviet leadership was trying to change its hard-line image while attempting to retain for itself the stature of the world's other superpower—which meant that it should assume a position parallel to the United States in any Middle East peacemaking—it would be only logical to work toward normalization of its relationship with Israel. The absence of normal relations clearly prevented the Soviets from assuming the role of anything resembling that of an honest broker; but the furthest they were ready to go at this point was a meeting between the foreign ministers of the two countries on neutral soil. And so Shevardnadze and I met in Paris.

From the outset it was clear that Shevardnadze wanted this to be a good meeting. He thanked me for the help Israel had extended to the victims of the recent earthquake in Armenia, and for the efficient way Israel had handled the Aeroflot passenger plane that had been hijacked to Israel. I could not wish for a better opening. I replied, "We, unfortunately, have had considerable experience with terrorists and have learned how to deal with them," but this drew no reaction. He had brought with him a very modest ration of "good news": the Israeli consular delegation would now be allowed to work out of the Israeli Embassy building, which had been abandoned when the Soviets severed relations in 1967. Also, our consulate would be allowed to widen its activities to include some political matters, thus receiving a measure of political recognition that had been denied us until now.

Shevardnadze evidently thought these were steps of some significance to be greeted by pleasant surprise on our part, whereas it was difficult for me to fathom just what lay behind these minuscule improvements in a relationship that was completely out of step with the changed image Gorbachev was trying to fashion for the Soviet Union. In response, I suggested that in the absence of diplomatic relations, we should institutionalize the exchange of views and information between Israel and the Soviet Union. Shevardnadze promised to consider the suggestion and reply within the next ten days. No reply was ever received.

In this case, as in other subsequent meetings between us, anything that was raised or even agreed upon spontaneously was not followed up by him or implemented. He evidently lacked the authority to override the opposition he must have faced back home. What was more, he spent considerable time trying to convince me that Israel should talk to the PLO, and then suggested that I might be invited to the Soviet Union to conduct such talks with the PLO there. He seemed disappointed and uncomprehending when I rejected this suggestion. After the meeting, we were met outside his office by a large crowd of reporters. Shevardnadze, all smiles for the cameras, shook hands with me for their benefit. He described our meeting in very positive terms and spoke of the improvement in Israeli-Soviet relations. Of course I agreed. After more than twenty years of the deep freeze, this meeting was a minor sensation.

The meetings with Dumas, Shultz, and Shevardnadze were only the prelude to meeting Ismat Abd el-Meguid, the Egyptian foreign minister, a meeting that I hoped would facilitate the new Israeli policy I was about to initiate. In a luxuriously appointed sitting room at the Egyptian Embassy, Abd el-Meguid awaited me—gracious, smiling, and very friendly. An elderly gentleman, suave, a diplomat's diplomat, he spoke perfect English. He knew all about me, obviously courtesy of Egyptian Intelligence. That I was a hawk, had opposed the Camp David agreements, and was the apparent heir to Shamir in the Likud; and since it looked like the Likud was going to stay in power for a long time, I was the man to woo. Who knows, just as Begin had at Camp David, I might at the appropriate moment throw overboard my hard-line positions and agree to concessions that would surprise everybody.

In the presence of the Israeli and Egyptian ambassadors, we had a lengthy discussion of the means to advance the peace process in the Middle East, and of course Abd el-Meguid wanted to talk about Taba —that tiny speck of land next door to Eilat on the Red Sea, about one square kilometer in area, the "last grain of sand" of the Sinai Desert which Egypt claimed that Israel still owed it under the Israeli-Egyptian peace treaty of 1979. Ariel Sharon, Israel's defense minister during the evacuation of Sinai, had ordered that Taba not be turned over to the Egyptians, claiming that the international boundary between Egypt and Mandatory Palestine ran west of Taba, even though the demarcation line between Egypt and Israel as recognized by both sides between the years 1948 and 1967 ran east of Taba. In the meantime Israeli investors had put up a five-star hotel in Taba, turning it into a major tourist attraction on the Red Sea, and now there was the added issue of the compensation that would have to be paid to the hotel owners if Israel were to withdraw from the area.

Although I had opposed the terms of the Israeli-Egyptian peace treaty, once the treaty was signed I considered it foolhardy for Israel to retain this microscopic piece of land by devious and ill-conceived arguments, an attempt that was bound to strain relations with Egypt that had been established at so heavy a price. Now I had the job of disentangling Israel from this mess.

After much wrangling the Taba dispute had been submitted to inter-national arbitration, which after lengthy deliberations supported Egypt's claim to the area. Faced by the new Likud-led government, Egypt was now concerned that Israel would not carry out the arbitration tribunal's decision. "Once the Taba matter is settled, the sky's the limit in the state of Egyptian-Israeli relations," Abd el-Meguid promised me, when I complained that the Egyptian government was doing everything possible to contain relations between our two countries at the lowest possible level. I made it clear that there was no question in my mind that we had to comply with the decision of the arbitrators, even though I knew that it was going to be a hard pill for Shamir and Sharon to swallow. Encouraged, Abd el-Meguid suggested that we meet again for breakfast in my hotel. I saw this as no small gesture on his part considering his seniority as foreign minister in attendance at the Paris conference. He was evidently placing high hopes on me.

Two days later he came to my suite at the Paris Hilton, ostensibly for breakfast, but actually to keep working on my ego. For an hour and a half, over coffee that was turning cold, he maintained that I was the man of leadership and courage the Middle East had been waiting for; I could bring peace to the area if I would take matters into my hands. I told him that it was my intention to do all I could to advance the peace process, but that I needed his help, and that it was important that the Israeli public see that Israeli-Egyptian relations were improving from their present frozen state. As for Taba, to which he kept returning in the conversation, I told him not to worry; once a few technical details were cleared up, Israel would implement the decision of the arbitrators. I invited him to Israel, stressing the importance of such a visit, and he promised to come sometime during the next few weeks. We parted the best of friends, but each of us with his own thoughts on how best to advance the peace process.

When my turn came to address the Chemical Weapons Conference on Disarmament, I reminded the audience of foreign ministers and their aides of the Jewish experience with German chemical warfare during World War II, and the more recent use of chemical warfare by Arab armies in our immediate neighborhood:

> As Foreign Minister of Israel I come to the conference with a greater sense of concern and urgency on the issues being discussed here than any other delegate. Not only because millions of Jews were killed in gas chambers during World War II, but also because the two countries that have used chemical warfare in recent years—Libya in the fighting in Chad, and Iraq on a massive scale against the Iranians as well as against their own Kurdish villages—are located in the region in which we live and insist that they are in a state of war with Israel.

My words obviously made little impact. In the years that followed, the Iraqis continued developing their chemical warfare capability, not only without hindrance from the world but with the active assistance of industries and specialists from some of the countries represented at the conference, whose representatives spoke so eloquently about the need to ban chemical weapons.

That evening an Iranian journalist wanted to interview me. After a meticulous check by my bodyguards he entered my hotel room, sat down opposite me with his tape recorder, and proceeded with a series of questions on Middle Eastern politics. Then there was one last question he wanted to ask me. "Since you Israelis destroyed the Iraqi nuclear reactor, why don't you go on to destroy their chemical warfare facilities?" "This is a job we leave to you," I answered.

Before leaving Paris, I met with Mitterrand. He had invited me, emphasizing that of all the foreign ministers attending the conference he was seeing only two—George Shultz and myself.

At the Elysée Palace, Mitterrand's *chef de cabinet* Jacques Attali ushered me into Mitterrand's presence. Mitterrand, who speaks no English, had an interpreter at his side. After I explained to him the problems that Israel was facing, he launched into an exposé of the Arab-Israeli conflict, concluding with the two principles that he said guided French policy: the Palestinians, whose legitimate representative is the PLO, are entitled to self-determination; and Israel has a right to secure borders. I was tempted to explain that there might be an inherent contradiction between the two principles, but thought better of it. At this point my aim was to temper the criticism that Israel had been subjected to these past few months and win a breathing spell for the new government. I told him that I thought it would be useful if he were to meet Shamir. He agreed immediately and gave instructions to invite Shamir to Paris for a meeting.

On the whole, my sojourn in Paris had been successful. I had explained the security problems facing Israel, the dangers we faced daily from terrorism, and most important, that the new Israeli government was preparing an initiative aimed at promoting negotiations that would advance the cause of peace. We had bought ourselves time, but not unlimited time. Now it would depend on us whether we would be able to utilize that time. That I knew was going to depend on Shamir's cooperation.

The following day, on my return to Israel, I had to get the inner cabinet's approval to implement the arbitration decision on Taba. Sharon strongly opposed my motion to accept the decision. He argued that Egypt had not fully complied with the terms of the peace treaty and therefore we were not obligated to accept the decision; he seemed to disregard that in agreeing to the arbitration, we had committed ourselves to accept their verdict. Most of the cabinet realized that we had no other choice, and the majority approved my motion.

My vote against the Camp David agreements had created the impression that I was one of the outstanding hard-liners in Israel, opposed to any concessions or compromise. Now I found myself arguing against Sharon and his supporters that on the Taba issued we had to face reality and could not renege on a commitment we had made. Some among the Israeli public may have come in for an additional surprise when I appeared on Israeli TV's weekly interview program and stressed the need for a peace initiative that would address the aspirations of the Palestinians in Judea, Samaria, and Gaza. Actually, these views attracted attention only after I stated them before a closed session of the Knesset's Foreign Affairs and Defense Committee. As was so often the case, what went on at the meeting did not remain secret and my words were leaked to the media.

By the beginning of February 1989, after six weeks in the job as foreign minister, I had, after long consultations with my trusted aide Salai Meridor, formed in my own mind the outline of a peace initiative. It consisted of five points: (1) a call for a meeting of the signatories to the Camp David Accords (Israel, Egypt, and the United States as witness) to review its status; (2) a call for meetings between Israel and every Arab country claiming to be at war with us; (3) a conference of the countries supplying arms to the Middle East together with the recipient countries to discuss ways of moderating the ongoing arms race; (4) a conference of the major industrialized nations to deal with means of alleviating the conditions of the Palestinian refugees; and (5) elections amongst the Palestinians in Judea, Samaria, and Gaza for representatives who would then negotiate with Israel their status and the status of the areas in which they resided.

I had taken up the matter of a peace initiative with Shamir a number of times, urging him to adopt the proposal immediately. Sometimes I found him reticent, at other times taciturn, and on occasion favorably inclined, although it was clear to me that he was far from enthusiastic. He would have preferred taking no initiative, but was beginning to accept my view that that was not a viable option. So now he was playing for time. Whereas I felt that possibly his upcoming visit to Washington, scheduled for the beginning of April, might be too late for announcing our peace initiative, Shamir was not at all sure that he would want to present it at that time, saying that he preferred to do so only after his return. I shared my impatience with the cabinet secretary, Eli Rubinstein, a close and trusted confidant of Shamir, who remarked with his inimitable Yiddish humor: "Nu, vos brent?" (So, where's the fire?)

In Paris I had made our case to Mitterrand, Dumas, and French Premier Michel Rocard; to Shevardnadze; to the Chinese foreign minister, Quian Quichen; the German foreign minister, Hans Dietrich Genscher; the Dutch foreign minister, Hans Van Den Broek; and the Canadian foreign minister, Joe Clark. Missing from the list was the British foreign secretary, who did not attend the conference. Since I felt it important to enlist British sympathy for our position, I arranged to meet Mrs. Thatcher in London in the middle of February.

At Ben-Gurion Airport before boarding the plane to London, I was approached by a man in the uniform of a TWA employee. I could see that his face and hands had been badly burned and were now disfigured. It was Abie Moses, a resident of the settlement of Alfei Menashe, located only a few kilometers across the "green line," as Israelis term Israel's pre–Six-Day War borders. A few months ago his car had been hit by a firebomb thrown by a Palestinian terrorist, killing his wife and five-year-old daughter. He and two more of his children were badly burned. A week before, another resident of Alfei Menashe, Albert Gerasi, was burned to death at almost the same location. "How long will this go on? Why can't you put a stop to this?" he asked me. What could I say except to assure him that every effort was being made.

The tragedy of the Moses family did not leave my thoughts all the way to London. At 10 Downing Street, after Margaret Thatcher and I had exchanged initial courtesies, I told her the story, and I could see that she was deeply touched. I must admit I was enchanted by her. The fact that she expressed her friendship for the Jewish people and Israel of course helped, but I found her a most impressive personality. Without the subterfuges of diplomatic language she told me of her admiration for what had been accomplished in Israel, of her abhorrence of terror and terrorist organizations. It was clear that her friendship for Israel was intimately bound to her great respect for Judaism. She had a very clear view of the difficulties and dangers facing Israel, and warned me that in the pursuit of peace we must be careful not to make any mistakes. There was little I could add.

Knowing of her good relations with King Hussein of Jordan, I did suggest that Mrs. Thatcher might be helpful in bringing him into the peace process. Although she was prepared to try, she was not optimistic, being well aware of the delicate relations that existed between Hussein and the Palestinian population in Jordan and the PLO's continuous attempts to intimidate him. She had been playing a signal role in pressuring the Soviet government to permit free emigration for Soviet Jewry, and I thanked her for her efforts. "The Russians are still anti-Semites," she remarked. As we parted, she extended a warm invitation to Shamir to visit her, even if it was only on his way to America or on his way back; if it were more convenient for him she would host him at her country home, Chequers. Greeted by reporters as I left, I said, "Israel has a friend at Ten Downing Street."

While in London I received notification from our consular delegation in Moscow that Arye Levin had been called to the Soviet Foreign Ministry and informed that Shevardnadze would be visiting the Middle East the following week, but that he would not be coming to Israel and would I meet him in Cairo. I replied that my agreement to such a meeting in Cairo was subject to the approval of the Egyptian government. I had no sooner returned to Israel than the Egyptian ambassador, Mohammed Bassiouny, called to tell me that I was invited to Egypt to meet with Shevardnadze, and that on that occasion Abd el-Meguid would also like to meet with me. I asked him to inquire if I could meet President Mubarak during my stay in Cairo. He called back within an hour to tell me that a meeting with Mubarak had also been scheduled, for Monday, February 20.

I could not help but think back to my previous visit to Egypt in the spring of 1981. I was then chairman of the Knesset's Foreign Affairs and Defense Committee, and came at the head of a Knesset delegation that was reciprocating the visit of an Egyptian parliamentary delegation to Israel a few months earlier. We had visited the sites in Cairo, Alexandria, and Luxor. I was appalled by the poverty, the dirt, the confusion; and like all recent Israeli visitors found it difficult to imagine that this country, seemingly so disorganized, had been able to mount the crossing of the Suez Canal in the Yom Kippur War. I evidently did not endear myself to our Egyptian hosts when during our discussions I suggested that we consider an exchange of territory so as to avoid uprooting our settlers in the eastern Sinai along Israel's border, and that the continued presence of the Israeli Navy in the Red Sea was now of common Egyptian-Israeli strategic interest. When I emphasized the tremendous price Israel had paid for the Camp David treaty by turning the entire Sinai peninsula over to Egypt, the Egyptian parliamentarians protested vehemently, saying that the Sinai was not Israel's in the first place and that we had returned to Egypt what in any case was rightfully its own. My reply that our rights to Sinai were based on the thousands of our soldiers who had fallen there as a result of repeated Egyptian aggression did not seem to make much of an impression.

Now, at Cairo Airport, we were met by Ismat Abd el-Meguid and his wife, carrying a bouquet of flowers for my wife. From the airport we drove to the Sheraton Hotel in Heliopolis. I had decided that the best way to carry out a free and open discussion with Mubarak would be for us to meet alone. I asked Abd el-Meguid to inquire if Mubarak would agree to that, and when I arrived for the meeting he informed me that Mubarak was agreeable. As I walked into his office, Hosni Mubarak came toward me, shook my hand, asked me to sit down, and within minutes we had dropped all formalities and were deep in discussion. I liked him from the start. He seemed like many senior business executives that I had met. No nonsense, strictly business; friendly and direct. He was elegantly dressed in a business suit and completely at ease.

I began by thanking him for permitting me to meet with Shevardnadze in Cairo; for the compensation that an Egyptian court had recently awarded to the families of the Israeli victims of the Ras Burka incident, where an Egyptian soldier had fired at a group of Israelis touring in the Sinai, leaving a number dead; and for the patience he had displayed during the interminable wrangling over Taba. Moving on to the peace process, I told him that the Egyptian-Israeli relationship should serve as a foundation for the negotiations. Mubarak's response was that Israel should agree to an international conference. "Let's have direct negotiations. That's how peace between us was achieved; what can the Soviets and Chinese contribute?" I said. He explained that the international conference could serve as an umbrella for direct negotiations and that it would help overcome psychological barriers. I suggested that maybe he could bring Jordan into contact with us by setting up a meeting with King Hussein. He was aware that Israeli leaders had met secretly with Hussein in the past and said that he would try to arrange a meeting between Hussein and myself.

I explained that Israel continued to be concerned about the possibility of another attack from an Arab coalition on its east led by Iraq and Syria, and that therefore Israel needed defensible borders and a minimum of strategic depth. He replied with complete assurance: "You have nothing to worry about over Iraq. They have learned what war is all about and they are not going to war again." To deepen the feeling of mutual confidence that seemed to be developing, I decided to share with Mubarak a message I had sent to the Iraqi dictator during my tenure as defense minister about five years earlier, when the Iraqis were taking a beating from the Iranians. Donald Rumsfeld, former U.S. secretary of defense, was shuttling between Middle Eastern capitals as President Reagan's special emissary, and after visiting me in Tel Aviv was going to proceed to Baghdad. Here was an opportunity to establish contact with Saddam Hussein. "Tell him that we in Israel have considerable experience in fighting wars and we might be ready to advise or even assist him, if he were prepared to establish contact between Israel and Iraq," I had said. When Rumsfeld returned, he reported that he could not elicit any kind of response from Saddam Hussein. As badly as things were going for him at the front, he was evidently not prepared for any contact with us. Only years later did I learn of the valuable assistance the Iraqis received clandestinely from the United States at the time, assistance that helped Iraq to stem the Iranian advance. Now I suggested to Mubarak that maybe he could help establish contact between Israel and Iraq; but he seemed noncommittal.

"The Syrians," Mubarak explained, "will not go to war against you. I know Assad well; he keeps talking of going to war against you once he has achieved strategic parity. He will never achieve it, it's all just talk. Nothing for you to worry about." This was the closest I had come to Israel's adversaries, Saddam Hussein and Hafez al-Assad: hearing Mubarak, who knew them well, speak about them so frankly. He was sanguine, and if we were to follow his advice we had nothing to worry about. Within less than two years it would turn out that he had been mistaken.

As for the Palestinians, Mubarak urged us to speak to the PLO. "I have had many talks with Arafat," he said, "and I've gotten him to moderate his positions. Now is the time to talk to him."

"There are more Palestinians in Jordan than there are in Judea and Samaria and Gaza," I responded. "Those living in the West Bank are Jordanian citizens. It is essential to draw Jordan into negotiations. In addition, we are looking for interlocutors among the local population who might best be elected democratically. The PLO is a terrorist organization that continues to practice terrorism despite Arafat's recent pronouncements."

To this Mubarak replied that Arafat did not have control of all the PLO operations, and that regardless of what Arafat said, terrorist operations would continue without his approval. He did not seem enthusiastic about holding democratic elections amongst the Palestinians, but I could see that he was really worried about the Intifada, maybe concerned that this kind of violence against authority might serve as an example to Egyptian troublemakers. "I wish I could wake up one morning and find that it is gone," he said. I told him I felt exactly the same way.

Before we parted, I reminded him that March 1989 would be the tenth anniversary of the signing of the Israeli-Egyptian peace treaty, and that this would be a good occasion for him to meet with Shamir, but Mubarak said only, "This isn't the right time. I had wanted to meet with him, but he keeps making these statements about not giving up an inch of territory. Under these circumstances I cannot meet him." We parted with a friendly handshake. I liked him. He was direct and I believe honest in the evaluations he shared with me. He was sincere in his desire to advance the peace process, but was obviously concerned with the Egyptian domestic scene, which seemed to place not inconsiderable constraints on his freedom vis-à-vis Israel.

My meeting with Shevardnadze was still two days away, so at the suggestion of our ambassador, Shimon Shamir, I drove out to see the experimental agricultural farm at Nubariye. Nubariye, located near the Cairo-Alexandria Road, is run by Israeli experts who are showing the Egyptians how to reclaim the desert using Israeli seedlings, computerized-drip irrigation, and other Israeli agricultural techniques. It was amazing to see what had been accomplished, and the admiration of the Egyptian workers for the Israeli instructors. A large tract of what used to be desert land had already been reclaimed and was now producing an abundance of vegetables and field crops. At Nubariye I was joined by Yousuf Wali, Egypt's minister of agriculture and deputy prime minister. He was full of praise for the project and generally a great admirer of Israel. On the way back to Cairo, he explained to me that the Cairo-Alexandria Road used to be called the Desert Road, but now that a number of enterprising Egyptians had bought up land along the road, brought in Israeli experts, and applied the methods that had been demonstrated at Nubariye, the bordering areas were desert no more. The Nubariye project is one of the best-kept secrets in Egypt. Trade between Israel and Egypt is practically nonexistent. The Egyptians make it difficult for Egyptians to visit Israel. Ten years after the signing of the peace treaty, it was still a very cold peace.

The following morning I drove to the Soviet Embassy on the banks of the Nile. Shevardnadze was standing at the top of the steps to greet me. I went up—two steps at a time—to shake his hand. We moved inside; he was accompanied by his interpreter and two other gentlemen who kept their silence throughout our meeting, and I was joined by Binyamin (Bibi) Netanyahu, whom I had appointed deputy minister of foreign affairs; Yeshayahu Anug, our deputy director general; and Arye Levin, who had come down from Moscow. "Well," I said, "if Mohammed doesn't come to the mountain, the mountain comes to Mohammed," referring to the fact that during his tour of the Middle East Shevardnadze had visited all the countries in the region except Israel and that therefore I had to come to Cairo. I described the assistance that Israeli agricultural experts were rendering to Egypt in the Nubariye project. He responded by expressing his hope that the day was not far off when Israel would provide that kind of assistance to the Soviet Union.

Then we went at it. He started by telling me that the Middle East was a powder keg, that war could break out at any minute and it was therefore imperative to bring peace to the region. This was just the opening I was waiting for.

"You know," I said, "you made a mistake by not coming to Israel on this visit. In Israel you would have found that there is hardly a family that has not lost somebody in the wars we have had to fight to defend ourselves against Arab aggression. Then you would have seen that nobody needs to preach to us about the need for peace. Nobody yearns for peace as we do. If the area is a powder keg it is because of the bellicosity of Arab rulers and the vast quantities of arms that are being shipped to them, much of it by the Soviet Union."

Shevardnadze urged me to agree to an international conference and talks with the PLO. "Why do you oppose an international conference?" he asked. "You know," I said, "Jews like to answer a question with a question; why do you oppose direct negotiations?" As for the Palestinians, I gave him a lecture on Palestinian demographics, explaining that there were 650,000 Palestinians who were citizens of Israel, who voted in our elections and were represented in our parliament; that there were more Palestinians in Jordan than there were in Judea, Samaria, and Gaza; and that therefore addressing the Palestinian problem required negotiations with Jordan and with representatives of the Palestinian population in the territories, not the PLO.

When he replied that all of the Arab countries recognized the PLO as the representatives of the Palestinian people, I called his attention to Syria, which supported groups opposed to Arafat, and to Jordan, which had still not forgotten its battle with the PLO in "Black September" of 1970. I knew I had him at a disadvantage, since his knowledge of the Middle East and its problems was superficial, and what little he knew had probably been drilled into him by his Middle East experts.

"Since you broke relations with us over twenty years ago we have had no contact, no opportunity to exchange views and information," I went on. "No wonder there is such a gap in our evaluations of the situation. Why don't we set up an Israeli-Soviet committee of experts on the Middle East and begin a systematic exchange of views that hopefully will lead to us finding some common ground?" Without hesitation, he agreed. As we parted, he announced to reporters on the steps of the embassy building that we had agreed to set up such a committee; but again nothing came of it.

Just as I thought that our meeting had ended, he seemed to remember something he had forgotten to tell me: "Tomorrow I am going to give a speech in Cairo where I shall announce our readiness to renew diplomatic relations with Israel if Israel would agree to an international conference and contact with the PLO." I suggested that he should not include this announcement in his speech, telling him that we believe in the universality of diplomatic relations between nations, relations that should not be made contingent on agreements on policy. When he explained that the Soviet Union had to take into consideration opinions in the Arab world and bring about circumstances so that the Arabs would understand the renewal of relations with Israel, I asked in amazement whether the Soviet Union, one of the world's two superpowers, allowed others to set conditions for Soviet policy. Shevardnadze's response was immediate: "Nobody can dictate to the Soviet Union." "You know," I said, "Israel is a much smaller country than the Soviet Union, but nobody can dictate to us either." The following day he gave his speech, including the part that I had asked him to omit.

Within a few days of my return from Cairo, Abd el-Meguid telephoned to inform me that Mubarak had met with King Hussein at Emperor Hirohito's funeral in Tokyo and, as he had promised me, had asked the king to meet with me. The king had agreed.

That same week the Likud won a sweeping victory in the municipal elections. Our victory showed to all that the Likud's power was growing, and that friend and foe alike would have to deal with the Likud for some time to come.

As I reviewed my first two months as foreign minister, I felt that we were making progress. It looked as though we had won ourselves a breathing spell that would permit us to launch our peace initiative. I had established a working relationship with Mubarak, and I was looking forward to meeting King Hussein. Our relations with the Soviet Union were beginning to thaw. Now I needed Yitzhak Shamir's cooperation to further our diplomatic moves. But when I reported to him the results of my visit to Cairo and the arrangement Mubarak had made for a meeting with King Hussein, Shamir seemed cool and unenthusiastic. He was not going to "beg" for a meeting with Mubarak, he said, and as for the peace initiative, he still wanted to think about it.

How was I going to get this "reluctant dragon" to lead Israel's peace initiative? This was a challenge that was to confront me again and again in the months to come.

The Peace Initiative

Shamir called a meeting in his office in preparation for my visit to Washington in early March 1989. Our brain trust consisted of Dan Meridor, the young minister of justice and a rising star in the Likud; Ehud Olmert, minister without portfolio, who had entered the Knesset at the age of twenty-nine and had in the ensuing fifteen years made a name for himself as one of Israel's smartest politicians; Bibi Netanyahu, who had served as Israel's ambassador to the United Nations, where he had become a familiar and popular face to millions of U.S. television viewers; Eli Rubinstein, who had been an aide to Moshe Dayan, had been at Camp David, and was a particular favorite of Shamir even though he was not a Likud member; and Yossi Ben-Aharon, whom Shamir had borrowed from the Foreign Ministry to become director general of the prime minister's office. All of them knew the United States well and had extensive contacts in Washington and in the American Jewish community. I brought to the meeting my aide Salai Meridor, who was Dan Meridor's younger brother.

We sat around the low rectangular table in the prime minister's office with Shamir, as always, in the armchair against the wall, the position that Begin had chosen for himself at such meetings. An elderly lady brought in Shamir's tea and lemon, as well as tea, coffee, fruit juice, and cookies for the rest of us. The participants gave their various suggestions for my upcoming meetings in Washington, while Shamir silently sipped his tea. I was the last to speak. "We will not find the sympathy and warm friendship in Washington that we have been used to these past years. They are going to play hardball with us, and if they feel that they have the political backing for it they will try to cut our balls off without mercy." There were no notetakers and I permitted myself to speak freely.

Shamir lost his temper. He was usually pretty good at controlling it, but when he got going he would clench his fists, raise his voice, and give vent to his feelings without regard to those of others. "If there is one thing I cannot stand it is fear," he exclaimed. In fact, fear was the furthest thing from my mind. I simply wanted to make sure that none of us had any illusions about the reality we were facing in Washington.

It took only a few days to see that my appraisal had unfortunately not been far off the mark. I left Israel on El Al's midnight flight, which landed at JFK Airport at about 5:00 A.M. Sunday morning, March 12. When I arrived at the Regency Hotel in Manhattan, the *New York Times* was waiting for me in my suite. On the front page was a report by the *Times* diplomatic correspondent, Thomas Friedman, entitled: "PLO and Israel to Get Bush Ideas on Mideast Peace." It began:

> The Bush Administration plans to ask Israel and the Palestine Liberation Organization to take steps to ease tensions in the Israeli-occupied West Bank and Gaza Strip to lay the foundation for peace talks, a senior Administration official said. The official said the Administration's suggestions for Israel will be presented on Monday when Israel's Foreign Minister, Moshe Arens, meets with President Bush, Secretary of State James A. Baker 3rd and national security advisor Brent Scowcroft.

The report went on to list a number of suggestions for Israel and the PLO to bring about a relaxation of tension in the area. The senior administration official was quoted as saying, "We should take our time, till the ground carefully and only move when we think there is a reasonable chance of success." Further on, Friedman reported that "the Bush Administration may also discuss with both the PLO and the Israelis some general ideas it has about what the 'final status' in the occupied territories should be . . . ," and he ended with: "The Bush Administration is expecting Mr. Arens to convey all these ideas to Prime Minister

Yitzhak Shamir in the hope that when Mr. Shamir comes to Washington in the first week in April for a meeting with President Bush he will bring with him some serious proposals along these lines."

I had heard that Baker had made a name for himself in Washington as an expert at leaking information to the press, and I had no doubt that it was Baker who was hiding behind the guise of the "senior Administration official." And yet I was shocked. This was an outrageous contravention of all diplomatic practice. The foreign minister of a newly elected government has flown 5,000 miles to meet with the secretary of state of a new administration to open discussions on a matter crucial to his country and important to the United States, and the secretary of state preempts him by leaking to the press on the eve of their scheduled meeting what he intends to say to him, or maybe more to the point, the lecture he is about to deliver. Moreover, reference to discussion at this time of the "final status" of the territories was in clear contravention of the Camp David Accords.

For a moment I thought of canceling our meeting. After all, I already knew what Baker was going to say to me, and I could readily assume that he had little interest in what I was going to say to him. But I concluded that I was obliged to make an effort, however futile it seemed, to get our message across.

The next morning I took the shuttle to Washington. In his office, Baker greeted me courteously and we sat down on a couch alongside each other. "I received quite a welcome with that story that was leaked to the *New York Times* yesterday," I opened. Baker said that he had had nothing to do with that report, but saw nothing particularly wrong with it.

I decided to try to get the secretary to understand our position. Pointing out that stability in the Middle East was a common objective for the United States and Israel, I stressed the need for our working in concert if this objective was to be achieved. Baker nodded agreement. I told him that the new Israeli government was in the process of formulating a peace initiative, that we needed a little more time, and that it was important that Washington should lend us support in the meantime. I decided not to present the initiative itself, leaving that for Shamir's upcoming visit to Washington, and not having as yet received his consent to it.

Baker nodded here and there, now and then raising some doubts, and left me with the clear impression that he would await our initiative.

In the meeting later that day with President Bush, which Baker attended, I went over the same ground, stressing the need to find interlocutors amongst the Palestinians in the territories, and that giving in to PLO terrorist intimidation tactics would be self-defeating. Bush seemed surprised when I referred to the PLO's continuing terrorist activity, and asked whether we could substantiate that. When I told him that we had all the necessary evidence, he asked that one of our counter-terror experts be sent to Washington so that the evidence could be presented there. (A few days after my return to Israel, we were informed by the State Department that there would be no need to send our expert to Washington.) The President raised the question of Israeli settlements in the territories, leaving no doubt of his objection to further settlement activity. My reply that Shamir faced political pressure on this issue from some of his coalition partners and that over a hundred thousand Israelis already lived in Judea and Samaria so one or two additional settlements were not going to make much difference obviously did not satisfy him. Of the many meetings that I had attended in the Oval Office, this was the coldest.

When Baker and I met with reporters in the lobby of the State Department at the conclusion of our meeting, Baker's review of our discussion bore almost no resemblance to the story leaked to the *New York Times* the previous day. There was no mention of the PLO or of "final status" discussions. "I reaffirmed our desire in the weeks and months and years ahead to work closely with Israel in the search for peace," he concluded.

But now began the anonymous background briefings. On the following day the *New York Times* carried a story about my meeting with Baker that bore equally little resemblance to what had actually taken place. According to the *Times*,

> Secretary of State James A. Baker 3rd today gave Israel the first broad outline of the Bush Administration's approach to settling the Palestinian-Israeli conflict, a senior State Department official said. Mr. Baker told the Israeli Foreign Minister, Moshe Arens, that Washington believed the best way to break the deadlock in the Middle East was through a two tier peace process: Israelis and Palestinians would take specific and immediate steps to reduce tensions between them in Israel and the occupied territories, and at the same time begin a general discussion of a "final settlement" for resolving Israel's security concerns and the Palestinians' quest for national self-determination. . . . Baker said we need some general commitments from Israel and the Palestinians to a final settlement.

Along the way, a small hint was given as to the true nature of our meeting. "Mr. Baker did not ask Mr. Arens at this time to take any specific steps to ease tension in the territories," but this was immediately followed by an explanation, "Such general steps . . . have already been outlined to the Israelis."

Then came the thinly veiled threat:

The senior State Department official said Mr. Baker had made it clear to Mr. Arens that when Prime Minister Yitzhak Shamir comes to Washington in the first week of April, the Administration expects him to bring specific proposals for improving the atmosphere in the occupied territories, as well as general ideas about how Israel sees the "final status" of the West Bank and the Gaza Strip. . . . We didn't expect Arens to give any definitive proposals, but we do expect Shamir to, a senior State Department official said.

But there was more to come. The day following our meeting, during which I had explained the efforts we would be making to locate interlocutors among the Palestinian population in the territories, that the PLO was trying to intimidate the local population by terror tactics in an attempt to prevent such contacts, and that we did not intend to submit to these tactics, Baker appeared before the House Appropriations Committee. When asked whether it was part of U.S. policy to promote direct negotiations between Israel and the PLO, he responded: "It is an element of our policy to promote direct negotiations which can be meaningful between Israelis and Palestinians. Now, if you can't have direct negotiations that are meaningful, that do not involve negotiation with the PLO, we would then have to see negotiations between Israel and representatives of the PLO. It may be that you can have meaningful negotiations that do not involve the PLO."

It must have been clear to Baker that this statement would strengthen the PLO's stand. Reporters sought me out immediately to solicit my reaction to "Mr. Baker's comments today about the possibility of eventual Israeli talks with the PLO." I replied truthfully, "He did not say anything like that to me."

Before leaving Washington, I called Baker and told him that his statement before the House committee was not consistent with our discussion of the previous day and that it would encourage local Palestinians to spurn any Israeli overtures and direct them to the PLO in Tunis. Baker replied that he had not meant to put any obstacles in our way but had merely answered a "hypothetical" question. A "senior State Department official" expanded on this to Friedman: "While he was not trying to send any signals, Mr. Baker 'knew what he was saying.' He did not wake up this morning with any regrets. The Israelis have to understand that this is a new world."

The "new world" the State Department was talking about was a world in which the Bush administration had decided to assume a confrontational posture toward Israel, its longtime ally and friend. I could only assume that the insistence on discussing "final status" at this time —despite the Camp David agreements that called for such discussion only after the second year of a transitional autonomy phase for the Palestinians, which would hopefully produce the climate to make such discussions productive—was an indication that the "final status" it was promoting was a return of Israel to the lines that existed prior to June 1967. The administration knew that this was the only "final status" that might be agreeable to the PLO and the Arab world.

I had anticipated this change in U.S. policy from the Bush administration, but I had not expected that discussions and consultations anchored on the common values and mutual trust that had characterized the relationship between the United States and Israel over the years, even at times of disagreement, would now take a back seat to a web of leaks, distorted background briefings, and public pronouncements of a provocative and confrontational nature by the new secretary of state. I could see that these tactics were designed to put the new Israeli government on notice as to the way in which the wind from Washington was going to blow for the next four years, and to discredit me personally.

Baker brought some strong cards to the confrontation that he was staging. America was a superpower, while Israel was one of the smallest countries on the globe. Israel received $3 billion in aid from the United States annually, and acquired much of the weaponry it needed for its defense there. And, perhaps most important, American political and diplomatic support added significantly to Israel's ability to deter renewed Arab aggression. But the Bush administration would have to learn that Israel would not be bullied or pushed around.

It was clear to me that the only possible constraint on the Bush administration's tactics toward Israel was domestic politics. Henry Kissinger had once said that Israel had no foreign policy, only domestic politics; this is true of all democracies whose politicians want to get reelected. It is certainly true of the United States. If Bush and Baker were to realize that there was public opposition to their bullying tactics, then they would be likely to relent, certainly as election time approached.

Now that I saw the change in U.S. policy toward Israel taking shape and began to get a measure of Baker's position, I realized that we would have to fortify support for Israel in the Congress and among U.S. public opinion. The administration's policy might find a resonant echo among those American Jews who were not sympathetic to the policies of the Likud-led Israeli government, and present a dilemma for those supporters of Israel who would hesitate to take a public position contrary to that of Washington. Should that turn out to be the case, there would be little restraint on the new policymakers in Washington.

I spent the next day on the Hill meeting with congressional committees and with individual members of the Senate and House, then flew to New York to appear before the Conference of Presidents, now chaired by Seymour Reich. I spoke to them of the shift in perceptions that had been induced by the media coverage of the Intifada, which had successfully switched the focus from the Israeli-Arab conflict—in which Israel appeared as little David—to the Israeli-Palestinian conflict, in which Israel was being made to appear as Goliath. I explained that the two had to be seen in the same context, that Israel still faced the danger of renewed aggression by a coalition of Arab armies. And I spoke about the need to get negotiations going and that the Israeli government was formulating an initiative with that aim.

Upon my return to Israel toward the end of March, I attended the Jewish Solidarity Conference in Jerusalem. Hundreds of Jewish leaders from communities around the world had come to express their solidarity with Israel at this hour. There had been considerable concern that the conference would serve as a forum for dissent from the policies of the Israeli government, but this was not the case. Even those attending who did disagree with Israeli policy in the territories seemed to realize that an expression of solidarity with Israel had to take precedence over everything else this time.

I had a series of conversations with Shamir in preparation for his visit to Washington, doing my level best to explain the severity of the situation. Unless we came up with a credible initiative, the United States was likely to join the chorus for an international conference, possibly even initiating consultations with the five permanent members of the UN Security Council. I described the increasing pressure we would be under to talk to the PLO, and that in my view only a call for democratic elections in the territories would successfully meet that challenge. Sometimes I felt that I was talking to the wall; at others he seemed to be vacillating between moods of gloom and defiance. A few times he suggested that I accompany him on the trip. I had no particular desire to join him since I did not know what he was going to say when he got there.

A few days before his departure I came to Shamir's office in the evening, bringing Netanyahu along for support. That night Shamir was in a defiant mood. Evidently encouraged by the Solidarity Conference, he talked about mobilizing American Jewry to face "a threat to the Jewish people's very existence. Baker is against us; a new hangman for the Jewish people has arisen." The following night he called me at home in a more reasonable mood, struggling with the five-point initiative in his own mind and seriously considering presenting it to Washington.

The American press, echoed by the Israeli press, was already full of what Washington expected of Shamir when he got there. It looked as though they were digging a hole in Washington for Shamir to fall into upon his arrival. Rumors were also surfacing in Israeli newspapers that Finance Minister Shimon Peres had a peace plan of his own which he was going to disclose after Shamir's return from what was generally assumed would be an unsuccessful trip. This, of course, was not intended to strengthen Shamir's hand when he got to Washington.

On Sunday, April 2, after the weekly government meeting, Shamir invited Peres, Rabin, and me to his office in order to brief us on what he intended to present in Washington. We took our usual seats around the coffee table, Shamir in the chair up against the wall. Despite my many discussions with Shamir, I had no idea what he was going to say. After some preliminaries, he told us that he intended to raise four points. Without referring to them as a peace initiative, he outlined all but the point dealing with arms control from the five-point initiative I had proposed, with one additional modification. He seemed to have had difficulty with the idea of holding elections among the Palestinians in Judea, Samaria, and Gaza, proposing instead that a list of Palestinian delegates for negotiations with us should be composed by Jordan and/ or Egypt, and only failing that would elections be held. Rabin seemed satisfied; it was clear to me that Shamir had discussed the matter with him, and that Rabin had vetoed the point dealing with arms control. Peres kept his own counsel. And I, though disappointed that the initiative had been somewhat emasculated, thanked God for small favors.

I had given Shamir five pages of explanation in English covering every one of the points of the peace initiative that I thought might be useful to him during his Washington visit. I advised him that, regardless of President Bush's reaction to his presentation, he should upon leaving the meeting, while standing on the White House steps, announce to the assembled reporters that after considerable thought and deliberation he had formulated this initiative in order to advance peace in the Middle East, and then read out the points of the initiative one after another.

In the meeting with Bush on April 6, Shamir presented the four points. Bush seemed to respond favorably, and after their meeting in the Oval Office Shamir read out the contents of the peace initiative to waiting reporters. As might have been expected, the point dealing with the Palestinian elections drew almost all the attention. Among the American Jewish community, Shamir received an enthusiastic reception. On the whole his trip, contrary to the many pessimistic predictions, had been a success.

Shamir returned to Israel full of confidence. He felt that he had hit it off with Baker, but had his reservations about Bush. Generally, he was in a very optimistic mood, convinced that it was going to be smooth sailing in our relations with the United States from now on. He would not agree with my assessment that despite this initial success, we would still feel lots of pressure from Washington in the months to come.

I told Shamir that it was essential that we now exploit our initial success to the full. Special envoys should be sent immediately to the important capitals of the world to present and explain the peace initiative. He gave my idea only lukewarm support. We did send Netanyahu, who was in the United States at the time, to Ottawa, and had Rubinstein and Ben-Aharon meet with a number of ambassadors at the United Nations. But these contacts lacked the drama that I thought we should provide at the moment.

The initial response in the Arab world was negative. President Mubarak, who had gone to Washington in the wake of Shamir's visit, at first said that he was prepared to consider the idea of elections among the Palestinians, but he also said that he saw Israel's initiative as a futile exercise. The PLO announced that it rejected the idea of elections. Shamir's visit had evidently put the ball in the Arab court.

When I called in the Egyptian ambassador to Israel, Mohammed Bassiouny, to brief him on the initiative, he said to me, "Why do you need elections?" After Mubarak had returned to Cairo and consulted with other Arab countries, he had concluded that Palestinian elections were not a useful idea. Instead, Bassiouny suggested that we should allow Egypt and the United States to select the Palestinian delegation. Mubarak had given an interview to the Egyptian daily *Al Mussawar* in which he declared that as long as Shamir was Israel's prime minister, there was no chance of progress toward peace. I suggested that Bassiouny tell Mubarak that it was important for him to correct the impression he had created, and that the best way to do that would be for him to hold a meeting with Shamir, or if it was easier for him, to arrange for a tripartite meeting together with Bush.

Bassiouny explained that as long as Shamir continued to make pronouncements that he was not ready to give up an inch of territory, it would be difficult for Mubarak to attend such a meeting. Although I tried to stress to the Egyptian ambassador that Mubarak could justify a meeting with Shamir to Arab public opinion by explaining that he wanted to put the Arab case to Shamir face-to-face, it was to no avail; only the Americans would be able to get Mubarak to agree to sit down with Shamir.

I was not surprised by Arab opposition to the election proposal; after all, democratic elections were far from the accepted norm in the Arab world, and elections among the Palestinians might give the population in other Arab countries ideas. Their disregard of the other three points of our initiative was also not unexpected. But it put them on the defensive: should Mubarak agree to a meeting with Shamir, Jordan and Syria, as well as other Arab countries, would be pressured to begin direct negotiations with Israel.

Turning next to an international effort to help rehabilitate the Palestinian refugees, I called in the ambassadors of the "Seven"—the United States, Japan, Germany, France, Italy, the United Kingdom, and Canada—to present the essential details of the physical and economic conditions of the Palestinian refugees, with particular emphasis on the conditions in Gaza. But when I asked them to transmit our proposal for a rehabilitation program to their governments, I drew a complete blank. Governments that were busy criticizing Israel were evidently not prepared to make an effort to alleviate the human tragedy of the Palestinian refugees.

That week Bill Brown, the U.S. ambassador who had become a good friend from the days when he served as deputy chief of mission at the American Embassy in Tel Aviv some years ago, came to see me, bringing me a "Dear Misha" letter from Baker. The letter contained a series of detailed proposals for holding elections among the Palestinians, while ignoring the other three points of our initiative. Perusing the letter in Brown's presence I saw that Baker had decided to jump the gun, and rather than await our ideas on the subject, to confront us with his own proposals. I told Brown that there was no better way to magnify differences of opinion on the subject and create an atmosphere of tension between us. It would have been far better, now that Shamir had presented our peace initiative, to await our ideas on its implementation, and then respond with comments or counter-suggestions. To Baker, I replied in a "Dear Jim" letter:

> . . . We are actively engaged in working on the details of Prime Minister Shamir's four-point initiative that was presented during his recent visit to Washington. Every one of the points—meeting of the Camp David signatories, normalization of relations with the Arab countries at war with Israel, an international effort to rehabilitate the Palestinian refugees still in refugee camps, and election of representatives of the Palestinian population in Judea, Samaria, and Gaza—will not be easy to implement. But we are convinced that a concerted and intensive effort will lead to parallel progress on all of them.
>
> Your advice and assistance are greatly appreciated. The Administration's approval is of great significance. I am convinced that if the Prime Minister's initiative will enjoy the support of other peace-loving countries and if the Arab world will respond positively, Prime Minister Shamir's initiative will turn out to be a milestone in the Middle East peace process.
>
> I am looking forward to seeing you on my next visit and discussing the points you raised in your letter and our own ideas on the subject. . . .

I used the opportunity of Brown's visit to call to his attention the ongoing shelling of the Christian quarters of Beirut by Syrian Army forces. It was clear that the Syrians were making another of their many attempts to take over Lebanon, and they were prepared to use any and all means, as long as they could get away with it. In 1982 they had organized the assassination of the Lebanese president-elect, Bashir Gemayel, who was on close terms with Israel. In May of 1984, when I was defense minister, they succeeded in torpedoing the Israel-Lebanon agreement, which George Shultz had achieved after shuttling back and forth between Beirut and Jerusalem, by letting the new Lebanese president, Amin Gemayel, know that if the agreement were ratified, he could expect to meet his brother's fate. "If the Syrians learn that the world lets them get away with the shelling of residential areas," I told Brown, "just as the Iraqis have gotten away with the use of chemical weapons, a terrible precedent will be set: in the Middle East you can presumably get away with anything." I could see that Brown took my concerns seriously, but I was not sure they would be taken seriously in Washington.

The peace initiative had not as yet been presented to the government and would need formal approval, obtained by majority vote, for it to become official policy. Shamir asked the government secretary, Eli Rubinstein, to draft the text and to coordinate it with Peres, Rabin, and myself. Shamir had instructed Rubinstein that it was most important to clear it with Rabin. As long as he had Rabin's backing, Peres would be prevented from breaking up the government, and Shamir would enjoy the support of most of the other Labor ministers and thus be assured of a majority at the government meeting. Working closely with Rabin, while occasionally meeting with Peres and me, Rubinstein finally came up with a long and complicated document that included the principle of autonomy for the Palestinians in Judea, Samaria, and Gaza as a five-year interim arrangement, just as it appeared in the Camp David agreements, and called for election of Palestinian representatives to negotiate the details of the autonomy regime. It also contained the three other elements of our initiative, but the document was devoted chiefly to autonomy and Palestinian elections.

I urged Shamir to propose that the Palestinian elections be held at the municipal level in Judea, Samaria, and Gaza, and that the elected municipal leadership then also constitute the delegation for negotiations with Israel. It would be relatively easy to hold such elections since the laws and regulations covering municipal elections were mostly in place, and such elections had been held in Judea and Samaria in past years. On the other hand, if the elections were to be held with all the territories as a single constituency, we would be faced with the problem of arriving at agreement on election modalities and procedures. Rabin, however, was against municipal elections. In arguing the subject with me, he emphasized that most Palestinian municipalities were now being run by Israeli Army officers, much of the Palestinian municipal leadership having been fired or deported in the last few years, and that he had no desire to return the running of these municipalities to Palestinians. I thought this argument rather incongruous, considering the fact that we were about to embark on a policy designed to lead to self-government for the Palestinians. But he was adamant, and Shamir, feeling that Rabin's support was essential, was prepared to accept Rabin's position.

On Sunday, May 14, Shamir brought the peace initiative to the government meeting for discussion and vote. I opened the debate by explaining the difficulties Israel was currently facing in the international arena: that we were becoming progressively isolated under a diplomatic offensive aimed at returning us to the 1967 lines; that the PLO had become very active politically and was scoring significant diplomatic successes. To those concerned with the risks they thought our initiative might entail, I said that they should consider that the risks of *not* taking an initiative were far greater. The purpose of the initiative, I explained, was to put the ball in the opponents' court, to return the focus of world attention to the Arab-Israeli conflict, to update the Camp David Accords to which Israel was in any case committed, and to create conditions for the start of negotiations that would hopefully lead to agreements that would bring peace to Israel.

The debate went on for hours. Twenty-six ministers were seated around the long table on the second floor of the prime minister's office, the windows overlooking the Judean Hills, a large picture of Theodor Herzl, the founder of Zionism, on one of the walls. Shamir sat at the center of the table, occasionally gaveling the meeting to order, while ministers consumed gallons of tea and coffee, conversed with their neighbors, or left the cabinet room to take care of ministerial business or leak the contents of the discussion to the media. Occasionally Israel radio would report a minister's speech even before he had made it, his aides having previously leaked the text.

There was some opposition on the left, from those who felt that the initiative had not gone far enough. The major opposition, however, came from the right, whose most forceful spokesman was Ariel Sharon. In his view, the initiative would bring down a catastrophe on Israel; it would encourage terrorism and open the road to another war. When the vote was held, we had a solid majority for approval of the initiative. Twenty for and six against. Two of the opponents were from the left: Ezer Weizman and Rafi Edri, the two Labor ministers without portfolio. On the right, the opposing votes came from three Likud ministers, Sharon, David Levy, and Yitzhak Moda'i, and from one of the two National Religious party ministers, Avner Shaki.

On that day a triple alliance—a troika—was born that was to bedevil

Shamir and the Likud for many months to come. Sharon, Levy, and Moda'i began a rebellion against Shamir, accusing him of leading Israel to destruction. They came to be known as the *Hishukaim;* like the hoops of a barrel, they claimed, they were going to "constrain" Shamir. They would not resign from the government; on the contrary, they would stay in so as to make sure that Shamir would not stray from "the strait and narrow" and make concessions that to their minds would endanger the State of Israel or compromise the rights of the Jewish people to the Land of Israel.

Ariel Sharon had been Israel's most illustrious general, who had helped snatch victory from the jaws of defeat during the Yom Kippur War when he led his division across the Suez Canal into Egypt. Like other successful generals before him, he was too big for politics. He held himself in high regard but had little regard for other politicians, whether in his own or rival parties. He had succeeded in pressuring Begin to appoint him minister of defense. It was Sharon who supervised the evacuation of the Sinai and the destruction of the Israeli settlements there. He led Israel into the Lebanon War, and was forced to resign from the Defense Ministry after the Kahan Commission's inquiry into the Sabra and Shatila massacre.

Although I had not agreed with the commission's conclusions and had no designs to become defense minister, it was clear that Sharon was going to bear me a permanent grudge when Begin asked me to return from Washington to assume the post that Sharon had to vacate. He had made something of a comeback and was now minister of trade and industry, but he was still frustrated at not being at the very top, or at least returning to the Defense Ministry. He had challenged Shamir for the Likud leadership in 1984 but had lost in the Herut Central Committee vote. But that did not keep him from proclaiming that he continued to see himself as contender for the position of prime minister. It was clear that as long as Sharon had not attained that ambition, he was going to make life uncomfortable for anybody in a leadership position in the Likud.

David Levy had had a meteoric rise on the Israel political scene. He came to Israel from Morocco in his teens, worked as a building laborer, entered local politics in his hometown of Bet Shean on behalf of Labor, was discovered by Herut leaders who at the time were looking for somebody who could help gain votes among the large number of Moroccan immigrants, and established himself as part of the Likud leadership by virtue of the following he developed among the many newcomers from Arabic-speaking lands. Not having had an opportunity to complete his formal education, he was nevertheless quick to learn all he felt he needed to know to make his way in politics. He had been minister of absorption, was now minister of housing, but made no secret that he was aiming higher than that. At the last Herut Convention Levy had proclaimed himself a worthy heir to Menachem Begin. Now he was frustrated and disappointed that he had not been named foreign minister. Although in the past he had not been known for his hawkish views, he now joined Sharon and Moda'i in attacking the peace initiative as a "sell-out."

Yitzhak Moda'i belonged to the Liberal branch of Likud. Highly educated, with a powerful intellect, modesty was not one of his strong points. He had fought his way up the ladder of the Liberal party hierarchy, developing a reputation for erratic behavior and leaving many enemies behind. He had been finance minister in the first National Unity government but was forced out of that position after he publicly hurled insults at Shimon Peres, who was prime minister at the time. Moda'i, too, had announced on a number of occasions that he was a contender for the position of prime minister and was obviously dissatisfied with his current position as minister without portfolio. The coalition with Sharon and Levy evidently seemed to him a good vehicle to fight his way to the top.

I did not believe that the troika sincerely opposed the peace initiative. All three had been members of Begin's first government and had voted for the Camp David Accords. Our initiative did not go beyond these accords, except for the proposal that we negotiate the modalities of Palestinian autonomy with elected delegates of the Palestinians. And yet I found it hard to accept that they were going to fight this supremely important decision only to advance their own political ambitions. But that seemed to be the sad truth.

Containing a preamble and some twenty clauses, the May 1989 initiative was now Israel's official blueprint for peace. Based on the Camp David Accords and UN Security Resolutions 242 and 338, and on the assumption of a national consensus, the document opened with a declaration of Israel's "yearning for peace," going on to express opposition to the establishment of "an additional Palestinian state in the Gaza district and in the area between Israel and Jordan," and refusing to negotiate with the PLO or accept any change in the status of Judea,

Samaria, and Gaza other than in accordance with the government's basic guidelines. Following the relevant parts of the Camp David Accords, the initiative proposed elections among the Palestinians for a representation to negotiate a transitional period of self-rule—with Israel continuing to be responsible for security, foreign affairs, and all matters concerning Israeli citizens in Judea, Samaria, and Gaza—and later negotiations, starting three years after implementation of the interim arrangements, toward a permanent solution, each side then presenting whatever proposals it saw fit.

At my insistence, it also contained the three other "neglected" points: reconfirmation of the Camp David Accords; an "enlarging of the circle of peace in the region," primarily by the termination of the state of war by the Arab nations (including an end to the Arab boycott and establishment of diplomatic relations); and Israel's willingness to participate in an international endeavor to rehabilitate the residents of Arab refugee camps in Judea, Samaria, and Gaza.

Four days later, I was off to the States again to address the annual AIPAC policy conference in Washington, to meet with the Conference of Presidents in New York, and then back to Washington to keep appointments with Baker, National Security Adviser Brent Scowcroft, and U.S. Secretary of Defense Richard Cheney. I had, of course, already met Brigadier General Scowcroft, who, from the start, struck me as profoundly indifferent to Israel. There was a certain heartlessness about him; and much later, during the Gulf War, his openly expressed lack of empathy with Israel was to become a source of concern. I looked forward to meeting Dick Cheney, who would become first a friend and then, though neither of us could have foretold this, a colleague. But chiefly I was relieved that we had kept the promise I had made to Baker. "I told you that we would produce a peace initiative," I said to Baker as we shook hands in his office. "Here it is. Now what we need is your unqualified support." "You have it," said the secretary with a broad smile. He was especially pleased, he said, with the Palestinian elections. I told him that the other three points were equally important; the four, in fact, were intended to be mutually reinforcing, and I gave him a letter from Shamir to the president, asking Bush for his support for the proposed international effort to rehabilitate the Palestinian refugee camps.

In my meeting with Baker, he listened attentively as I brought up one topic after another. We spoke about the situation of Soviet Jewry and I stressed the need for relaxation of USSR emigration restrictions for Soviet Jews, and our desire that the Soviets permit the Israeli consular delegation to issue the visas to Israel rather than having the Dutch go on doing it. Baker said this was important and that he would at once put it on his list. Then I moved to the situation in Lebanon. "Coming in the wake of the precedent set by Iraq in the use of chemical warfare with nobody stopping it," I said, "the stage is being set for potentially terrible things in the Middle East." "Yes, but what can we do?" Baker asked. "The international community must step in," I replied, and said that I thought that the Syrian dictator Hafez al-Assad should be told that he would not be allowed to continue such actions. We shook hands again upon parting; it had been a very good session. There had been dialogue and understanding between us, I told the press, and we had obtained the administration's wholehearted support for Israel's peace initiative. For the first time in weeks, it seemed possible to me that we were on the right track. But I had underestimated Baker once again.

On May 22, while both Shamir and I were abroad, James Baker, addressing an audience of over one thousand American Jews at the AIPAC conference in Washington, dropped a bombshell. Stating that "American support for Israel is the foundation of our approach to the problems, the very, very difficult problems of the Middle East," he buttered up the crowd by praising Israel as a vigorous democracy, telling a little story about the "strong working relationship" he had established with Shamir, reaping applause for stressing that negotiations must be face-to-face and that neither the United States nor any other party ("inside or outside") could dictate the outcome. As to the initiative, he described the United States as welcoming "these Israeli ideas . . . the Israeli government . . . has given us something to work with. It has taken a stand on important issues. . . . Palestinians have it within their power to help define the shape of this initiative . . . and its essential elements." Having damned it with faint praise, he turned from the initiative to the heart of the matter, as seen by the administration.

"For Israel," Baker said, "now is the time to lay aside once and for all the unrealistic vision of a Greater Israel. Israeli interests in the West Bank and Gaza, security and otherwise, can be accommodated in a settlement based on Resolution 242. Forswear annexation; stop settlement activity; allow schools to reopen; reach out to the Palestinians as neighbors who deserve political rights."

His words, the tone in which he had spoken, the message that the initiative was all right as far as it went but that this was nowhere near far enough and that Israel was going to have to accept the principle of land-for-peace, was met, I was told, by almost total silence in the audience. There was more: admonitions to the Arabs, particularly the Palestinians, that they must speak with one voice for peace, "practice constructive diplomacy," recognize Israel as a partner in trade and human contact, understand that violence would not work and that "no one" would deliver Israel to them. But these homilies were only incidental to Baker's main and now barely concealed purpose: to put the Israeli government on the defensive and to accentuate U.S. criticism of Likud policies.

Within the course of less than an hour, in front of an all-Jewish audience deeply committed to Israel's well-being, Baker had completed a dazzling variety of missions calculated to prove that, to use his own words, "the world is changing." He had significantly strengthened the hard-line opposition to Shamir within the Likud; publicly discredited, or at least severely embarrassed, both Israel's prime minister and its foreign minister by making it appear that neither—but especially I, who had just met with him—had understood what had been said to us on our recent visits to Washington; conveyed to the Arabs, not least to the PLO, that Israel would be made to toe the line, but that it was up to them to facilitate the process by comporting themselves more sensibly; and signaled to the Labor leadership that better times lay ahead.

I wrote to Baker to express my astonishment. It wasn't the letter I would have sent had I felt free to tell him what I really thought of his tactics, of how shabbily he was dealing with Israel's life-and-death struggle to attain peace at long last, of how little he knew or bothered to learn about the country. Instead, I pointed to the inconsistency of his AIPAC speech with "our discussion held in your office only a few days earlier [when] you assured me of your wholehearted support for Israel's peace initiative without hinting at the 'visions' of a permanent settlement that you presented at AIPAC. . . . Your speech came at a time when Israel had launched an important peace initiative and was looking for your assistance in enlisting support for it. I am not at all sure that your remarks will engender much support, whereas I am concerned that they will raise Arab expectations, harden Arab positions and make Arab acceptance of our peace initiative less likely." Equally troubling, I wrote, was the presence in his speech of "several new elements, as well as the absence of traditional elements of American policy regarding Israel's most vital interests and its security."

Back came a long "Dear Misha" missive. After the prescribed "very much regret" and "in no way intended" and "now more than ever before you and I have to engage in a spirit of mutual trust and confidence," the secretary got down to "explaining" how much progress had already been made. "It is important," he wrote, to recall that . . .

within five months . . . with resolute American leadership and creative Israeli thinking, the bases of moving forward to negotiation have been altered. There is no longer a question of the immediate convening of an international conference [nor] an assumption that a Palestinian state is a foregone conclusion simply because of a PLO announcement . . . and there is no basis on which to believe that the strategic relationship between Israel and the U.S. can be shaken by any party including the PLO. I am personally committed to strengthening the bonds of strategic cooperation. . . . Together the U.S. and Israel have worked to shape a negotiating process to be launched by fair and free elections [and] understand the importance of this concept; [and] have offered the Palestinians to move through a democratic process to negotiations on the key issues. . . . This is an opportunity that they and other Arabs should not miss. . . .

Then he came to the point:

In our public diplomacy, and [most recently] in my speech of May 22, we have sought to define our own views on some issues of greatest concern . . . in doing so we have sought [neither] to break new ground nor to focus attention on final status issues. . . . We have sought to convey the need for realism. . . . There is nothing new or different about recent statements by U.S. or Israeli officials . . . we both seek a constructive and positive Arab and Palestinian response to a workable process. . . . As we move ahead, let there be no doubt that President Bush and I are firmly committed to Israel's security and to advancing the peace process in a way that recognizes this fundamental reality.

Since his letter clarified nothing and did not in any way alleviate my apprehension as to his real goals, I let him have what I thought was the last word. But another letter on the same theme, written almost immediately afterward, was to make more waves in Washington than I ever could have done. Early in June, in an extraordinary display of support and collective acknowledgment that there had been a turnabout in official U.S. sympathy for Israel, ninety-four of the one hundred U.S. senators signed a letter to the secretary of state asking that the administration "strongly and publicly" endorse the Israeli peace initiative.

The unprecedented number of signatories astonished even AIPAC. In their letter, the senators stated their belief that the elections proposed by Israel represented a first step "towards a just and lasting peace," and stressed that the U.S. role in convincing others of the merits of the plan was vital. "Israel's proposals have not always received the consideration they deserve by other parties to the conflict or by the international community at large. To prevent that from occurring now, the United States must be fully supportive, both in fact and in appearance. While every detail of Israel's proposals may not yet be entirely in place, a strong endorsement by the U.S. would help ensure their serious consideration." It also informed the administration that in the opinion of the overwhelming majority of the members of the Senate, it was necessary "to keep in mind that Israel will be asked to give up politically what it won militarily by defending itself against attacks from outside Israeli borders in which thousands of Israelis died. Those aggressors, except for Egypt, remain in a state of war with Israel to this day. . . . Israel is not simply asked to make peace with the Palestinians . . . the decisions Israel makes will greatly affect her ability to defend herself against other Arab enemies."

There could be no misreading the message to the administration, or the implied rebuke. It was reported to me that Baker was genuinely taken aback by the letter and the fact that ninety-four senators had signed it, the more so since only hours before its release, he had informed his audience at a National Press Club luncheon that Congress was "not very interested" in the entire issue and that he had only received three letters about his supposedly controversial AIPAC speech —"two very positive and one that I would characterize as slightly negative."

The real question, however, was not the extent of the administration's discomfiture but rather how, if at all, it would react to what it might well dismiss as yet another display of manipulation by Israel's well-placed American friends. As to the reaction by Israel, within the Likud it was as predicted: Sharon, Levi, and Moda'i immediately created an uproar, insisting that the initiative be brought before the party's Central Committee for discussion in depth, claiming that government decisions were not enough, that Israel was being sold down the river by a combination of evil forces that included Shamir and myself, while Moda'i clamored for Shamir's resignation. After a while, the shouting subsided; it was agreed that sometime in June the Central Committee would meet, though later the date was pushed back to the start of July.

That summer, the peace process faced new threats from home and abroad, some anticipated, others not; and there was reason to fear that it might not survive its infancy. In July, just before the scheduled meeting of the Likud Central Committee, the three "constrainers" paid a call on Shamir, insisting that not one but two motions be put to a vote: the May initiative, plus a second motion specifically incorporating four "additional" principles with which presumably they hoped to hobble the original initiative, as well as to show the Americans what was what: the Intifada should be crushed; the Arabs of East Jerusalem should be prohibited from participating in the elections (whenever these were held); there must be no division of the western part of the Land of Israel; and no contact with the PLO.

Shamir assured them that all four points were incorporated in the speech he was going to deliver at the meeting, and that there was no reason for a separate vote, and no need for them to be concerned. It was finally agreed that one motion would do, but that it would explicitly identify these four elements, and as such it was presented by Shamir to the Likud Central Committee and approved. I thought Shamir should not have compromised, and that he had made a rather serious mistake, bred of his extreme dislike of confrontation: unwittingly he had helped to create an impression inside the Likud, as well as in the general public, that he had "given in" to the trio and that the initiative had been resultantly and effectively "constrained."

The Labor party responded at once to what it chose to view as an altered climate. Rabin began to mutter that under the "new" circumstances, perhaps it should consider leaving the government; Peres and some of his associates openly declared themselves ready, willing, and able to do so. Dissension was everywhere in the air. The Likud simmered; the Labor party boiled. Nonetheless, when Shamir decided to take the unusual step of putting the initiative to the vote in the government for the second time to correct any mistaken impression that the Likud Central Committee meeting might have left, it fared approximately as it had done in May: Sharon, Levi, and Moda'i against, joined this time by Ezer Weizman; everyone else in favor. The initiative was saved and a major government crisis averted, for the time being.

What now? Nothing much had changed. The Intifada blazed un-curbed; Palestinian leaders with whom I talked told me they dared not take any steps without PLO approval and were clearly frightened; we had committed ourselves to political rather than municipal elections which we might, at this stage, have unilaterally tried to get under way; the Arab world had not responded to the initiative; and Israel's overall security situation was not improved by new Iraqi-Jordanian military cooperation, particularly in the air. How were we going to keep the peace initiative alive? But it proved to possess some life of its own.

In June, Egyptian Minister of State Boutros Boutros-Ghali, who had accompanied Sadat to Jerusalem and was later to become UN secretary general, visited Israel for two days to see, as he put it, "what Egypt can do . . . because time is not on our side. We need a new momentum in favor of peace." He brought with him a "message of friendship" for Shamir from President Mubarak, voicing Egypt's willingness to play an active role in the peace process. But since, on the same visit, Boutros-Ghali also stressed Egyptian support of the Intifada ("a very important expression of self-determination . . . throwing stones is not violence but you [meaning Israel] are counter-attacking with real violence") and announced that without the formal and active participation of the PLO, there could be no peace process, I did not think the offer was likely to be a positive development and said so. I also repeated what I had told Mubarak himself: what was really needed was a Mubarak-Shamir summit. Instead of that, by coming to Israel, Boutros-Ghali had demon-strated to Washington that Egypt, far from rejecting the initiative, was doing its best to modify it—and concurrently had shown the Arab world that Mubarak was standing guard over the rights of the Palestin-ians. I could see where and how this exercise in diplomatic agility was to Egypt's advantage, but how did it benefit the pursuit of peace?

Within weeks, I had a partial answer: Mubarak floated his own ten-point plan, presented to Washington via a traveling U.S. congressman in Cairo (Congressman William Gray), who was kind enough also to convey the text to Jerusalem, something the Egyptians had refrained from doing. Of the ten points, seven dealt directly with the preparation for, and the procedures during, the proposed elections. One called on Israel to agree to the land-for-peace formula; another demanded that all settlement activity be halted; the third required Israeli agreement to the participation in the elections of Arabs from East Jerusalem. "A way to implement the Shamir elections proposal," Baker was to call it later;

but that, of course, was absurd. None of these three points was acceptable to the government of Israel—as Mubarak well knew. By the beginning of September, however, the Labor faction in the Knesset, and the
Labor ministers, would begin to press for discussion of the Egyptian
ten points. I could not understand why; no one had formally notified
us of the existence of these points, as I told the Foreign Affairs and
Defense Committee on September 12. Why should we allow ourselves
to be sidetracked? What about the Israeli initiative? What was happening to that?

In the afternoon of the 12th, Shamir asked to see me. Rabin, returned
from a visit to the States, had just reported to him on a meeting with
Baker during which Baker had told him about the Mubarak points
("not an initiative; the Egyptians just want some explanations") and
asked for Israel's reaction. No notes had been taken at the meeting, nor
had Shamir or I been informed that it would take place. It was very
strange. Why would Israel's minister of defense hold one-on-one un-
scheduled, unrecorded talks with the U.S. secretary of state behind the
backs of Israel's prime minister and foreign minister? The answer was
hard to believe but inescapable: Mubarak had transmitted his proposals
to Bush, who had passed them on to Baker, who in turn had chosen to
transmit them not to me but to Rabin for what could only be political
reasons. It was neither the first nor the last time that Labor ministers
tried to subvert a government in which they served; but it was certainly
the first time that any U.S. administration had directly intervened in
Israeli internal affairs to further a policy of its own. Hostile and devious
speeches were one thing; active secret interference in the domestic
policies of a friendly nation conducted at the secretary of state–minister
of defense level quite another.

The next day, Shamir, Peres, Rabin, and I met, and Rabin, supported
by Peres, made his demand: either the government responds positively
to the Egyptian proposal or Peres and he might have to "draw conclusions." What proposal? So far we had seen nothing in writing. Well,
said Rabin, his voice rising, at least we must accept Mubarak's invitation
to come to Cairo to meet the Palestinian delegation for negotiations on
election modalities. Invitation? Evidently Mubarak's letter to Baker had
contained a four-point proposal relating to the elections and calling for
a PLO delegation (or, if not that, then a PLO-authorized delegation) to
meet with an Israeli representation in the Egyptian capital. I suggested
that there was no need for hurry; I would be seeing both Mubarak and

Baker at the UN General Assembly in a week or so and would be able to hear in greater detail from them about this Egyptian proposal. Rabin became very agitated. "An answer has to be given at once," he said, his face reddening; if not, he would go to the media and present his opinions publicly. He was willing to wait for a day or two but no longer.

Had Rabin also been dealing with the Egyptians behind our backs? When he had reported to Shamir on his talk with Baker there had been some mention of a possible meeting between Mubarak and himself, something hinted at in the press a few weeks before, and Shamir had then asked Rabin about that, only to draw a blank. All this talk about a meeting in Cairo when we had seen no invitation of any sort. Obviously a very tangled web was being woven, and Peres and Rabin knew more than they were prepared to reveal either to Shamir or to me.

We did not have to wait long for the next development. Within twenty-four hours, Baker phoned. He wanted to tell me how greatly he looked forward to meeting me in New York and to explaining "exactly where we stand now." Yes, and there was something else; before Rabin had arrived in Washington, President Bush had received "this letter" from Mubarak about setting up an Israeli dialogue with the Palestinians. "I would, of course, have conveyed the message to you, but since Rabin happened to be here, I gave it to him," Baker said, adding that he hoped this had not caused any complications.

Then he went on to say that the four Egyptian points were not being presented on a take-it-or-leave-it basis, everything was open to discussion, nothing was "locked in concrete." I told him that we had seen the four points but not within the context of the letter that Mubarak had apparently written to the President. "It would be a good thing, Jim," I said, "if we could see the letter itself." "There wasn't much in the letter," Baker replied, but he would ask the Egyptians if it was okay to send us a copy.

As for the points that specifically mentioned the PLO, I reminded him that Israel would not deal in any way with that organization. Yes, he had already told the Egyptians that these "suggestions" could not be cast in terms of PLO membership or authorization. Perhaps, I said, when I came to New York, he, Abd el-Meguid, and I could get together. Baker thought that would be fine, though it would be good if we could give him "some input" on our reaction to the "four points" before our meeting in New York. I told him I expected to see Mubarak there too and that I would be able to hear from him exactly what the Egyptians had in mind. "Great," said Baker, "but please try to get back to me before then." I promised to talk to Shamir and then call Baker to let him know whether we could provide him with the "input" he wanted. I said nothing about the fact that when I asked to meet with Bush on that same visit to the States, my request was not approved, though a presidential meeting had been scheduled for Peres. It was not less significant, I thought, that Baker had said nothing to me about any of this.

Two days later, at the next meeting of what the local press called "the gang of four," I reported on Baker's phone call. Rabin and Peres flew into a rage. There was no need to wait. Did I think I held the monopoly for speaking on the government's behalf? What was I going to say? Why not respond to the Egyptian invitation now? We went through the whole routine again. What invitation? To whom? Where was it issued? I said that I had asked Baker for a copy of the Mubarak letter to Bush, and Peres at once said sharply that there was no need for that either. "Why is it so important to see the words 'Dear Mr. President' on top of a letter?" he snapped. Subsequently, I saw the contents of the Mubarak letter to Bush. It included references to members of the Israeli cabinet who were in contact with the PLO—at the time this was illegal—and who were likely therefore to support the Egyptian points, and in retrospect partially explained Rabin and Peres's extraordinary behavior.

In the middle of this rather heated meeting, a note was sent in to Rabin; after reading it, he announced that there were "indications" that Mubarak might invite him for a meeting in Cairo. A few minutes later, another note was brought in to me. Ambassador Bassiouny was on his way to Jerusalem and would be most appreciative if I could see my way clear to receiving him right away. I replied that I would.

When we met, Bassiouny told me that he had just returned from Cairo, having been summoned there by Mubarak. The president was ready, if we agreed, to invite an Israeli and a Palestinian delegation to Cairo to talk about the election proposal; he himself would determine the composition of the Palestinian delegation, which would be made up entirely of Arabs living in Judea, Samaria, and Gaza, and there would also be two other Palestinians from abroad who would be chosen in coordination with us. There wasn't a word about Rabin, Peres, or letters to Bush. The Americans could be invited too if we wanted, but then the Russians should also be asked to come. The ambassador—adding that Mubarak had put much pressure on the PLO (including inviting Yasser Arafat to Cairo) in order to secure its approval—made no attempt to hide the obvious: in Cairo we would be presented with a list of PLO-approved names. And one more thing: Mubarak would meet me at the United Nations in New York on September 29.

It was the first official communication we had received about Mubarak's proposal; someone, perhaps Baker, must have alerted him to the possibility that propriety had been overstepped. For symmetry's sake, Bassiouny had been directed to convey the same message to a number of other people, to Peres and presumably also to Rabin, though the ambassador did not burden me with these facts.

On September 19, I flew to the States to discover that wherever I went, Peres had preceded me, arriving a day or two earlier, meeting the people I was to meet and appearing before audiences I too was to address, but bringing with him a very different message: that in reality there were two plans, the Shamir plan and the Mubarak plan. The latter had won Labor's support because of the two it seemed the more likely to lead to peace. He made it clear that a worthwhile alternative existed to the May initiative. As for the government's speaking in two voices, Peres unhesitatingly informed the *New York Times* that he had not come to the United States to "argue with Arens." If there was something I wanted to know, "he can give me a ring and I'll give him an answer." It had been in order to avoid such displays of government disunity, which did Israel little credit abroad, that Shamir had ordered a list of government policy guidelines to be drawn up "for the use of ministers meeting Baker and Mubarak," but even that didn't cramp the finance minister's anti-government rhetoric.

My first stop was Los Angeles. I had barely settled down in the hotel when the phone rang. It was Baker. First, I should know that the tripartite meeting—Abd el-Meguid, Baker and myself—had been arranged. Then he wanted me to know that his own view of the Egyptian proposal—the four points about which Mubarak had written to Bush, and the ten points Congressman Gray had delivered in Israel, having in the meantime evidently been elevated to a "proposal"—was that it constituted an acceptance of Israel's peace initiative. I could hardly believe what I was hearing. But this was not the time or the place to start a discussion.

Bush and Baker were reported to be "deeply concerned" about the fate of Israel's initiative and the conflicting statements being made by

Peres and myself. "We continue," Baker told a news conference, "to be committed to the Israeli election proposal [and] to view the Egyptian ten points as an acceptance, in effect, by Egypt of this proposal."

It was, of course, nothing of the kind. How could it be that Baker did not understand this, or understand that the Mubarak proposal was unacceptable to the government of Israel? In Israel, Rabin lauded the Mubarak plan as a "great and important step" in furthering the peace process, brushing aside charges that agreeing to the Cairo talks was tantamount to negotiating with the PLO, and ridiculing the Likud for its opposition to the plan. Shamir meanwhile crusaded against it in speech after speech, reiterating the Likud's view that Mubarak's invitation was "an invitation to enter into talks of capitulation" with those "who wave the banner of the Intifada." "If accepted," he warned, the Mubarak proposal would eventually require Israel to agree to "unacceptable principles," i.e., territory for peace and the participation of East Jerusalem Arabs in the proposed elections. Moreover, it ignored the vital interim arrangement during which each side could build up confidence in the other before negotiating the final status.

At the same time, in Egypt, Mubarak was also on a crusade. Encouraged by Labor and abandoning all customary channels of diplomatic communication, the president of Egypt appeared on television to appeal to Israelis directly that they press their government to accept his invitation. This was followed by another special event, only slightly less dramatic: the convening of a press conference for Israeli journalists in Cairo at which Arafat, flanked by Mubarak's personal aide, called upon the people of Israel to negotiate with the PLO, following Israel's withdrawal from the territories.

It stood to reason that most of the conversations people held with me at the UN General Assembly either began, or ended, with the peace initiative. But the most extraordinary of these meetings—in fact, perhaps the most extraordinary I have had anywhere—was the quarter of an hour or so that President Bush agreed to grant me between the reception and the dinner he was holding at the Metropolitan Museum of Art for the foreign ministers attending the Assembly. With all the formality with which one is traditionally escorted to the Oval Office, I was led to a cluster of marble statues where the president of the United States and his secretary of state stood awaiting me. There were no chairs near us; this was going to be a stand-up meeting. Nonetheless, the other amenities were observed. As at the White House, a "photo opportunity" was organized before the "meeting" began: the three of us grouped at the base of the fig-leafed figure of a naked youth: the president, glass in hand, all smiles; Baker, attentive at his side; I, trying not to be distracted by the surroundings or the fact that, somewhere beyond us, distinguished men and women from all over the world were waiting for their dinner.

I suppose those few minutes were intended to compensate me for Bush's meeting with Peres at the White House, but under the circumstances, all I could contribute to the session was that Israel was on the verge of a serious coalition crisis because, or so it was being made to appear, Mubarak wanted to deal exclusively with Labor. "But it's important," Bush said, "that the National Unity government continue." "Yes," I replied, "but what can you expect when Mubarak invites Rabin to Cairo? Maybe he doesn't understand how it looks, but it's a public snubbing of Shamir. I can't, at the moment, think of an American analogy but I'm sure there is one." "Oh, I know one," said Bush instantly, looking pleased with himself. "It's like Gorbachev inviting Ted Kennedy to Moscow." "No," I said, "it's even worse," and caught an enigmatic smile on Jim Baker's face. It was not entirely impossible, I reflected on the way to dinner, where I was seated next to his very charming wife, that even Baker was fleetingly embarrassed by the public snub that had just been administered to me.

The next afternoon, before I addressed the General Assembly, I met, as scheduled, with Baker in his hotel suite. Just the two of us, and I spoke my mind. We must base our efforts, I said, on two principles: first, that there would be more frequent communication between the parties linked in the peace process, unencumbered by the kind of political noise we were having now; and second, that we restrict ourselves to talking about specifics, not catch-alls such as the Egyptian ten points. In other words, damage containment, because damage had been done. We had a coalition crisis on our hands, which had to be repaired forthwith; a message should be sent around to everyone involved that, in Israel, Shamir was the man to talk to. Baker listened without interrupting me, just nodding now and then as if in accord with what I was saying; but when I told him it was important to arrive at a consensus among the United States, Egypt, and Israel on the election modalities, he shook his head. He didn't think that "would fly." How about the United States, Egypt, and Israel jointly composing the Palestinian delegation, he asked. I said, "How about telling Mubarak to meet with Shamir?"

We bargained briefly. Baker said, "Can I tell Mubarak that you agree to a U.S.-Egypt-Israel effort on the composition of the Palestinian delegation?" I said, "That will need government approval." He added that "we are trying to remove the cause of any unnecessary noise in the system such as, for instance, not letting Arafat come to the United Nations."

A little later on, from that General Assembly podium, I spoke once more of Israel's peace initiative:

> We call on all nations to support it and on the Arab world to respond favorably to it . . . not to attempt to wring concessions from Israel that relate to the permanent settlement. Our immediate objective must be to put an end to violence and to get negotiations going . . . if the representatives of the Palestinian Arab population will come to the negotiating table cognizant not only of the rights of the population that will have freely chosen them but also of Israel's rights and legitimate concerns, there is an excellent chance that negotiations will lead to agreement. I urge all member-nations of this organization to lend their support to Israel's continuing efforts to end warfare and bloodshed in the Middle East.

Then I named them one by one: " . . . I call on the representatives of Algeria, Bahrain, Djibouti, Iraq, Jordan, Kuwait, Lebanon, Libya, Mauritania, Morocco, Oman, Qatar, Saudi Arabia, Somalia, Sudan, Syria, Tunisia, the United Arab Emirates, the Yemen Arab Republic and the People's Democratic Republic of Yemen to utilize the opportunity of our presence at the UN General Assembly and meet with me to discuss how we can move from belligerency to peace, from hostility to friendship. The peace process requires courage, patience and perseverance. We expect your support." Even if they had not all walked out demonstratively before I began to speak, no one would have answered this call. I knew that, but it had to be made, and I also knew that we would go on making it until there was some response.

My "reunion" with Shevardnadze centered mainly on the problems of Israel's delegation in Moscow, which was having a very rough time: six people dealing with a mountain of work, ten thousand immigrant visas per month, poor communications with Israel, everything made difficult for them. He wrote it all down, said he would see what could be done, and promptly brought up the question of some Soviet property in Israel that had not yet been restored to his government. Would I see what could be done about that? We hardly talked about the peace process. Shevardnadze suggested that we meet with the PLO in the Soviet Union, together with representatives of the USSR and the U.S. governments, and I told him that I did not think this would speed up the peace process much, so we dropped the subject.

A meeting of a very different nature took place in New York that week. It was my encounter with Britain's new foreign secretary, John Major, who seemed to have forgotten that Britain had ceased to be the Mandatory power in Palestine over forty-one years ago and whose only questions to me were: "When will you finally leave Lebanon?" and "How long do you think you can sustain your present position?" "The problem with Israel is that it is growing," he continued. I asked him if he had ever been to "the area"; would he like to visit? He looked down his nose at me. Maybe, he said disagreeably, but only if he could also visit other places. Such arrogance and unpleasantness I had never encountered in any of my diplomatic dealings. When we parted, I asked him to give my best regards to Mrs. Thatcher and be sure to tell her that we had gotten along famously.

As soon as I turned up at Mubarak's Waldorf-Astoria suite, his earlier visitors, Boutros-Ghali and Abd el-Meguid, rose from their chairs, greeted me hastily, and vanished. Mubarak didn't even give me a chance to sit down; the moment the door closed behind his guests, he turned to me. "What are those statements you're making?" I assumed he was talking about statements I had made regarding his refusal to meet Shamir. Within seconds, we sat there like old friends and we talked for a long time. I spoke of Israel's anxiety lest the Iraqis might want to retaliate for the 1981 bombing of their nuclear reactor ("You've nothing to worry about as far as Iraq is concerned," Mubarak said authoritatively) and told him he had brought on a coalition crisis by inviting Rabin to Cairo. ("I can't understand why," Mubarak said. "He's a member of the Shamir government. I meet you; I meet him; I meet Peres.") I suggested that he call in Bassiouny for a quick rundown on the Israeli political scene. Actually, just the day before, I had commented to Baker that I thought perhaps Mubarak didn't understand how coalition governments work, and Baker, who understood this all too well, had said matter-of-factly, "Of course he doesn't; he's a dictator."

Mubarak asked what I thought he should do. "Meet with Shamir," I said, "then everyone will know that you are dealing with the National

Unity government." "Yes, although such a meeting would have to be very well prepared," Mubarak answered. "But we could talk about the ten points if I knew there was agreement on some of them and agreement to talk about the others." Then he smiled. "Maybe I should call Shamir?" I said, "Fine, I have his number right here. It's the eve of Rosh Hashanah, the Jewish New Year. I know he'll be at home."

I got through to Shamir immediately. "I'm sitting here with Mubarak, who would like to talk to you," I said to the prime minister. "Oi veh," said Shamir, and they talked. Mubarak told Shamir that he didn't want to bring down the National Unity government, and that he wanted to deal with Shamir, and to take this opportunity of wishing him a happy New Year.

I asked Mubarak why, when he had spoken at the General Assembly, he had not mentioned Israel's initiative or the election proposal. In fact, he had stated that the PLO was the sole legitimate representative of the Palestinians with which Israel must negotiate, after which should come an international conference to deal with a comprehensive peace settlement. "I can't talk at the UN about everything that's on my mind," he replied, meaning, I deduced, that his speech had been intended primarily for Arab consumption. As though he had read my thoughts, he said again that "not everything has to be spelled out," that he agreed with Baker's idea about how the list of "acceptable" Palestinians should be composed, and that we should not be "anxious" about the "outsiders" because the Palestinians outside of Israel "who had made all that money in Kuwait and Bahrain" would not want to return, nor would the others. "Nothing to worry about," he said with his usual self-assurance.

The day I left the United States, Baker phoned to say that Mubarak, who had met with President Bush in Washington, was "prepared" to be very responsive to our concerns and agreed to a coordinated approach on the composition of the Palestinian delegation. Also he would send Abd el-Meguid to Israel in the near future. I told Baker that Mubarak seemed ready to meet with Shamir. Well, said Baker, even a blind hog will find an acre of corn. Then he went on to say that a possible result of such a meeting would be some agreement between Shamir and Mubarak which would be short of what the Egyptians wanted, and that they would arrive at a statement confirming that a dialogue would take place between Israelis and Palestinians with respect to the elections. The agenda for the dialogue would be the elections and the interim arrangements. "No," I said, "the agenda has to be only the elections. The interim arrangements are something to be negotiated with the people who are elected."

"How about our saying that the agenda will be the election proposal in accordance with Israel's peace initiative?" asked Baker.

"That's fine; that's just what we want," I replied.

CHAPTER 4

Telephone Diplomacy

I returned to Israel the morning of October 4, feeling satisfied with the understandings I had reached with Baker. In the afternoon I reported to Shamir on the secretary's agreement that the agenda for the Israeli-Palestinian dialogue would consist of "the election procedures in accordance with Israel's peace initiative," and suggested to him that we accept the American proposition for determining the composition of the Palestinian delegation. There was a certain reticence in Shamir's reaction; he neither agreed nor disagreed, but simply asked me to report at the Likud ministers' meeting the following morning, and thereafter at the meeting of the inner cabinet, where Peres and Rabin would also report on their recent trips.

By the time we met the next morning we had been presented with an Egyptian initiative, which came as a total surprise to me but, it seemed, was no surprise to Peres. Bassiouny had transmitted to Peres, Rabin, Shamir, and myself an invitation to begin negotiations with a Palestinian delegation in Cairo, the composition of the delegation presumably being determined by the PLO and the agenda seemingly unlimited. The invitation was actually delivered to Peres and Rabin at a meeting of the Labor party ministers the previous night, giving them the opportunity to decide right then and there that they would enter a motion to accept the Egyptian invitation at the inner cabinet's meeting in the morning.

The invitation was a radical departure from the understandings I had reached in Washington. The unprecedented manner in which it had been submitted, without any prior coordination with our Foreign Ministry, and Labor's immediate acceptance even before their ministers had been briefed by me on my meetings with Mubarak, Abd el-Meguid, and Baker in Washington, were an obvious indication of a coordinated effort by Peres and the Egyptians to bypass the agreement I had secured.

When the Likud ministers met at eight-fifteen in the morning, the story of the Egyptian invitation and Labor's decision to propose that the invitation be accepted had already been broadcast on the morning news. The meeting became quite stormy. Sharon, Levy, and Moda'i demanded that the Likud ministers oppose the Labor proposal. They were not placated by the agreement I had reached with Baker regarding the composition of the Palestinian delegation and the agenda of the proposed dialogue.

At the inner cabinet meeting, everything started off as planned: Rabin and Peres reported on their respective trips, and Peres also announced that he would enter a motion to accept the Egyptian invitation received the previous night. I reported on Baker's proposal, instantly running into crossfire from both blocs, the more ferocious onslaught mounted by members of my own party. The "constrainers" were in an uproar. Was there really such a U.S. proposal? If so, why had it not been submitted in writing? How could I have failed to ask for a written text? Sharon, Levy, and Moda'i demanded to see the proposal with their own eyes. They were joined by some of the Labor ministers in casting doubts on the veracity of my report.

That night I telephoned Baker from my home. I had by now realized that there was little room for unlimited trust in this game, and asked two members of our young guard, Dan Meridor and Ehud Olmert, to listen in on the conversation and take notes. I told Baker of that morning's inner cabinet meeting and the request that he provide his proposal in writing. "I know," he interrupted. "It's all been reported to me, but I understand that you said at the meeting that the agenda would consist solely of the election proposal."

I reminded him of our last conversation on the phone when he had called me in New York from Washington. "That is what you and I agreed upon," I said. "Tell me exactly what it is that you want to see in writing," he said. So I dictated to Baker (and he said he was writing it down): " 'The composition of the Palestinian delegation will be determined by the U.S., Egypt, and Israel. Each side will have the right to veto. The Palestinian delegation will discuss with the Israeli delegation the electoral procedures as proposed by Israeli's peace initiative.' That," I said, "is what you and I agreed and what you said to me on the phone, and what they want to see in black and white." It would take a few days, Baker said; he would have to talk to the Egyptians.

When the inner cabinet continued its meeting the next day, I read from the minutes taken at the New York "tripartite" meeting Baker's urging that we consider his suggestion that "the U.S., Egypt, and Israel will come up with an acceptable list of names"; from the record of a Baker press conference held on October 2 the same suggestion, to which he then added "that would give . . . Israel a chop on the people in the occupied territories who would be representing the Palestinians"; and from a cabled dispatch sent by Moshe Arad, Israel's ambassador in Washington, the report of a conversation with the assistant secretary of state for Middle Eastern Affairs, John Kelly, in which Kelly stated that the U.S. position on the agenda of the proposed meeting was "the same as that of the Israeli government." I also reported on the previous night's telephone conversation with Baker and that he had said it would take him a few days to get his proposal in writing to us. That must have sounded strange to the assembled ministers, who had heard on the morning news that a "high State Department official" had told the Israeli radio's correspondent in Washington, Oded Ben-Ami, that Baker had not been asked for his proposal in writing by me.

When I finished, Shamir amazed me. "All right," he said, "then there is no American proposal; in the meantime let's go on with our discussion." Peres wanted to put the Labor proposal to a vote, and a discussion ensued. When my turn came to speak, I began with what I thought was the heart of the matter, an appeal for unity, basing it on the assumption that Labor and the Likud had a common interest in moving the peace process forward. It was up to us to look again at the Palestinian factor, which was in many ways the most intractable in the overall Arab-Israeli conflict. "The real choices before us are limited," I pointed out; "we can perhaps go on looking for other solutions, maybe some eventual arrangement with Jordan, though the Palestinian population has no desire to be ruled or represented by King Hussein; we could annex the territories as we did East Jerusalem and the Golan Heights, giving the Palestinians the option of Israeli citizenship, with all the problems that would entail. But nobody is suggesting that now. What remains, therefore, is to implement the decision we made when we launched the initiative: to hold elections so we can, at long last, begin to communicate with elected representatives of the Palestinian population in Judea, Samaria, and Gaza . . . a concession, if you like, requiring us to recognize this population and its grievances and aspirations, but without recognizing the PLO.

"This is an hour for caution, discretion, and unity," I went on to stress. "If we are to be effective in the crucial days ahead, we must speak with one voice, keep the debate among ourselves in this forum, do whatever we can to ensure the best possible conditions for Israel and, together, stand guard over Israel's vital interests . . . rather than bicker in public or belittle our initiative for the benefit of others. . . ."

When the discussion ended, Shamir asked the Labor ministers not to put their motion to a vote. Since the inner cabinet was evenly divided between Likud and Labor, there could only be a tie, which would mean that the motion had failed.

"I know," Peres replied, "that strictly speaking you are right, but once this vote is taken we are going to have a new political situation in Israel." No one asked him to spell out the meaning of this dramatic statement, because it was clear that for the past weeks he had done everything possible to maneuver the government into just this situation, and now he seemed confident that he held the cards for forming a new coalition, and that the vote on this motion might well be the starting point.

Shamir finally relented: the vote was held and the result was 6–6. The Labor ministers—my plea for unity disregarded—streamed out of the room to inform the press that a onetime opportunity to advance the peace process had been missed by the Likud.

In the afternoon, I called Baker to tell him what had transpired at the meeting. Once again, he seemed to know what I was going to say. "The Egyptians feel that they can get more through the Labor party," Baker interjected. "I'm trying to work on them to see if we can get something agreeable to all sides." When I expressed the hope that we might be able to repair the damage once we received his proposal in writing, I was astonished to hear him say, "I didn't understand that you were asking for something in writing when you spoke to me yesterday."

Was this simply a misunderstanding, or was there more here than met the eye? And why were the Labor ministers so certain that I would not be able to present Baker's proposal in writing? I thought that it would be inappropriate to tell him that I had a written record of our previous conversation, but simply repeated to him the contents of that conversation, emphasizing the reason I had asked him to send me his proposal in writing, and that I had dictated to him the two elements of the proposal.

"Look, we have to clear the air. I thought that we had established an atmosphere of mutual trust, and now I see it's nothing of the sort," I said. "Don't worry about it, it's okay, there's really no problem here," was his response.

Baker went on to identify the two issues that he thought required agreement: the agenda and whether the Egyptians would be able to hold preliminary discussions with the Palestinian delegation. He didn't mention the issue of the composition of the Palestinian delegation. "Could the dialogue begin with the Palestinians making an opening statement?" he asked, to which I replied, "Maybe." Baker added that he detected some reluctance on the part of the Egyptians to stay engaged. "But I'm going to keep at it, I'll talk to them," he said. I could only assume that the Egyptians were already well informed about yesterday's meeting and had been disappointed that the Likud ministers had not given in to Labor's onslaught.

Three hours later Baker called me with a brand-new proposition, the previous one now entirely forgotten. "This is a real effort that I'm making," he said, and started to read out a five-point proposal:

1. The U.S. understands that because Egypt and Israel had been working hard on the peace process there is agreement that an Israeli delegation should conduct a dialogue with a Palestinian delegation in Cairo.
2. The U.S. understands that Egypt cannot substitute itself for the Palestinians and will consult with the Palestinians on all aspects of the dialogue. Egypt will also consult with Israel and the U.S.
3. The U.S. understands that Israel will attend the dialogue only after a satisfactory list of Palestinians has been worked out. Israel will also consult with Egypt and the U.S.
4. The U.S. understands that the Government of Israel will come to the dialogue on the basis of the Israeli Government May 14 initiative.

The U.S. further understands that the Palestinians will come to the dialogue prepared to discuss elections and negotiations in accordance with Israel's initiative. The U.S. understands, therefore, that the Palestinians will be free to raise issues that relate to their opinion on how to make elections succeed.
5. In order to facilitate this process the U.S. proposes that the Foreign Ministers of Israel, Egypt, and the U.S. meet in Washington within two weeks.

He admitted that he had already spoken to Abd el-Meguid about the proposal, who had told him that he would have to talk to Mubarak and the Palestinians about it. I could see the Egyptian hand in the formulation, which deviated significantly from the agreement Baker and I had reached in New York that had been approved by Mubarak at the time. "I have no reaction as yet from the Egyptians," Baker continued. "Will you please talk to the prime minister and give me your reaction as soon as you can? I'm going off to Texas for the weekend; my mother is sick and I'm going to visit her." He went on to say that he had "jumped hard" on Abd el-Meguid. "I told him, don't play party politics in Israel." Then, after urging me to go to work on this and not let any time go by, came the bombshell—"Should I communicate this to Rabin?" Keeping my cool, I told him it would be better if he did not, but I had to assume that Rabin might already have seen it.

In the evening, I met with Shamir to discuss Baker's new proposition. I also asked Meridor and Olmert to attend. We agreed that it deviated significantly from his original proposal, which he evidently was not prepared to submit to us in writing, and that we could not accept it as it was. I tried to reach Baker all evening; he finally reached me at 11:30 P.M. "Look, Jim," I told him, "we have problems with your draft; this is some distance from what we agreed to in New York. We will send you our suggested revisions." "Okay," he replied, "tell me what you agree to, and then I'll call Abd el-Meguid and tell him that we are close and try to get agreement out of him." Then he entered into dangerous territory: "Egypt seems to want to stall the whole process until Wednesday; they thought they had somebody in your government who was more accommodating—I told them to drop it." Peres? Rabin? Probably both. And what were the Egyptians expecting to happen by next Wednesday? Almost as if he were reading my thoughts, Baker continued: "I would like to work this out with you and Abd el-Meguid. When will I have your response?" "I'll send it to you in a day or two," I said.

Our response to Baker's five points once again stressed that the government of Israel wished to proceed with the peace initiative but would not deal with the PLO. If the PLO was in, Israel was out, and there should be no "misunderstanding" about this between the United States and Israel. Therefore the composition of the Palestinian delegation would have to be agreed upon in advance by Israel, Egypt, and the United States, and the Cairo agenda must consist solely of the election procedures in accordance with our peace initiative—within which context the Palestinians would be free to raise issues, make suggestions, and convey ideas. Shamir approved the text and I asked Salai Meridor to call Baker's assistant, Dennis Ross, and read it to him, since Baker was away in Texas.

That evening was Yom Kippur eve, the holiest day in the Jewish calendar, a day set aside for prayer, atonement, forgiveness, and fasting. At the synagogue in Savyon, someone came over to me to point out that one of the prayers for that day was for a year of "negotiation and peace."

The day after Yom Kippur, October 10, I was attending a dinner in Tel Aviv in honor of the departing Dutch ambassador when a call from Baker came through. He said he had received our suggestions for changes in his draft and expected to receive a "redraft" from Abd el-Meguid as well, who, he said, wanted to include Mubarak's ten points. "You know the Egyptians are consulting with the Palestinians, want to continue to consult with them, and want it mentioned in the draft," Baker said.

I knew full well that meant the PLO in Tunis, but he was not about to say that. "Why does this have to be spelled out in your draft?" I asked.

"Well," Baker said, "you have certain needs and Egypt has certain needs; our document gives you both. I suggest we come to an agreement so that we can have the dialogue."

"But why not go back to the agreement that we had in New York?" I pursued.

"Look, I didn't pretend that I was speaking for the Egyptians in New York."

"But Mubarak agreed, he told me that he agreed to your proposal, and you told me that when he met with the president he gave his agreement," I said.

Baker just said: "Look, if we redraft this document we won't get closure." And then he again brought up Rabin. He knew, as well as I, that there was little justification for substantive relations between the defense minister of Israel and the U.S. secretary of state. Perhaps he sensed that I suspected such a relationship had already been established.

"I haven't talked to Rabin. Would you object if I talked to him, if I let the Labor party see the draft?" Baker asked.

"I don't think you ought to do that; as you know, once the Likud agrees, Labor will automatically agree. If it now gets into the hands of Labor it will just cause complications."

Then Baker returned to the draft. "You know the Egyptians want to talk to the Palestinians."

"Why do you have to spell that out in your document? We need less wording, not more—the less wording we have in the document the easier it is going to be to come to an agreement."

"Look, according to my document you are not sitting down with the PLO. We want to see this thing proceed; so why don't you make an effort?"

"I'll talk to the prime minister, but I suggest that you think about reducing the wordage in the document."

Baker said he would think about it, but could not get the Labor party off his mind. "Maybe I should talk to Labor. I'm concerned I might get a negative knee-jerk reaction from them because they have not been consulted." I explained that in the Israeli government there was only one foreign minister, and that was me. At the end of the conversation he urged me to come to the meeting of the three foreign ministers, saying that if it did not work out to my satisfaction I could always leave. But I let him know that I was not about to get trapped in a situation where the burden for the dialogue not taking place at the last minute, or breaking up, would be on Israel.

I had decided to tell the Egyptians how I felt about their latest maneuvering, but first I asked our ambassador in Cairo, Shimon Shamir, to come to Jerusalem to give me his evaluation of what was going on there. Shamir, a professor of Middle East History fluent in Arabic, had been appointed to his post by Peres when he was foreign minister, and had offered to resign when I assumed office. I had asked him to stay on because I valued his knowledge of Egypt, his contacts there, and his judgment. He had met with Abd el-Meguid the day before coming to see me and discussed the subject of the Israeli-Palestinian dialogue with him. His impression was that the Egyptians had gotten cold feet about the agreement that was reached in New York and decided to send their invitation prior to the meeting of our inner cabinet, in a last-minute attempt to sidetrack that agreement.

Bassiouny arrived at my office looking innocent and eager to please. Without the usual courtesies, I admonished him for interfering in internal Israeli politics, telling him that Egypt should be interested in the continuation of the present coalition government so that we could progress with the peace process. Bassiouny denied any wrongdoing and insisted that creating a rift between Likud and Labor was the furthest thing from his mind. He was communicating first and foremost with me, he claimed. "If you had a new proposal," I told him, "you would have done better bringing it to me first, instead of presenting it simultaneously to Peres, Rabin, Shamir, and myself the night before the inner cabinet meeting. I could have told you what the chances are of the invitation being accepted and maybe guided you in its formulation. As a veteran diplomat, you must have known that it is accepted diplomatic practice to coordinate an invitation before it is issued." He listened to me with a crestfallen look; I think he could tell that I did not fall for his explanations. I assumed he had only followed instructions from Cairo and could only hope that my message would have some effect when received there.

Although I had suggested to Baker that the best way to reach agreement would be to shorten his document, we were beginning to move in the opposite direction, discussing side letters to provide sufficient assurances to make the basic document palatable. Dennis Ross had broached this possibility to Salai and it looked like it might be the only way to avoid an impasse.

Knowing that the Sephardi religious party, Shas, was the weak link in our coalition and that Peres was actively courting them, I asked the man who set the tone in that party—Aryeh Deri, the minister of the interior—to come see me. Deri, the youngest minister in the government, was also considered one of the ablest, and an acknowledged master of the political game. Our conversation made it clear to me that Shas had no intention of abandoning the benefits the party derived from membership in the government, and would join Peres in a Labor-led government if Peres were to succeed in putting it together. Deri's explanation was that in recent meetings with Shamir he had gotten the impression that Shamir did not want to advance the peace initiative.

I decided that the time had come for a talk with Rabin, and I went over to the Defense Ministry to see him. It felt a little strange walking into my old office and seeing Rabin sitting behind what used to be my desk. He was in a good mood. Saying that he could not speak for Peres, Rabin emphasized that he was opposed to breaking up the government. He said that he certainly would like to see an improved version of Baker's five points, encouraging me to try to obtain the best possible document for the Israeli-Palestinian dialogue. He opposed participation in the delegation of Palestinians from the "outside," but did not care if Palestinians who had been expelled participated because they were, in effect, still residents of the area.

Rabin added that he favored the participation of Jerusalem Arabs in the elections, because this was consistent with his overall view regarding the permanent solution of the conflict. "I want," he said, "to establish the precedent that Arabs living in Israel who are not Israeli citizens vote in elections outside Israel, not in Israel itself." We tossed that around for a while, but I said it wasn't really relevant since what was under discussion were elections for Palestinians who would negotiate with Israel on the future status of the population they represented. For Arabs from East Jerusalem to take part in such elections would mean that the government of Israel regarded the status of Jerusalem as negotiable—which it was not. And Rabin appeared to have no objection to the idea of the side letters. I suggested that he talk these matters over in some depth with Shamir because it would be good for the prime minister to know that Rabin agreed that we should try to speak with one voice on the issues we faced.

During the next few days, I was in and out of Shamir's office a lot; I could see the strain he was under, that his entire being was alerted to what he perceived as the dangers surrounding Israel, and that his intuition dictated digging in, not following any course that he felt might injure Israel then or in the future. All around him, even within his own government, there were people who wanted to push Israel back to the 1967 borders, and he was not about to cooperate in that effort. As far as he was concerned, Baker's five points were nothing but attempts to have us sit down with the PLO. "We don't need that dialogue right now," he said, "certainly not as presently envisioned." But whatever he said to others, or to himself, he knew that he might not be able to sustain the course he wanted, and that the government would probably fall, with Labor succeeding in forming a narrow-based alternative and the Likud going back into opposition after thirteen years in power. At any rate, it was difficult to discuss the dialogue with him. I urged him to speak to President Bush. Although Shamir put it off for a day or two, on October 17 they talked. Nothing very important was said, but Shamir described it as a "good" talk in which they had agreed that there must be more contact between Washington and Jerusalem, and that I should speak to Baker about this.

Baker and I talked the next day—a long conversation, forty minutes, weaving back and forth over much the same ground. Baker said it was difficult to make any changes in the five points, but he was ready to consider minor changes if we submitted them; and he would give us assurances on the two major points of concern to us, though they would have to be "discreet." But wouldn't it be a good idea (I thought not) to have each of the parties make an opening statement without constraints? I also said that I didn't know if these assurances could be kept discreet, to which Baker said, "Well, then don't use the word 'assurances.'"

What Baker most desired, I thought, was success; and what he most feared was failure ("I don't want to get burned," he had said). Perhaps he really wanted peace for the Middle East and for Israel, but what he wanted more was to bring it off, and he took great care not to become too intimately associated with any aspect of this venture that might end up a fiasco. It was both strange and disturbing to me that Baker had no curiosity at all about Israel, what it looked like, how Israelis lived. "I'm not coming to Israel," he said. Perhaps one of his people could come or we could send someone to Washington, I suggested. "Too much visibility," he said. I promised to consider the deal he was proposing— the five points plus assurances—but that wasn't enough for him. He put in a call to Shamir, telling the prime minister that while he wasn't sure the five points could be changed, he was ready to give the assurances. But Shamir wasn't going to settle anything on the phone, so Baker had to agree to our sending someone to Washington, although he told Shamir that this would have to be done in "total secrecy." Shamir didn't ask why and Baker refrained from any explanation.

Following a few more rounds on the telephone, it was decided to put things into writing. Israel had two suggestions for amendments to the five points, as I wrote to Baker on October 23.

> These changes are minor textual modifications but are essential to Israel. . . . They fall into two straightforward categories which will come

as no surprise to you. . . . Any suggestion or implication that Israel meet with Palestinians selected directly or indirectly by the PLO . . . flatly contradicts the spirit and the letter of the American-endorsed Israeli peace initiative. Accordingly I recommend a return to your original suggestion that the Palestinian delegation [to the dialogue] . . . be determined by Egypt, the United States and Israel. And . . . given our shared commitment to democratic principles, you will understand that substantive issues can only be negotiated with freely elected Palestinian representatives. An Israeli-Palestinian dialogue makes sense if it advances elections. If it does not, it contradicts the Israeli peace initiative and ill-serves the cause of peace. In order to be sure that the Israeli-Palestinian dialogue is not deflected from the elections, the dialogue must be directed only at the election procedures. The proposed revisions are the minimum required to make sure that the five point framework cannot be interpreted in a manner inconsistent with Israel's peace initiative.

I ended with the plea: "Let us move together, quickly and decisively, [for] free elections among the Palestinian residents of Judea, Samaria and Gaza, elections which hold so much promise of reversing the tragic spiral of hostility in this region. . . ." Shamir approved the letter for sending off through the good offices of Bill Brown, and I left for Brussels and a meeting of Israeli ambassadors to the European Community countries to discuss relations between Israel and the Community.

On my second day in Belgium, Baker phoned me, sounding quite upbeat. He had spoken to Abd el-Meguid and "worked" with him on the composition of the Palestinian delegation and removing the word "negotiations" from the agenda. He would call me back in a day or two to let me know how he fared in his attempt to persuade the Egyptians to accept these modifications.

At week's end, he was on the phone again, this time to tell me that he was going to be traveling but hoped to have everything "tied up" by November 1. Obviously he hadn't made much headway with the Egyptians.

On November 1, I was in the Knesset replying to a Labor MK's berating of the Likud for various sins of omission and commission, when Baker called once more. He was in California (it must have been 3:00 A.M. there) on his way to Australia; he hadn't been able to sell the Egyptians his original suggestion about the composition of the delegation being determined by Israel, Egypt, and the United States, but I should know that this was the meaning which he himself would attach

In an election campaign debate with Labor's Ezer Weizman in September 1988.

With Prime Minister Yitzhak Shamir at a meeting with Israeli Arabs. Their support for the Likud surprised everybody but me.

3

With Prime Minister Margaret Thatcher in London in February 1989. After our meeting I told the waiting press that Israel had a friend at 10 Downing Street.

At a meeting with Egyptian President Hosni Mubarak in New York on September 29, 1989. The atmosphere was friendly, agreement was reached, but problems arose shortly afterward.

5

Soviet Foreign Minister
Eduard Shevardnadze
suggested Israel meet with the
PLO in Moscow. I declined
the invitation.

Addressing the UN General
Assembly in September 1989,
I invited the representatives of
all the Arab nations present to
meet with me to discuss
Israel's peace initiative. All
twenty delegates walked out.

6

At a trilateral meeting in New York with U.S. Secretary of State James Baker and Egyptian Foreign Minister Ismat Abd el-Meguid in September 1989.

Air force, navy, and ground troops lined up to salute Israel's new defense minister on June 12, 1990.

9

With President George Bush at the White House on February 11, 1991, during the Gulf War. The enemy of our enemy did not turn out to be our friend.

10

German Foreign Minister Hans Dietrich Genscher offered his support during a visit to the Defense Ministry at the height of the Gulf War when Israel was under attack by Iraqi Scud missiles.

11   The destruction caused in Israel's urban centers by Iraqi Scuds had not been seen anywhere in the Western world since World War II. One of eight Scuds launched against Israel on January 25, 1991, landed in a suburban neighborhood of Ramat Gan.

With Lieutenant General Ehud Barak, my choice as chief of staff of the IDF.

I met with U.S. Secretary of Defense Dick Cheney after the Gulf War to discuss security and arms control in the Middle East. We kept in regular contact during the war via a secure telephone link the Americans had dubbed "Hammer Rick."

Shamir and I met with Jim Baker in October 1991 in preparation for the historic Madrid Conference. Whatever else happened, nothing would alter the fact that the Syrians, Jordanians, Lebanese, and Palestinians were officially going to meet with Israelis to talk about peace.

15

Reviewing an IDF exercise in Judea. To my right is Major General Danny Yatom, commander of the Central Region, and behind me, my aide Colonel Shimon Hefetz.

With new Prime and Defense Minister Yitzhak Rabin, Chief of Staff Ehud Barak, and Colonel Hefetz at the changing of the guard at the Defense Ministry, July 14, 1992. I was a private citizen for the first time in eighteen years.

16

to the points as currently written. As for the word "negotiation," he had suggested that it be replaced by "negotiating process." He would send the "redraft" to Egypt and to us, and hoped that we would both have answers for him by the time he got back to Washington on November 8.

When he finished this exposition, which didn't impress me as having advanced anything, I told Baker that there was no use thinking that concessions would be wrung from Shamir when the White House was so obviously procrastinating by not fixing a date for him to meet with Bush, although the prime minister was due to visit the United States on November 15 to address various Jewish organizations. Withholding an invitation until the very last minute was a clear instance of the administration's punishing Shamir and/or members of his government for refusing to accede to the president's or the secretary of state's wishes. Nor had any attempt been made to conceal this fact. "It has to be a two-way street," Baker said. "You haven't given us anything so far." But, he added with his customary caution, it wasn't his decision to make; the White House decided these matters. That night, the "redraft" came. It said pretty much what Baker had said to me on the phone, and Bill Brown, delivering it, commented that the United States was not going to let the PLO play any role in the process.

Next day, the Likud ministers, minus the "constrainers," met to agree that we could accept the five points as now amended, provided there was agreement on the assurances. On November 3, Shamir and I met with Rabin and Peres at Peres's Tel Aviv apartment; Peres had just been discharged from the hospital and was a bit subdued. My impression was that he would accept anything suggested as long as he wasn't odd man out. Rabin agreed that the assurances were very important. Eli Rubinstein was asked to draft a summary of the assurances to see if an agreement between us could be reached on them, even though, in the background, the "constrainers" beat away on their drums, demanding that the five points, never mind the amendments, be rejected out of hand.

In Cairo, Mubarak (who had just met with Arafat in Geneva) announced that only the PLO could accept or reject the five points and that Egypt was merely a conduit, not a spokesman, for the PLO. I called Baker in Australia and read Mubarak's statement to him. "Things were beginning to move fairly well here," I said, "until this bombshell was thrown at us. So Egypt is not a partner and it is indeed with the

PLO that we are engaged. I hope you agree that this is not helpful?"
Baker said that he did agree and asked that I send him the exact text of
Mubarak's statement and he would then speak to Abd el-Meguid about
it.

By the time the assurances we wanted had been drafted in Washington, which took a few days, the five points had turned to six—the
addition being that the United States would publicly support Israel's
position should we decide that there was any contravention of what had
been agreed upon. The Alignment had produced its own version of the
points, with only trivial differences between the two texts. And there
were more diatribes against the points and assurances by Moda'i,
Sharon, and Levy. But on November 5, the framework (always assuming
that the assurances would be forthcoming) was accepted by the government. When all was said and done, an important step had been taken
in the right direction: the way was now more or less open to a dialogue
with the Palestinians, without Israel having to negotiate with the PLO
or retract any part of its peace initiative. When I handed Bill Brown a
copy of our decision, he smiled broadly and said: "This is a historic
moment," and I told him that we would probably have a succession of
such historic moments in the months to come.

My schedule involved considerable travel, but wherever I was in the
first half of that November, the points, the assurances, and Baker's
communications followed me. We spoke on the phone when I was in
Tokyo and he was in Australia. He told me he was glad the government
was going along with his proposal and that he was drafting a letter to
me containing the assurances. It arrived on November 10, while I was
still in Japan. It was not exactly what we had anticipated. Opening with
"I am sensitive to the reality that these issues relate to critical questions
of survival and well-being," repeating that he hoped the assurances
would "remain out of the public eye," Baker wrote that "there will be
no surprises regarding with whom Israel will sit," nor would anyone
"force Israel to sit with anyone you feel unable to sit with." But, "at the
same time . . . the U.S. cannot become the guarantor of any Palestinian
on the list or of any position a Palestinian on the list might take. To
avoid surprises and to work out the 'satisfactory' list, I see, as I have
said to you, a clear link between Point Three and Point Five of the
framework, the meeting of the three foreign ministers in Washington."
The substantive issue in the dialogue, he continued, would be the elections and how to get to them. "However I have also indicated to you

and Ismat [Abd el-Meguid] my understanding that each side will have the opportunity to address broader issues of its own choosing in opening statements."

The "assurances" were non-specific and familiar: continued U.S. support for the general principles of the Israeli government peace initiative and for a policy "designed to bring about the kind of peace that will ensure Israel's security, promote Israel's recognition and acceptance throughout the region and enhance Israel's well-being." The letter ended with the statement that "the President is looking forward to discussing the peace process with the Prime Minister during their meeting next week" (the reward, I supposed, for the cabinet decision), and a line to the effect that Baker was waiting for a definitive response from the Egyptians. Despite its final words ("Misha, as the result of your cabinet's decision, we stand on the brink of an important opportunity to scale the walls of hostility and rejection that have divided the Middle East far too long"), the letter served only to heighten my growing concern.

What perturbed me was not the measure of warmth or coolness or even the sincerity of Baker's letter or the circumstances surrounding the graceless invitation to Shamir, but Baker's backsliding (between September and November) from the positions he had originally taken in favor of positions that were closer to those demanded by the PLO. In the course of the past three months, at Baker's instigation and probably under his personal guidance, a new game had begun. The United States had stopped pretending that the discussions were trilateral among itself, Israel, and Egypt. No one, Baker included, was making much effort anymore to conceal that it was not Egypt's response to the new version of Baker's points that everyone was awaiting, but that of the PLO, a fact which Baker apparently counted on our being able to deduce for ourselves—as we had now done. Mubarak had been telling the truth. Egypt was only a "conduit" to the PLO; and Baker had known this all along.

So the masks were off everywhere. No one looked better without them, but it was easier to breathe, and healthier for us to know who was who, not only in Washington and Cairo but also at home. There remained no doubt in my mind that there was collusion between Peres, perhaps also Rabin, and the Egyptians (much of it probably made possible by Bassiouny), in addition to whatever contacts Peres and his people were maintaining, in defiance of the law, with the PLO. Nor did much remain surreptitious about Peres's parallel attempts to establish an alternate narrow-based government while still a member of the inner councils of this one. It would be, I thought, nothing short of miraculous if the National Unity government survived these various machinations long enough to achieve, even partially, what only less than half a year ago it had set out to do.

I needed to let Baker know how we felt about the co-option of the PLO into the contacts and negotiations. Writing to him on November 20, I listed the steps Israel had taken thus far to arrive at an agreed formula for the dialogue, and expressed my personal dismay at "certain developments which threaten to set back the prospects for free and open elections among the Palestinian residents of Judea, Samaria and Gaza. . . . " I added that at every point in the discussions between us, "we have emphasized the unacceptability of negotiations with the PLO. In the contentious world of Israeli political life, [this] is one of the few unifying principles . . . the foundation on which the National Unity Government was established and the Cabinet's approval of the five points explicitly based. The extent that U.S. actions have created the impression that the PLO has been co-opted into what started out as Israeli-Egyptian-U.S. consultations, these actions are a source of deep concern to us." I signed the letter knowing that it would have very little impact on Baker.

The notes in my diary around that time reflect the progress of my anxieties.

November 21: Much going back and forth between the PLO Executive in Tunis and Cairo . . . it looks as though the PLO has rejected Baker's "redraft," although as of today Egypt has not yet transmitted this answer to the U.S. Or is Israel being taken for a ride? This seems not impossible: what is being said to the PLO, partly through the Egyptians but mostly by the Americans, is contrary to all our understandings with them.

November 23: Nothing has as yet been heard from the Egyptians . . . but we know that [they] are working on the PLO to provide at least a positive-sounding answer . . . while at the same time Baker is pulling all stops out to have promises passed on to the PLO to assuage [it] and he expects them to come around with an answer the Egyptians can transmit. Over the past two weeks, what began as a U.S.-Egypt-Israel contact has turned into a U.S.-Egypt-Palestinian contact. . . .

November 24: Shamir back on Friday. He was raked over the coals in

Washington. . . . I suppose that they think that maybe they can get him to push the peace process forward by pressuring him and maybe he hopes that the Americans will give up and leave us alone. But I believe that if the Baker proposals don't produce a positive result, we will have to find other ways.

December 3: It is now close to four weeks since Baker sent the letter to Abd el-Meguid and myself asking for principal agreement on the five point proposal, and until today the Egyptians had not replied. But apparently the PLO has finally come up with an answer, though rather ambiguously couched. It does not include a positive response to Baker's five points.

No wonder Baker had still not heard from the Egyptians. According to our information, the PLO had gone back to long-discarded first principles: it had insisted on being the sole representative of the Palestinians in the Israeli-Palestinian dialogue; that Palestinians from "outside" also be brought in; and that the dialogue be held under international auspices as a prelude to the international conference—all points unacceptable to Israel, as everyone knew.

So who would move next, and in what direction? I could be certain of only one thing: Baker would phone me soon. And in the late afternoon of December 4, the call came through. He was aboard Air Force One, returning with President Bush to Washington from Brussels after having reported to the NATO ministers on the Bush-Gorbachev Malta Summit.

"I just wanted to let you know what transpired at the summit regarding the Middle East," Baker said. He told me that Gorbachev had been very optimistic about the possibility of peace in the Middle East and that Bush had seized upon the opportunity to raise the question—as Shamir had asked him to do—of Soviet diplomatic relations with Israel. Gorbachev had not given the president an unequivocal answer, but Baker's impression was that it was only a matter of "when," not "if."

That was the good news, although I had my doubts about the advisability of resuming diplomatic relations at this particular stage because I suspected that U.S.-USSR coordination was among the last things we needed just then. The bad news was that there was no answer yet from Egypt. Baker had spoken to Abd el-Meguid, who had promised a reply within forty-eight hours. ("I think we are getting close, but we are not there yet.") And, yes, there had been "some kind" of note from the PLO, not that the United States was looking for their response but their

101

acquiescence would be good. Anyhow Baker had not spoken to the PLO, nor had his associates. "If the Egyptians don't give me a positive answer," he said, "I'm going to drop the whole thing. I have other things to do."

Then he said, "Hold on a minute," and in a flash, the president was on the line. "Mr. Minister," Bush said, "we just wanted to report to you on the Malta Summit. I am behind the secretary of state's efforts. Please give my best regards to the prime minister." That was all.

There was a sudden spate of unfriendly statements from Cairo. Abd el-Meguid told the Israeli ambassador that there was no point to coming to Israel just for a cup of coffee, this after he had told me in New York that I could expect him within the next ten days to two weeks. All we could figure out was that there was friction between the Egyptians and the PLO, and that the Egyptians had refused to pass the PLO's negative response on to Baker, fearing (with some justification) that the messenger would be blamed.

On December 6, Baker phoned: a response had come from the Egyptians in a private note. The language wasn't all he would have "liked it to be," but Mubarak was prepared, in the main, to go ahead on the basis of the five points, having consulted the PLO and even received a PLO text. "Do you have any idea what is in the PLO text?" I asked. Baker said, "No, none." He only knew that the Egyptians had referred to "some needs and observations of Egypt and the Palestinians," to be taken up in the course of discussion but which weren't spelled out. "What they are doing," Baker said, "is reserving a place holder. But now we can move ahead." The United States was encouraged by the Egyptian response, and he would announce this at a briefing and say that everyone intended to go on working hard.

I said that it did not sound to me as though this was the formal acceptance of the five points that he had requested. Baker quickly suggested that we send Salai Meridor to Washington to "visit with" Dennis Ross and thrash all this out, the visit to be kept "totally private." And, he added, since he would like the entire National Unity government involved, he thought Salai should be joined by a "representative" of Rabin's and he was going to suggest that to Ambassador Brown.

Late in the evening, Brown came over with a précis which, in referring to the PLO, merely stated that there was a separate text but offered no additional elucidation. Again, we had to sort out alternatives. Should we make a row about the PLO's "needs and observations"—and its role in relation to the Egyptians—and demand the explanations to which Israel was certainly entitled? Or should we just buy Baker's statement that Egypt had, in principle, approved his points? I thought the latter course was preferable to letting ourselves in for another round of confrontations in which we would ask to see the text of the Egyptian message and get turned down. Shamir agreed, and I phoned Baker with our version of the "good news."

I also took the opportunity to explain why a separate State Department invitation to someone from Rabin's staff was a bad idea. "There is no question involved here," I said, "of hearing both sides. There aren't two sides. Israel has one government; one Foreign Ministry; one foreign minister; and only one official voice. However, your message has already reached Rabin, who appeared on television last night to say that a great step forward has been taken and Israel can now proceed with the meeting of the three foreign ministers—though the prime minister has still to commit the government to this."

"Sorry about that, A 'busted signal,' " said Baker, and launched into how appreciative he was of everything that I had done. I said that I appreciated his appreciation, but whatever I did was because I thought it was in Israel's best interest, since it was we who needed peace more than anybody else.

Later, I met with Rabin. I told him I thought we were in the middle of a PLO offensive aimed at active participation in the peace process, attending the dialogue, and then holding forth not about elections or the peace initiative but about a Palestinian state and the "right of return." It was up to us to see to it that this did not happen and that Israel did not find itself trapped in some form of negotiation with the PLO. What made this all harder, I said, was the subversive behavior of people in his party, notably Peres and his young disciples, who were assiduously operating behind the government's back, whether in talks with Egyptians, contacts with the PLO, or the continued leaking of classified documents to the media. "It has to be stopped," I said. Rabin didn't argue.

When we met in Shamir's office on December 8, both Peres and Rabin put forth the idea that no one need, or should, go to Washington prior to the foreign ministers' meeting, but I insisted that this was the right time, perhaps the only time, left for us to clarify our position and to try to get Baker to see things the way we did so that no surprises would await us in Cairo. Also I thought that Baker wanted a working-level session on the assurances; in effect, he had said tell me what you need, and what your positions are, and that made it an invitation to be accepted. Shamir backed me up, suggesting that Eli Rubinstein be sent to the State Department.

A few days later, I appeared before the Knesset Foreign Affairs and Defense Committee. Everyone, regardless of political affiliation, seemed very upset by the news that the Egyptians had received a communication from the PLO and passed it on to Baker.

I went through my paces again. Israel had only three options as far as the Palestinian population of Judea, Samaria, and Gaza was concerned: first, we could dig in and stonewall; say that we wouldn't talk to the PLO, that there was nothing to talk about, and leave it at that. I doubted that this was a viable option or that we could sustain that position for long but it existed. Or, we could agree to talk to the PLO, which would be calamitous for Israel, and probably irreversible. Or, we could talk, via their elected representatives, to the 1.5 million Palestinians in Judea, Samaria, and Gaza—which was what we were trying to do. If it turned out that the Egyptians were functioning exclusively as couriers for the PLO and had nothing of their own to contribute, or if the tripartite course was not going to lead anywhere, then we would look for other avenues through which to further the peace initiative. But we had no intention of abandoning the search. The tension abated, though I did not hide the fact that Israel's relationship with the U.S. administration was undergoing a change for the worse.

Neither the Mubarak-Shamir meeting nor Abd el-Meguid's projected visit to Israel had been mentioned for weeks. On December 4, former U.S. Secretary of State Cyrus Vance, in Israel for a conference on Science and Government at the Weizmann Institute, had come to see me. He had visited Syria, where he met with Assad, and Jordan, where he met with King Hussein, and was going to Egypt that evening. We talked about the peace process and the fact that the Egyptians with whom, not so long ago, we had been very close to agreement seemed to have gotten cold feet and to be fronting for the PLO. I hoped Vance was going to take this up in Cairo.

After a few days, I called in Bassiouny in the hope of discovering what had gone wrong, but he only said, characteristically, that he couldn't even "imagine" what grounds I might have for thinking that anything had changed. Elsewhere, however, there were changes that no one could deny: the collapse of Romania heralding—though we couldn't yet know it—the end of the Communist bloc and the Warsaw Pact, thus reinforcing the shift of the Eastern European nations away from their automatic support of the Arabs over the past twenty or thirty years. And, above all, almost unbelievably, there was the likelihood that hundreds of thousands of Jews would be allowed to leave the USSR for Israel. Israeli public opinion, divided on the subject of the future of Judea, Samaria, and Gaza, was unanimous in the determination that nothing be allowed to hamper the wave of immigration. The travails of the peace process, even the continuing toll of the Intifada, receded for a while from the forefront of Israeli consciousness in a surge of joy over the prospect of the fulfillment of such a long-hoped-for dream.

There was also a change in the composition of the government. On December 31, at the tail end of an uneventful government meeting, Shamir announced that he was firing Ezer Weizman, then science minister, for having been in contact with the PLO, via messages to Yasser Arafat. For some of the ministers, Shamir's statement came as a shock; others had been told months ago about Weizman's contacts. Shamir had decided to wait for the new budget to be approved in the cabinet before taking action. But the week before, he had informed Rabin, Peres, and me of his intentions, suggesting that Peres persuade Weizman to resign. Given the many years that we had all known each other, the experiences we had shared, the depth of our common commitment to Israel's security and well-being, it was natural that Shamir, however furious with Weizman, should look for a way to soften the blow. But Peres was not prepared to get involved, perhaps because he himself was not entirely innocent in this regard. So Weizman had received no warning of what was to come, and Shamir's few curt words were devastating.

The Labor ministers at once went into a huddle, emerging to insist that Shamir retract his decision. I did not think they would, or could, allow themselves to quit the government over what had just taken place, but for forty-eight hours it was touch and go. In the end, a deal was struck. Dan Meridor and Rabin got together. Weizman, though ousted from the inner cabinet, was permitted to stay in the government; and the Labor party stayed too. For a while, Weizman's reputation suffered badly; most Israelis, myself included, felt that he had behaved unpardonably, but like so much else, that scandal too is now water under the bridge.

The year 1990 began with a bang: the vast political, social, and economic construct of the USSR and its satellites lurched and crashed;

new expectations arose from the ruins of a once-omnipotent and ruthless ideology. At the Foreign Ministry, there was intense activity; many of the East European nations were already seeking diplomatic relations with us. By the middle of January, the Hungarian foreign minister had visited Israel, the Czechs were on their way, the East Germans had contacted us, and I had scheduled a February visit to Poland. There were also other pressures and calls to action—the certainty now of an immense wave of immigration from the USSR, each week's crowded flights bringing more Jews than those of the week before (by April, ten to twenty thousand men, women, and children were arriving in Israel each month), and mounting concern over the fate of the thousands of Jews in war-torn Ethiopia, who were also waiting to be brought to Israel. But the peace process remained central and Baker's demand for a response to the redrafted letter was not among the least of the pressures.

A new blow-up was in the making; Eli Rubinstein had brought a revised draft back to Israel and it had been leaked to the press. On January 10, Baker called, raging. He was chiefly angry with Shamir's "director general," Yossi Ben-Aharon, for having publicly blamed the United States for the absence of any action and demanding assurances that the PLO would not be involved. "I'm really at the point of pulling the plug," Baker said in his steeliest voice. "We deal with you privately and we don't get responses and then we get comments like this which make me wonder whether we ought to keep this up."

I didn't even know what he was talking about so I was at some disadvantage, but he explained, fuming, that he was quoting from an interview which Ben-Aharon had given in Jerusalem the day before. I told him that this was not the prime minister's position. "I would sure appreciate it," Baker said, "if somebody would . . . make it clear that the Israeli government does not stand behind what Yossi said in that interview." I promised to get some sort of statement.

He calmed down a bit and we talked about leaks. I reminded him that he wanted to deal with "representatives of both sides, or components of the government, the end result being that . . . the government secretary has to report to four people all the time which makes the problem of leaks much more difficult," which didn't upset him as much as I thought it would—although he was hardly entitled considering his own record to make much fuss on that score.

Not only was Baker not about to alter his basic attitude toward the government of Israel but neither was Mubarak or the Labor party. Once more ignoring accepted procedure, the Egyptian president extended an invitation to Peres about which I learned thanks only to one of Peres's zealous assistants, who had passed the information to Eli Rubinstein. Peres had not said a word about it either to the prime minister or to me. The plan was for Peres to go to Prague (neatly preceding me there) and from there travel on to meet Mubarak in Cairo. Peres didn't even pretend that his responsibilities as finance minister were in any way involved in this journey.

I had just heard about this when Baker phoned me on January 16 to let me know that Abd el-Meguid was coming to Washington. He wanted to be sure, he said, that I knew that he intended to do nothing behind our backs. They would probably talk about the peace process, but the visit, which was at Abd el-Meguid's request, was to be primarily about Egyptian economic problems. What about that trilateral meeting? I asked. I'm still waiting for answers from you and the Egyptians, he said, and I couldn't nail him down to a date. He also wanted me to know that Rabin was coming to Washington but they had set no date for a meeting.

A long-scheduled week's trip to Portugal and Spain at the invitation of the foreign ministers of those countries came as something of a relief for me; for once I was glad to get away. Peres had announced at a press conference that he had the votes necessary to form an alternate government, presumably suggesting that he had the religious parties lined up, or perhaps just trying to put psychological pressure on them, getting each one to believe that the others had already signed up with him. All of which highlighted the government's great instability. Before I left, Rabin said that he would be seeing Baker in Washington but would make no suggestions, merely listen to what Baker had to say. The visit to Spain and Portugal turned out to be useful, interesting, and pleasant; it was not often that I could spend time abroad without hearing criticism of Israel. Even King Juan Carlos went out of his way to demonstrate friendship.

I was due to return home on January 24. That morning, Shamir's office called me in Madrid: the prime minister had to see me as soon as I got back. In Jerusalem, Shamir told me that Baker had phoned him the night before to complain about the leaks, and to tell him that he had met with Rabin and that he wanted to hold the trilateral meeting of the foreign ministers in very short order, i.e., before he went to Moscow on February 3. He also asked Shamir some "unclear" questions relating to the composition of the Palestinian delegation, questions about Arabs from East Jerusalem and Arabs who had been expelled in the past. "But you don't have to answer," he had told Shamir. "I'll call Arens tomorrow night and get the answers from him."

The call from Washington didn't come that night or the next, by which time the Likud was making last-minute preparations for the Central Committee meeting on February 7, with Shamir at last determined to insist on a clear-cut vote of confidence, as I had pressed him to do, so that order could be restored to the party. Meanwhile, Baker had taken to calling Shamir. He had received a positive response from the Egyptians about the trilaterals and wanted to set the date. "Call Arens," said Shamir. "I want your approval first," Baker replied.

I didn't have to wait long for my phone to ring. On January 31, Baker called me with the information that there had been this "very positive" response from the Egyptians: they were ready to have two Palestinian "deportees" in the delegation who could return to wherever they lived, or to the territories, once they had been named to the delegation. I understood that "return to the territories" meant annulment of their status as deportees, but what I couldn't understand was what question had been asked to which this was the answer—and by whom it had been asked. I put it to Baker: "Is this the answer to a question that Rabin asked you when he was in Washington?" "You could say that," Baker replied, "but after all it is a subject that has been raised before." He had discussed it, he said, with the prime minister when Shamir visited Washington.

He went on to say that he had gotten a "positive response" from the Egyptians on the issue of Arabs with dual residences serving on the Palestinian delegation. Had Rabin brought that up too, I asked. Again Baker said that this wasn't a new issue. He had worked very hard to get the Egyptians to agree and now, "let's get on with the trilaterals." That meeting couldn't take place, I explained, before the Likud Central Committee had its meeting, and Baker said he understood that, but it would be a good thing if I provided him with a positive Israeli response to the Egyptian answers. I said I would talk to Shamir, but warned him that cabinet approval would probably be needed. When I queried him about the assurances, he said it would perhaps be best to send us the final version after the Central Committee had met. We stopped talking about who would do what first and went on to his suggestion that we

108

should hold the trilateral meeting in Europe, perhaps in Geneva on February 11.

So we had been wrong about Rabin, our great hope for holding the coalition together, as I told Shamir next morning. His raising those issues, coming up with those "questions" in Washington, had helped to cement the Egyptian-American relationship and to strengthen the existing bonds between the Egyptians and the PLO. Now, Baker expected the government to come up with a positive response to "questions" which Rabin had led him to believe Israel had asked. It took months for the truth to emerge: Rabin had not just entered into discussions with Baker, but had entered into a secret agreement with him about the composition of the Palestinian delegation, even picking by name the Palestinians he thought should serve on it, making as sure as he could that the real nature of his visit to Washington was not revealed to Shamir or to me. Had Rabin thought that his deception would remain secret? What really mattered was that, when asked, Rabin had categorically denied ever having raised any questions at all with Baker. As for Baker, it took more than fleeting awkwardness for him to feel in the wrong.

"All right," he said, the next time we spoke, "why don't you give your responses to those questions?" I asked for the questions again, and Baker repeated them. I said that we would consider them, but I thought they could be phrased in a more general manner: Would Israel agree to having deportees on the delegation; and would Israel agree to have East Jerusalemites on the delegation? It was the principle, not the details, that had to be decided; nor should the phrasing of the questions imply Israel's prior agreement. Anyhow, we should talk face-to-face; we hadn't done so in a long time and I knew he had had extensive talks with Abd el-Meguid when the latter was in Washington.

Baker said he would be happy to sit down and talk, and he started to plan our next meeting. I could almost hear his mind clicking the dates and locations into place as he suggested that maybe the plane in which he was flying to Moscow on February 8 could pick me up in Prague, where I was scheduled to be, and we could go on together to Switzerland where he hoped to meet Abd el-Meguid. How many seats would we need? Maybe four, I said, because my wife was coming along. "I'll get back to you on the logistics," I said.

When I phoned back, I reminded him that I still would not have a final Israeli response because there was not going to be another government meeting before my departure, and it was the prime minister's opinion that such a response could only be given as the result of a cabinet meeting. The edge was back in Baker's voice. Couldn't I leave a proxy with the prime minister? If the prime minister and I agreed on a response, wasn't it a foregone conclusion that the government would also approve it? I told him I had to be present at the government meeting when these matters were discussed and anyhow I was not keen on the Egyptian positions. "In that case," he said stiffly, "I think we can make no further progress. So that's that."

I said that I thought his attitude was unreasonable. "Here you present us with the Egyptian positions, and the moment we say we don't think we can accept them, you declare that the whole thing is over. Why the ultimatum? You have always known that for Israel the two most basic issues are how to keep the PLO from being involved in the negotiations, and the non-negotiability of Jerusalem. These two points are integral to Israel's peace initiative, which you are on the record as supporting."

"They are not Egyptian positions," Baker snapped. "They are American positions, and this is not an ultimatum, but if you reject them, I don't see where we can go from here. You'll have to come up with a reasonable alternative and I doubt that such exists."

"I think we can, but we have to talk about all this," I said. "Do you still want a trilateral meeting?"

Baker said he didn't want "all that media attention" given to a meeting that might be perceived as unsuccessful. I said something more about the two of us meeting to talk. He indicated that the telephone would be an adequate substitute for a face-to-face meeting.

He was very angry. He had managed to reach an agreement on crucial issues with Rabin and with the Egyptians, thus also with the PLO, and was now being blocked by what was popularly known in his, and other, circles as Israeli intransigence. I, for my part, hung up feeling that I would have to go on doing and saying whatever I could to keep the peace process from breaking down irretrievably, and the government of Israel from falling apart.

On the evening of February 4, as I was about to speak at one of a series of meetings being held daily in preparation for the meeting of the Central Committee, I was notified that a bus filled with Israeli tourists had been attacked on the road to Cairo; there were ten dead and seventeen wounded. Abd el-Meguid, to whom I spoke twice, sent a letter at once, expressing the condolences of the Egyptian government. Baker also phoned, but with an additional item to discuss: perhaps we should meet in Europe after all. But the pieces couldn't be put in place, so it would have to wait until the middle of the month, after the Central Committee meeting.

The End of National Unity

Prior to the meeting of the Likud Central Committee, which was rescheduled to take place at the Tel Aviv Fairgrounds on February 12, 1990, Shamir and I held numerous meetings with three of the Likud's young ministers—Ehud Olmert, Dan Meridor, and Ronni Milo—in an attempt to forge a strategy to overcome Sharon's refusal to coordinate the meeting with Shamir. In disregard of established tradition, Sharon, chairman of the Central Committee, ignored Shamir's role as elected leader of the Likud and arbitrarily set both the date of the meeting and its agenda. He hoped to demonstrate that the Central Committee did not support the peace initiative. Fearing a repeat of what had transpired at the previous meeting, where the maneuvering of Sharon, Levy, and Moda'i had created the impression that additional "constraints" had been imposed on the initiative, Shamir asked that this time the agenda consist of a vote of confidence for him and his policies. Sharon refused. Shamir had no choice but to call for such a vote himself, by a show of hands, at the conclusion of his address at the meeting.

Sharon opened the meeting with a long oration blasting the Shamir government for its many mistakes and in particular its failure to put an end to Arab terrorism. He concluded by saying that he was unwilling to continue to share the responsibilities for the government's failures

THE END OF NATIONAL UNITY

and was therefore resigning. Then he called on Shamir to address the three thousand Central Committee members assembled in the large hall.

Shamir approached the speaker's stand to the right of the long table on the stage facing the audience, with Sharon seated in the center and the rest of the Likud ministers to his right and left. He spoke about the political situation, the difficulties he was having with the Labor party, and his determination to guard Israel's vital interests while pursuing the peace initiative. Then, without missing a beat, he asked for the vote of confidence. Sharon, seeing a wave of hands go up, jumped to his feet and began shouting into the microphone before him that this vote was not on the agenda. But seeing that a large majority kept their hands raised, Sharon then asked those who wanted to see an end to Arab terrorism to raise their hands. Within seconds the meeting was in an uproar, Shamir and Sharon each shouting through his own microphone, simultaneously calling on the audience for support in a stereophonic cacophony, Central Committee members arguing among themselves and then walking out of the hall in disgust.

When Shamir and I met the following morning, it was clear that Sharon, Levy, and Moda'i would prevent orderly decision making in Likud party forums whenever they disagreed with the majority opinion. Only a party convention, the adoption of a constitution, and the election of new officers could bring an end to their subversion of Shamir's authority and the disarray which their tactics had brought to the Likud. But that would take time.

On my way to Bonn the next day, I had difficulty pushing the scene I had witnessed at the Central Committee meeting out of my mind and concentrating on the business at hand. The heads of the European Community were scheduled to meet the following week and on their agenda was a resolution of the European Parliament, seconded by the Commissioners of the Community, to impose economic sanctions against Israel as a demonstration of the EC's displeasure with Israel's policy toward the Palestinians. It was ironic that in trying to head off this move I should have to turn to Bonn, but I knew I wouldn't find a sympathetic ear in Paris, London, or Rome. There I could expect only pious sermons on human rights, self-determination, and calls to leave the "occupied territories." Unlike their colleagues, the West Germans seemed to feel they had no right to preach good behavior to Israel.

The first heavy snow of the year had fallen in Bonn the day of my arrival, but the police had succeeded in clearing the streets from the guesthouse to the Foreign Ministry, where Hans Dietrich Genscher awaited me. The newspapers that day reported on the visit of the East German prime minister to Bonn, while the editorials already anticipated the reunification of the two Germanys. After discussing that subject ("unification," not "reunification," Genscher corrected me), the recent request by the East German government to establish diplomatic relations with Israel, and the changes taking place in the Soviet Union, I turned to the issue of the EC sanctions. "It should be clear," I said, "that Israel will not give in to the punitive measures that have been proposed; we are a people who have sacrificed thousands of our sons in our defense and to assure our continued security—we are not going to be brought to our knees by economic sanctions. Such measures can only encourage Arab extremism, and thus impede the peace process."

Genscher raised his hand in protest: "You need go no further. I agree with you fully and will do all I can to block the imposition of sanctions against Israel by the European Community." I received similar assurances from Chancellor Helmut Kohl later in the day. Encouraged, I returned to Israel, only to learn the following week that economic sanctions against Israel had not been blocked at the meeting of the leaders of the Community.

On Saturday, February 17, I met with Shamir in preparation for my meeting with Baker, which had finally been arranged for the following Friday, February 23, on my way back from Mexico City. The usual problems of such a meeting were compounded by Peres's latest machinations and the rumors he was floating that he had already assembled an alternate coalition. I had no doubt that this news was simultaneously being received in Washington. Shamir, however, assured me that Peres had so far not been successful.

Only a few hours after I landed in Mexico City, as I was about to deliver a lecture at the institute run by the Mexican Foreign Ministry, Shamir telephoned to inform me that Moda'i and four other Knesset members, also former members of the Liberal party, had deserted the Likud and set up an independent Knesset faction. Shamir was agitated. "This move has a destabilizing effect on the government," he said. "When you see Baker, please tell him that all bets are off—we now have to wait until the situation clears up, and in the meantime we cannot provide any answers to questions he may want to raise."

I had been looking forward to my visit to Mexico, partly for the opportunity to strengthen relations with an important country, but especially because I admired the far-reaching economic reforms carried out by Mexico's President Carlos Salinas, who was doing in Mexico what the Likud had talked about but not implemented in Israel. But wherever I went, in meetings with the president, the foreign minister, and other dignitaries, I was followed by reports that a full-blown coalition crisis had developed back in Israel, and that Peres and Rabin were now working in a coordinated manner in an attempt to undermine the government of which they were both members.

Until now Shamir had made every effort to placate Rabin, hoping that Rabin's aversion to Peres becoming prime minister would set the basis for an alliance that could keep the coalition on an even keel. Now it seemed that this strategy had been exhausted. Peres and Rabin were making it known that they expected Shamir to respond positively to Baker's initiatives and questions, and that if he failed to do so, they would topple his government. It was obvious to me that a web of surreptitious contacts had been woven in recent months among Baker, Rabin, Peres, Mubarak, and the PLO, and that the focus now was on the composition of the Palestinian delegation, while holding the threat of bringing down Shamir's government over our heads.

When I arrived in Washington on February 22, I decided not to involve Baker in the Moda'i crisis, despite Shamir's instruction to use it as a pretext for stalling. I asked Salai to contact Dennis Ross in preparation for the next day's meeting with Baker, suggesting that Baker pose the following question: "Is the Government of Israel prepared to consider as candidates for the Palestinian delegation, residents of Judea, Samaria, and Gaza, on a name-by-name basis?" This, I thought, would make it clear that they would have to be residents of these areas, appearing in the Israeli population register, and therefore not residents of Jerusalem or of the Palestinian "diaspora," and that our approval would be required. When Salai returned to the hotel that evening after meeting Ross, I was pleased to hear that Baker had agreed to my formulation.

On the evening news I heard Baker testifying before the Congressional Committee on Foreign Affairs. The committee members were treating him with deference, prefacing each question—even when some criticism of U.S. policy was implied—with compliments on his performance as secretary of state. The Soviet Union was collapsing, the countries of Eastern Europe were turning to the West, the military intervention in Panama looked, for the moment, to have been successful, U.S. foreign policy was riding high, and Baker clearly enjoyed taking some of the credit. In his testimony on the Middle East, Baker reported on the very good contacts he had with the Egyptian foreign minister, that he had received positive replies from him, and that if the Israeli foreign minister would give equally positive replies in the meeting the next day, progress could be made in the peace process.

When we met the next day, Baker came right to the point, telling me that unless we moved forward in the process he would have to drop it. Knowing that I was revealing nothing new to him, I brought up the political problems facing the Shamir government: "Our so-called partners in the government are going behind our backs, carrying on parallel negotiations, giving away our positions before they have been made public. This makes it extremely difficult to make progress in what are in any case difficult negotiations. But make no mistake, if Peres were to bring down the government and succeed in setting up a narrow-based coalition led by himself, you should expect no progress in the peace process—the opposition he would face would simply paralyze him. Only a National Unity government can move the process forward." Baker said that he agreed and that he had told the Egyptians to stop meddling in Israeli politics.

I reminded him that so far we had had no response from any Arab government to our call for direct negotiations. King Hussein's positions seemed to be becoming more extreme from week to week, and now we were seeing an overt Arab effort to stop the immigration of Jews from the Soviet Union to Israel. "When I saw you on TV yesterday," I added, "one of the members of Congress told you that this was a continuation of Arab policy during the thirties, when they pressured Britain to stop the immigration of Jews to Palestine, and I heard you say that you were not acquainted with that history." Baker agreed that he had not been aware of that chapter in Jewish history. I recounted to him how the doors of Palestine had been closed to the Jews trying to escape Hitler's Europe, and how that had contributed to the scale of the Holocaust.

Baker told me he found my suggested formulation of the question he might put to the Israeli government on the composition of the Palestinian delegation acceptable. "However," he added immediately, "it should be clear that the list when finally approved by you should include two or three Palestinians who were deported or who have an additional address or business in Jerusalem." I decided not to reject his assumption on the spot, but rather told him that this was something that would have to be referred to the government for a decision. I knew that it would be a bitter pill for Shamir to swallow. However, considering that Baker had accepted my requirement that the delegates all be registered residents of Judea, Samaria, and Gaza, that they would have to be approved by us on a name-by-name basis, and that Peres and Rabin were breathing down our necks threatening to topple the government, I thought it the better part of wisdom not to make an issue of this at the moment.

I warned Baker that we must be prepared for the possibility that when the delegations met, the Palestinians might attempt to pose as PLO representatives, reminding him that in the past the United States had promised not to be party to any set-ups and that I would expect his support in such an eventuality. "Yes," he replied, "but you can't expect me to give you a blank check—on this issue you will just have to trust us." I told him that on this particular issue we could not proceed simply on trust, because the United States and Israel had different positions as regards the PLO. Baker astounded me by referring to the differences between us on settlements. "That's true," I countered, "but I don't see that that has anything to do with it." But he would not let up, emphasizing that the administration could not agree to settling the emigrants from the Soviet Union in the territories.

He was not placated when I stated that the government of Israel did not direct the new immigrants to any specific locations, and that only a fraction of 1 percent of the recent newcomers had settled in the territories. He kept pressing the point: "It would be very good if Israel were to announce that the new immigrants were prohibited from settling in the territories." The discussion was beginning to get a little heated as I explained that what he was suggesting was absolutely impossible. "The Government of Israel will not adopt a policy of preventing somebody from living in a certain area just because he's Jewish," I said. I was not sure whether Baker understood, or really wanted to understand, our position.

Next, I drew Baker's attention to the deterioration in the Israeli-Egyptian relationship since he had become involved in the negotiations. The expected meeting between Mubarak and Shamir had not taken place; despite his promises, Abd el-Meguid had not visited Israel; in fact, there had been no direct contact between us for the last few months. We had given the Egyptians everything, including the "last grain of sand" at Taba. There was nothing more we could give. I told Baker that when I had first met Abd el-Meguid in Paris just over a year earlier, he had promised me that once the Taba issue was settled, the Israeli-Egyptian relationship would blossom and the "sky would be the limit." "It must be very cloudy these days," Baker commented. I could tell he was not very eager to get involved. "That relationship is an essential part of the peace process," I went on, "sending signals to the other Arab states and to the Palestinians, and it is only U.S. leverage that can influence the Egyptians. The U.S., as signatory to the Israel-Egypt peace treaty, is committed to having Egypt meet its obligations under the treaty."

I had failed to arouse his interest. He was already thinking about the Israeli-Palestinian dialogue that he expected would take place shortly in Cairo, telling me that he intended to be present there and that he thought it would be a good idea for me to attend as well. Although I did not want to dampen his enthusiasm for what he evidently visualized as a big media event, I told him that staging it was a little premature and we could discuss it when the time came.

At this point Baker turned to the announcements of the names of the delegation members, suggesting, to my amazement, that the Egyptians announce the composition of the Palestinian and Israeli delegations. I could only guess the origin of that outlandish idea, which I rejected without further reflection. "Israel is a sovereign state, nobody else will announce the composition of our delegation—we will do that ourselves." Baker accepted that without a murmur.

Then he asked how I felt about the Soviets participating in the meeting in Cairo, and I rejected that idea too, telling him that the Soviet Union had zero experience in conducting democratic elections and could therefore contribute nothing to a discussion on election procedures.

We rode down the elevator to the State Department lobby to spend a few minutes with the waiting reporters. Baker described our meeting as "good and friendly," and then, in an unusual gesture of courtesy, he walked me out to my car. I did not realize at the time that this one-hour meeting spelled the beginning of the end of the National Unity government.

The 23rd was a Friday, so I took the shuttle flight to New York to spend the Sabbath there after the meeting. I spoke to Shamir briefly on the phone, telling him that I would give him a detailed report as soon as I returned. The following night I was on the El Al flight to Israel, with lots of time to think about my conversation with Baker. I was convinced that the government should reply positively to the question (on the composition of the Palestinian delegation) that I had formulated and that Baker had now posed, without rejecting the assumption he had added about nonresident Palestinians on the delegation. Having obtained his agreement to the Palestinian delegates being registered residents of Judea, Samaria, and Gaza, but not of Jerusalem, would make it clear that the elections to be discussed in Cairo were not going to concern Jerusalem. The alternative—answering in the negative—was bound to bring the coalition crisis to a head, probably toppling the government, possibly enabling Peres to assemble an alternate coalition. I wondered would Shamir see it that way as well?

Sunday evening, February 25, Salai and I met with Shamir at the almost deserted prime minister's office in the Defense Ministry compound in Tel Aviv. Shamir, seeming tired and withdrawn, listened to my report of the meeting with Baker and my recommendation that we reply favorably to what had now become "Baker's" question. "We should have no real problem, as long as we have nailed down the principle that no resident of Jerusalem can be a member of the Palestinian delegation," I said. He sat there, hunched over, sipping his tea. Aside from a few questions and some caustic comments, I could get no substantive reaction. Shamir had been having a tough time lately, taking flak from all directions—from Peres and Rabin, as well as from Sharon, Levy, and Moda'i—and he seemed fed up and maybe was even thinking of quitting; he was certainly in no mood to give me a positive response that evening. Since I was leaving for an official visit to Poland the next day, Baker was going to have to wait at least a week for our reply. Salai was to stay behind and prepare a detailed report for Shamir.

In Warsaw, where I was received at the airport by Foreign Minister Krzyszstof Skubszewski, I drove first to the Tomb of the Unknown Soldier to lay a wreath, then to the site of the Warsaw Ghetto to place a wreath at the memorial for the fighters of the Ghetto. That afternoon, I drove to Lublin and from there to Majdanek, the death camp, and later to the "ash planet"of Auschwitz where nearly 2 million Jews were tormented and murdered. For the Jewish people, Poland will forever remain the graveyard of multitudes who were abandoned to their murderers, first by their neighbors, and then by the rest of the world. I could go nowhere in Poland, see no one, engage in no official business until I had visited these sites. Only then was I able to turn to the mission that brought me to Poland: the establishment of a new relationship between that country and the Jewish State.

International telephone service in Poland was not all it should have been, but nevertheless I was kept informed of the growing crisis back home, which now included calls for Shamir's resignation. On March 1, I returned to Israel on a Tupolev transport flown by the Polish airline LOT, and met the next day with Shamir. I could see that he was struggling with himself, uncertain of how to handle the situation, how to reply to Baker's question, how to deal with the Labor party, or how to handle the internal opposition in the Likud. When I suggested that, in anticipation of the beginning of negotiations with the Palestinians, an agreement should be reached with the Labor party on the key elements of Israel's position, disengaging the negotiations from any Labor attempts to overturn the government, he seized upon the idea. But I suspected that he would have welcomed almost anything that would delay the tough decision he had to make.

That Saturday night, March 3, Shamir convened the Likud ministers at the prime minister's residence in Jerusalem. After we had taken our seats in the large living room on the ground floor, he asked me to report on my meeting with Baker the previous week. By now the substance of that meeting was well known, and I quickly launched into my analysis of the situation and the recommended course of action. "We are under the impression of the pressure being applied from Washington and by the Labor party, but let's for the moment assume that there was no such pressure, what would we do then?" Answering my own question, I said: "We would call for direct negotiations with the neighboring Arab countries, knowing well that they would probably present us with serious difficulties, and we would offer to hold direct talks with elected representatives of the Palestinian population in Judea, Samaria, and Gaza based on the Camp David agreements. We should not have any illusions about who might be elected, but would, nevertheless, hope that the democratic process would have a positive effect, the people elected having a feeling of responsibility to their constituencies. That is what our peace initiative is all about, and it has been a success so far. It has moved the international conference out of the way. It has, to some extent, pushed the PLO aside as the sole recognized representative of the Palestinian people.

"The U.S. has accepted the initiative," I went on, "although it has not been accepted by the European Community. The PLO would like to turn our initiative inside out, attempting to bring about direct negotiations between them and us on the PLO agenda. Baker wants to obtain PLO acquiescence to the dialogue by pressuring us to agree to Palestinian delegates from the 'diaspora' and from Jerusalem, and not limiting the agenda to election procedures, while trying to get them to accept the fact that they will have to stay in the background. We are standing by the principle that the Palestinian delegates must be residents of Judea, Samaria, and Gaza, that the PLO not be present, and that the agenda be limited to election procedures. Baker's 'assumptions' that the delegation, while being composed of people appearing on our population register for Judea, Samaria, and Gaza, include some deportees and/ or somebody with an additional address in Jerusalem is consistent with that principle.

"My conclusion," I said finally, "is that we should answer positively to Baker's question if, and that is a big if, we succeed in coordinating our negotiating positions with Labor and remove their constant threat to break up the government, which would make the negotiations impossible."

There was silence after I completed my remarks, and then, one by one, most of the Likud ministers expressed agreement with me. Moshe Nissim, the former minister of justice who had replaced Sharon as minister of trade and industry, emphasized the need to have Labor agree that the PLO would not be permitted to impose itself on the dialogue, and that the Arab population of Jerusalem would not participate in the Palestinian elections.

David Levy had all this time been glowering in his chair. Finally he spoke up. With a raised voice, he said this was a sell-out of all our principles, that we had surrendered to the PLO. Then he got up and left. To the waiting reporters, he said that the discussion had been meaningless, since the conclusion had been determined beforehand.

To my surprise Bibi Netanyahu followed Levy's line, arguing that unless we could get the Americans to adopt a position more favorable to us, Baker's assumptions should be rejected. It was already after midnight and Shamir, without expressing an opinion, announced that we would resume the discussion the following evening.

The week of March 4 was going to be stormy. It became clear that the fate of Shamir's government hung in the balance. On Sunday morning,

Shamir invited Peres and Rabin to his office and asked me to report on my meeting with Baker. They listened attentively, although they must have already known every detail. Shamir informed them that the Likud ministers had not completed their discussion, and that we would inform them of the Likud's position only afterward. Without another word, Peres and Rabin left. In a Knesset debate that afternoon I stressed our position to the Labor party. Before we could proceed with negotiations with the Palestinians, two conditions would have to be met: first, agreement that we would not allow the PLO to impose itself on the negotiations; and second, agreement that the Arab population in Jerusalem would not participate in the Palestinian elections. It was inconceivable, I told the Knesset, that the government should enter negotiations as long as there was a divergence of opinion in the Israeli government on these issues.

That evening the Likud ministers reassembled in Shamir's office— all except Levy, who stayed away. Our discussion continued late into the night. Finally, we decided to announce that the Likud wanted to move ahead with the peace process, but that doing so was contingent upon obtaining Labor's agreement on the issues of the PLO and Jerusalem.

When news of our decision was broadcast on the next day's early morning news, all hell broke loose. After a short meeting of the Labor ministers, they announced that they were rejecting what they considered to be a Likud ultimatum and, turning the tables on us, demanded that the Likud provide a satisfactory answer at the next day's meeting of the inner cabinet. Peres spoke openly of forming another government if the Likud's answer was not satisfactory. The most intemperate of the Labor ministers was Rabin. Appearing on television that week, he had worked himself into a rage, charging the Likud with insulting him and the other Labor leaders who had participated in the battles for Jerusalem by lecturing them on the steps to be taken to protect Israel's capital. This was outrageous, he insisted, especially since Likud ministers—such as myself, Nissim, and others—had contributed nothing to Israel's security. I had no doubt that this arrogance stemmed from deep-seated animosities between the rival pre-state underground organizations—the Haganah and the Irgun Zvai Leumi—culminating in Ben-Gurion's order to fire on the *Altalena*, the Irgun ship that had brought arms and volunteers to Israel's shores in July 1948. I had always suspected that, deep down, Rabin was convinced that anybody who did not participate in this ambush should not be counted among the contributors to Israel's defense.

When the inner cabinet met, Shamir chaired a long and heated debate; but insisting that the discussion should continue at next week's meeting, he succeeded in closing the meeting before the confrontation between Likud and Labor reached boiling point.

The religious parties were going to determine the outcome of this crisis, and the key to their behavior was Shas—the ultra-religious party that held six Knesset seats, whose constituency was the community of Israelis who had emigrated from Arabic-speaking countries. This party, a relatively new phenomenon on the Israeli political scene, appealed to the sense of pride in the community's Sephardi heritage and the feeling that it had been neglected by Israel's establishment. Its unchallenged spiritual guide and mentor was Rabbi Ovadia Yosef, a former Sephardi Chief Rabbi of Israel, and it was his word that was going to determine Shas's position in the crisis. A number of Likud Knesset members had suggested that I go to see him.

Late one evening, at 11:00 P.M., I rang the bell of Rabbi Yosef's Jerusalem apartment and was ushered into his book-lined study. He was wearing the traditional robes of Sephardi chief rabbis, a black and silver embroidered turban on his head and, as always, thick dark glasses. Sitting next to him was Aryeh Deri, the young minister of the interior who ran the day-to-day affairs of Shas. After a few introductory courtesies, partaking of the sweets and tea he offered me, I related my recent discussion with Baker. I emphasized the potential danger to Jerusalem and the necessity of arriving at a coordinated position with Labor before entering negotiations with the Palestinians. Rabbi Yosef asked if we could not give Baker a positive answer now, and only afterward establish a coordinated position with Labor. I explained why I thought that this would be putting the cart before the horse, but could not elicit an answer. When I left, long after midnight, I doubted our ability to keep Shas in our camp.

There was also still some uncertainty regarding Rabin himself. He did not want to break up the National Unity government, or to see Peres as prime minister, but he disagreed with the Likud about Jerusalem Arabs not voting in the proposed elections, and he did not want to be accused by his colleagues of having prevented Labor from coming to power. Quick thinking and a quick solution were needed. One possibility was put forth on March 10 at a meeting with Shamir, Dan Meridor, and Nissim, who suggested that the Likud try to form a narrow-based government without Labor. This would require Shamir, at the first opportunity (the forthcoming government meeting would be an appropriate occasion) to fire all eleven Labor members of the government and fill their positions with additional ministers from the religious parties, giving them an incentive to stick with the Likud. This idea, which seemed far-fetched at the moment, began to take root in Shamir's mind as the crisis wore on.

On Sunday, March 11, before the meeting of the inner cabinet, Rabin was on the radio sounding conciliatory. He felt that the National Unity government should continue if at all possible, and he put forward a new suggestion: the question of the participation of the Arab population of East Jerusalem in the Palestinian elections should be decided by a vote in the Knesset. At the meeting of Likud ministers just prior to the inner cabinet meeting, Nissim reported optimistically on the meetings he had held with representatives of the religious parties regarding the formation of a narrow-based coalition and our ability to mobilize the necessary votes to defeat the no-confidence motion scheduled for the Knesset session on Thursday afternoon.

The prime minister was authorized to fire ministers only at a government meeting, and if Shamir were to fire the Labor ministers at next Tuesday's meeting of the government, forty-eight hours would elapse before the vote of no confidence in the Knesset on Thursday, the time required by Israeli law for the ministers' dismissal to go into effect. Since the law also specified that once non-confidence had been voted in a government, its ministers were "locked in" and could not be fired, nor could they resign, the Labor ministers, if not fired in time, would continue as members of Shamir's government until a new government had been formed or till new elections were held. If they were fired in time and non-confidence was voted on Thursday, Shamir would continue as head of a "caretaker" government that did not include the Labor ministers until a new government was formed.

It was going to be a close call. Despite the prospects of being able to pull off this most unusual political maneuver, both Meridor and Ronni Milo thought we should be looking for a compromise formula with Labor. I could tell from Shamir's expression that he didn't agree.

At the cabinet meeting, Rabin, continuing in a conciliatory vein, proposed that the Israeli delegation at the Cairo talks walk out if the Palestinians were to announce that they represented the PLO. He also said that he opposed the inclusion of East Jerusalem in the area of Palestinian autonomy, as well as Jerusalem Arabs being candidates in the Palestinian elections, and whereas he favored their participation in these elections, he was prepared to have the Knesset decide this issue. I spoke about the need for unity, considering the difficult negotiations awaiting us in Cairo and the U.S. administration's position on East Jerusalem. There was little chance of moving the peace process forward by a narrow-based government, whether led by Likud or Labor, I concluded.

Shamir's tone was not conciliatory; he criticized U.S. policy, saying that it was an attempt to subvert the Israeli peace initiative. I could sense that entering the negotiations in Cairo was about the last thing he had in mind. Shamir insisted that there were still many things that needed to be discussed, and therefore he would not allow a vote to be taken at this meeting. Peres furiously insisted that, for Labor, a nonvote would be interpreted as a decision. He was still talking when Shamir closed the meeting and walked out of the room. The countdown toward the Knesset vote on Thursday had begun.

I was still hoping that a compromise could be worked out, and appealed to Shamir to meet with Rabin. Rabin's position was very close to ours, and only relatively minor modifications would be required for an agreement. But Shamir was becoming adamant. Nissim, whom Rabin had begun referring to as the gravedigger of the National Unity government, told me that he was advising Shamir against any kind of "compromise formula." He had been busy trying to convince the ultra-religious parties and the Torah sages who guide their parliamentary representatives to support the Likud in the vote of no confidence and to join a Likud-led coalition without Labor. Meanwhile, Shamir had rejected last-minute efforts by Zevulun Hammer, the minister of religious affairs from the National Religious party, to bring about a compromise solution.

This was the end of the National Unity government, a sad day for Israel. Many factors had brought us to this unfortunate state of affairs. Peres and Rabin had negotiated behind our backs and undercut the government's negotiating positions. The Egyptians had been in collusion, and Bush and Baker had encouraged them. The Likud was not blameless, either. Sharon, Levy, and Moda'i had done everything possible to put the brakes on our peace initiative, and had created the impression that the Likud was not serious about advancing the process;

and there were those in our party who supported them, apparently unable to agree to anything that seemed like a deviation from the party's ideology. Shamir, who had been fought by the "constrainers" every inch of the way, adhered to what had become unrealistic doctrines. I feared that the unwillingness of many in our own ranks to acknowledge the realities around us would sooner or later lead to the downfall of the Likud.

On Tuesday morning, March 13, Shamir called the Likud ministers into his office for a final consultation before the government meeting. But his mind was already made up. When I tried to suggest that there seemed a good chance of coming to an agreement with Rabin, who could probably get the Labor party to go along, he cut me off. The only question on his mind was whether he should fire only Peres that morning, or all of the Labor ministers. We trooped up to the government room on the second floor, where the other ministers were already assembled.

Shamir took his seat at the center of the table, next to Peres, and began reading from a prepared text. The ministers seated around the long table, straining to hear every word, realized that they were witnessing something unprecedented in Israel's political history: Peres, the deputy prime minister and finance minister, was being fired. Shamir was accusing him of having plotted the downfall of the government, pointing out that the decision taken by the Labor party on Monday, although vaguely phrased, was a clear indication that they intended a vote of no confidence in the government at Thursday's Knesset session. Then, quoting the relevant law authorizing the prime minister to fire government ministers, Shamir pushed the letter of dismissal over to Peres.

Peres, visibly shaken, his voice trembling, staring straight ahead and not looking at Shamir, hit back, accusing Shamir of being responsible for the dissolution of the government. The remaining ten Labor ministers, each in his turn, announced that they were resigning from the government, handing Shamir a prepared collective letter of resignation. As Shamir began to respond, Peres called out that he did not recognize him as prime minister. There were some minutes of confusion as arguments broke out before the eleven Labor ministers rose and left the room, leaving behind the fourteen ministers who, when the dismissal and resignation took effect in two days, would constitute the government of Israel.

In an instant, everything had shifted: Shamir had cut loose from an association he loathed but which he himself had created and for years had tolerated. Peres was only a step away from trying to assemble the alternate government he had striven so long to establish.

Now it became a race for the votes of the ultra-religious parties. Their 13 votes—6 Shas; 5 Agudat Yisrael, representing most of Israel's ultra-Orthodox communities; and 2 Degel Hatorah, which took its orders from the ninety-three-year-old Rabbi Eliezer Schach—were going to determine the outcome of the no-confidence vote on Thursday. I got talked into making the rounds of the rabbinical sages. Some lectured me on our rights to all of the Land of Israel, others on the need to advance the peace process. When it was all done, I realized that the rabbis of Agudat Yisrael could not forgive Shamir for having let their party down in the coalition negotiations after the last elections. Some insisted that as long as Shamir led the Likud they could not support it, while here and there it was hinted that if I were to replace him their support would be forthcoming. There was no doubt that the five Agudat Yisrael Knesset members were going to vote with Labor in the no-confidence vote, thus assuring that there would be at least 60 votes against the government, just one short of the number required to topple it.

When the Knesset went into session on Thursday, March 15, everything seemed to hinge on the votes of the two-man Degel Hatorah. While Peres and other Labor Knesset members delivered fiery speeches denouncing Shamir and his government, Shamir was busy negotiating with the Degel Hatorah representatives. As the debate proceeded and the vote approached, it looked as if they were going to vote with us and that the government would squeak through with a 60–60 tie. But at almost the last moment, a Shas delegation entered the Knesset bringing identical hand-written letters for Shamir and Peres from Rabbi Ovadia Yosef, calling for reinstatement of the dismissed Labor ministers, giving Baker a positive answer, and reaching agreement between Likud and Labor on Israel's negotiating positions. Whichever party did not accept these conditions would be considered by the rabbi as responsible for the breakup of the government. It was an ultimatum, most likely precoordinated with Peres.

Shamir hastily convened the Likud ministers in his office. By now it was clear that if Shamir were to reject the rabbi's letter, the government would not survive the vote. When I started telling Shamir that under the circumstances we had no choice but to swallow our pride and accept the conditions set by Shas, the alternative being a Peres-led government with Peres representing Israel in Cairo, Shamir was not willing to hear me out. He would not accept the terms of the letter, and he had no intention of going to Cairo because they were going to "break our bones" over there. If the Likud wished to accede, we would have to do it without him. He was frowning at me. To Meridor, sitting next to him, he passed a note suggesting that maybe he should hand in his resignation to the president. When it was suggested that Rabbi Ovadia Yosef would be insulted if Shamir did not at least pay him the courtesy of calling on him, Shamir agreed to go see him. We obtained a delay in the vote while Shamir hurried over to the rabbi's home, only to find Peres and Rabin already there. After an hour and a half he returned and informed us that his answer to the rabbi had been no.

There was great tension when the Knesset reassembled at 8:30 P.M. As the members' names were called by the secretary of the Knesset and they responded "for" or "against," it became apparent that five of the six Shas members had simply absented themselves from the vote, giving Peres his victory. The result was 60 for the no-confidence motion, and 55 against. Shamir's government had fallen, although it would continue as a caretaker until a new government had been formed.

The following morning I had a heart-to-heart talk with Shamir. "We are very near the end of the road," I told him. "Peres might have a hard time forming a government in which the religious parties and the far left sit together, but that does not mean that it cannot be done." I was not going to draw up a list of recriminations, but he had to know how I felt. This time, somewhat chastened, he listened without interrupting me as I told him that I was sure that nothing short of halting the peace process would stop the dialogue in Cairo from being held, if not with the Likud then with Labor, and that I could not understand why he was so agitated about it. He had known that we would face that kind of issue as soon as he decided, against my advice, to go for "political" elections that would require agreement on the Palestinian election procedures, rather than municipal elections, the procedures for which were already established. He appeared to have forgotten that we were free to say no in Cairo whenever necessary, as would be the case should any attempt be made to introduce other issues into the discussions. But he did not respond except to say that he was not even sure that the dialogue with the Palestinians was really essential.

I had made no headway; Shamir seemed to have no thought of stepping aside even after the blows he had taken. But he wanted to know what troops he had, and when the radio reported next day that "people within the Likud" were calling for his resignation, he phoned to ask if I was one of them. No, I said, he had my backing, though I could not—and do not to this day—understand how he envisioned a resolution of the Arab-Israeli conflict without meaningful contact with the Palestinians.

On Sunday, the president, Chaim Herzog, was going to begin the ritual prescribed by Israeli law of meeting with each Knesset faction and asking them for their recommendations about who should be charged by him with forming the next government. In anticipation of the Likud's meeting with the president, we met in Jabotinsky House in Tel Aviv on Saturday evening to come up with our recommendation for the next prime minister. Hundreds of Levy supporters, noisily demanding that he be chosen as the Likud candidate, had to be cleared from the room before the meeting could begin. While Shamir waited anxiously in Jerusalem, a seemingly endless debate developed, each of the thirty-nine Knesset members wanting to be heard again and again. While Levy tried to filibuster, demanding that the decision be postponed, most of those present, including Sharon and me, backed Shamir. At three o'clock in the morning we informed the press that Shamir would be our candidate.

By Tuesday, March 20, the president had completed the round of consultations with the Knesset factions. Shas had reversed course again and recommended that Shamir—not Peres—be charged with forming the next government. This resulted in sixty Knesset members recommending Shamir and sixty recommending Peres. By 9:00 P.M. the whole country was waiting to hear Herzog's choice. It was Peres. That evening he was invited to the presidential mansion, entrusted by Herzog to form the next government, and assigned the prescribed twenty-one days for the accomplishment of this task.

Could we keep the sixty-member bloc together, and thus block Peres's efforts to mobilize the minimum of 61 votes needed to support the government he was trying to put together? The answer might come the following Monday at Tel Aviv's Yad Eliyahu basketball stadium. There the venerable Rabbi Schach was scheduled to address a mass meeting where it was expected he would indicate his preference in the race between Peres and Shamir. Ten thousand of his followers, all dressed in black caftans, filled the stadium to capacity. After introductory speeches by his senior aides, the diminutive white-bearded rabbi stepped to the podium. The whole country was listening, maybe even a good part of the world, but his message was enigmatic. He spoke in a mixture of Hebrew and Yiddish, denouncing Labor's kibbutz movements for not knowing what Yom Kippur or the Sabbath were, what a ritual bath was, and for eating non-kosher food like pork and rabbits. The Jewish people, he said, had survived all their adversaries because they believed in God and because they studied the Torah—nothing else was important. He condemned those who knew nothing about the Jewish religion and furthermore did not want to know anything about it.

If most Israeli politicians had difficulty in interpreting the political meaning of this message, the religious community had no such problem: to them it was clear that the rabbi favored Shamir over Peres, and that Degel Hatorah and Shas Knesset members would not join a Peres-led government. Now Peres's only chance was to locate at least one defector in the Likud camp who would be prepared to support him. Next day I learned that this possibility was not far-fetched. I met Yitzhak Moda'i in his office in Tel Aviv, where he informed me that his five-man faction, which had defected from the Likud earlier that year and assumed the incongruous name of "The Movement for the Realization of the Zionist Ideal," was prepared to negotiate with Peres over the possibility of joining his government.

One man who did not seem to have been impressed by the political drama unfolding in Israel was Saddam Hussein. Speaking in Baghdad on April 1, he brought all of Israel back to Middle Eastern reality when he announced that he now possessed binary chemical weapons. "By God, we will make the fire eat up half of Israel if it tries to do anything against Iraq," he boasted. Coming from a man who had used chemical warfare in the past, this was serious. In fact, Iraq had become the largest producer of chemical agents in the world. Mustard gas and nerve agents such as sarin and tabun were being produced at large facilities in Samarra, Falluja, and Salman Pak that had been built using German and other West European technology.

On April 3, I called in Ambassador Bill Brown to emphasize the need for an appropriate response from the international community to this threat. "The absence of an unequivocal warning against the renewed use of chemical warfare is bound to encourage the Iraqi dictator," I told him, "leading him to believe that he can continue to get away with violating the accepted norms of civilized behavior; this is a danger to Israel, but not only to Israel—this kind of irresponsible behavior, if it goes unchecked, will end up being a threat to the whole region and to the world." I asked that urgent consultations be held between Israel and the United States on an appropriate reaction. Brown noted down my request, but it was to remain unanswered.

I did receive a response to a similar discussion I had with the Egyptian ambassador, Bassiouny. He called me at my home late one evening to tell me that he had a message from Mubarak assuring me that we had nothing to fear from Saddam Hussein, there was no need to escalate the tension, and not to worry. On April 4, the inner cabinet, now much reduced in number, received a briefing from IDF Intelligence on the Iraqi chemical warfare and missile capability and the missile launchers that had recently been built in western Iraq and were now pointed at Israel. From those launching sites, located near the H-2 air base, most of Israel was in the range of Iraqi Scud missiles.

The news from Baghdad did not in any way dampen Peres's efforts to put together a new government. That same evening Peres asked the Speaker of the Knesset, Dov Shilansky, to convene the Knesset on April 11, the date on which the twenty-one-day mandate was to run out, in order for him to present his government for the Knesset's approval. I was in Shamir's office when he received the news, and we both concluded that somehow Peres had succeeded in garnering his sixty-first supporter, but who? By next morning all Israel knew. It was Avraham Sharir, a former Likud minister whom Shamir had left out of the National Unity government, and who had joined Moda'i's defectors. He had gone into hiding after signing an agreement with the Labor party promising them his support in return for their commitment to appoint him minister in Peres's government, put him onto a "guaranteed" spot on their list for the next Knesset, and appoint him minister again if they were to form the government after the next elections. Two days later, Israeli newspaper readers read excerpts of a letter Sharir had written explaining his treacherous move. It included a long list of complaints against Shamir and the Likud leadership. And to top it all, the man who had been a member of the Sharon–Levy–Moda'i "constrainers" circle now insisted that he was convinced that a Peres-led government could bring about "true peace" with Israel's neighbors. It was a new record in hypocrisy.

But all was not lost. Two members of the Agudat Yisrael Knesset faction, Avraham Verdiger and Eliezer Mizrachi, made it known that they might be prepared to disregard the edict of the Council of Agudat Yisrael Torah Sages to support a Peres-led government. This left Peres with only 59 votes and Moda'i and his four cohorts holding the balance. The wooing of Moda'i by Labor and Likud began.

The night before Peres was scheduled to present his new government for Knesset confirmation, the Likud ministers, headed by Shamir, wrangled and bargained with Moda'i. His demands were outrageous: a senior government portfolio for himself and political plums for his associates, safe slots for them on the Likud slate for the next Knesset, and similar positions in the government to follow, if the Likud won the next elections. He threatened to go with Peres if his demands were not met. Perhaps Peres already had the votes he needed without Moda'i. Would Verdiger and Mizrachi really bolt from their party? Would Shas, which had already disappointed us once, do so again, in which case the commitments to Moda'i would be worse than useless? After an all-night session, the Likud ministers decided to give in, and at 5:00 A.M. they signed the document of surrender promising Moda'i all he had asked for.

That evening, Peres, confident that he had assured himself at least 61 votes for the following day's Knesset session, read out to a meeting of Labor's Central Committee the names of the ministers he had chosen to serve in his government. But next morning the drama that had kept Israelis in suspense for the past twenty-one days turned into a comedy of errors. The Knesset, called into session at Peres's request, had been scheduled to open at 9:00 A.M. and was to be devoted exclusively to the confirmation of the new government and the swearing in of Peres and his ministers. Peres's wife was in the visitors' gallery to witness the festive occasion. But the votes he had counted on were not all there. Although Sharir was now in his camp, Verdiger and Mizrachi, despite extraordinary pressure, were refusing to comply with the decision of their party's Torah Sages to support Peres's new government. With 119 Knesset members in their seats prepared for the vote of confidence, Peres had no choice but to request the Knesset speaker to reschedule the session to an unspecified future date. From the Knesset he proceeded directly to the president, from whom he obtained a fifteen-day extension to continue his search for the required number of coalition partners. There must have been considerable disappointment that day in Tunis, Cairo, and Washington, as long-held hopes for a more pliable Israeli government were put on hold.

Two days later, on April 14, Robert Dole, Republican Senate minority leader, arrived, heading a group of U.S. senators on a tour of the Middle East. Israel was not the senators' first stop; they had seen Assad in Syria, Mubarak in Egypt, and Saddam Hussein in Baghdad. In Iraq, the senators were offered a helicopter ride to the Kurdish area where, Saddam Hussein claimed, they could see for themselves that chemical warfare had not been used against Kurdish villages. But that day caution won out and they decided not to risk it. Dole refused my invitation for dinner that evening, but he came to my office the next morning to tell me that Saddam Hussein's threats against Israel were meant only as an indication of his response if Israel were to attack Iraq, and therefore were not to be taken seriously. I was astounded by Dole's reaction to the Iraqi dictator, who had started the war against Iran, had broken the international convention against the use of chemical warfare to which Iraq was a signatory, and was now threatening Israel.

With Peres trying to line up a coalition as background, and still seven days to go before the new deadline expired, the Likud Central Committee met in Jerusalem's convention center to approve the agreement with Moda'i. It was a vivid demonstration of how principles are thrown overboard in the quest for power. Shamir, in a long speech justifying the agreement, also made a last appeal to Sharir. Referring to him by his Russian nickname, he called out: "Abrasha, come home!" Sharir, who was probably glued to the radio somewhere in hiding, made no response. To my everlasting shame, I joined Shamir in appealing to the Central Committee members to approve the agreement. When the vote came, 70 percent, probably holding their noses against the stench, voted for approval. That very night Verdiger announced that he was submitting to the order of the Torah Sages and would support a Peres government. Now everything hinged on Eliezer Mizrachi, a Yemenite rabbi who was taking his marching orders from the Lubavitch Rabbi in Brooklyn.

The day before Peres's mandate was to expire, Vaclav Havel, the president of Czechoslovakia, and his foreign minister Jiri Dienstbier, arrived in Israel. I had met them both during my visit to Prague in early February when I went to reestablish diplomatic relations. Havel eagerly accepted President Herzog's invitation to become the first East European leader to visit Israel since 1967. A desert wind was blowing through Israel that day and Havel seemed to wilt as he stepped off the airplane. His first request was to be taken to the beach, and although I would have been happy to join him in a swim in the Mediterranean, I could not accommodate him, as President Herzog was waiting to receive him in Jerusalem. The following evening, Herzog gave a state dinner for Havel. Among the guests were Shamir, Peres, and many of the other participants in the political drama of the past few weeks, as well as Israelis who had come from Czechoslovakia—some before World War II, others who had made it after the war, and still others who had fled to Israel as Soviet tanks entered Prague in 1968.

At dinner there was only one subject of conversation—Yitzhak Moda'i. Moda'i, with a flair for showmanship, had announced that morning that he would reveal whether he was going with Peres or Shamir on the nine o'clock TV evening news. The tension was almost unbearable, everybody looking at their watches every few minutes during dinner. Shamir was pessimistic, believing that Moda'i was going to throw in his lot with Peres. But at ten minutes to nine a note was passed to him, informing him that Moda'i had chosen Likud. Within seconds the news had reached every guest as well as the waiters and kitchen personnel. Peres looked completely deflated—seven weeks of round-the-clock efforts to assemble a governing coalition had just gone down the drain. Even Havel, who within his two-day visit had begun to grasp something of the Israeli political crisis, turned to Herzog and asked what Moda'i's decision was.

That night, Peres announced that he had not been able to form a government; the following morning, Shamir was invited to the president's office and allotted twenty-one days to try to form a government.

By early May, concern was mounting over Hussein's blatant hostility toward Israel, the almost unanimous support that he seemed to be enjoying in the Arab world, and the lack of worry characterizing the attitude of the United States and Europe. Jordan had in recent months been developing an intimate alliance with Iraq, which included significant military cooperation. There were signs of closer ties between Iraq and Egypt, and Egypt joined Iraq, Jordan, and Yemen in the Arab Cooperation Council. As I told the Knesset's Foreign Affairs and Defense Committee, in the Arab world there had in the past been a correlation between military capability and aggressive intentions, with perceptions of increased capability feeding such intentions. The establishment of a united front, and the sense of increased power that would accompany it, might lead to new dangers for Israel.

On May 9, the inner cabinet met to review the Iraqi situation. Saddam Hussein had announced a few days earlier that he had given orders to his local military commanders to use chemical weapons against Israel if they were to lose contact with headquarters as a result of a military strike. It looked as though he was purposely escalating the tension, possibly creating a scenario that would provide an excuse for an attack on Israel, or else unwittingly injecting an element of instability into the situation, where an Iraqi commander could take the initiative in attacking Israel. Most disturbing was the fact that the United States was doing nothing to alert Saddam Hussein to the reaction he should expect if he were to use chemical weapons again. As a matter of fact, there had been no high-level contact between us and the Bush administration since my meeting with Baker back in February. They did not seem to be alarmed by Saddam Hussein's growing military capability or his bellicose pronouncements, and were probably avoiding contact with us in the expectation that any day Peres would replace Shamir as Israel's prime minister.

At the Foreign Ministry, I called in the senior officials to discuss ways of slowing Iraqi acquisition of non-conventional weaponry without provoking Saddam Hussein. There was no doubt in my mind that this madman, with one of the world's largest armies at his disposal, a vast inventory of missiles and chemical weapons, and who was moving rapidly to acquire nuclear weapons, represented an immediate danger not only to Israel and the entire Middle East but to the world at large. But without an internationally coordinated response there was little to be done but to await his next move.

I was dismayed to learn that just at this time the U.S. ambassador to the United Nations, Thomas Pickering, was working with the delegate of the People's Democratic Republic of Yemen—a country until recently on the State Department's list of countries engaged in terrorism —on the draft of a resolution to be submitted to the Security Council on the immigration of Soviet Jews to Israel and Israeli settlements in Judea, Samaria, Gaza, and East Jerusalem. I told Bill Brown how disappointed we were by the U.S. collaboration on a hostile document that referred to the Arab "right to return" and addressed the "illegality" of Israeli settlement in the territories and East Jerusalem. The Arabs at the United Nations eventually dropped the resolution, but it was an indication of the distorted priorities that had been established in Washington over the Middle East.

Adding to the tension was a speech President Mubarak delivered at the end of May at a meeting of the Socialist International in Cairo, which was also attended by Peres and a delegation of Israel's Labor party. In his speech, Mubarak said that the settlement of Soviet Jews in the territories, "and the subsequent expulsion of Palestinians from these areas," would bring the Middle East to the brink of a terrible war. Calling in Bassiouny, I told him that this was just the kind of talk that could provide Saddam Hussein with an excuse for starting a war, and expressed my hope that at the coming Arab summit in Baghdad, Mubarak would call on Arab countries to begin a process of normalizing relations with Israel.

Early in the morning on May 20, Ami Popper, a young Jew from Rishon Lezion near Tel Aviv, grabbed his brother's army rifle and rushed to the place on the highway where Arab laborers from Gaza waited every day to be hired by Israeli contractors for work in Israel. Shooting into the crowd, he killed seven of the laborers on the spot, severely wounding several more. Within hours, news of the murders set off an explosion of Arab anger throughout Judea, Samaria, and Gaza, as well as among Israeli Arabs, leading to rampages that claimed innocent victims of their own.

The Arab charge that the government of Israel was responsible not only for the killings but also for the violence that followed was taken up all over the world. The PLO demanded, and the United Nations agreed, that a special session of the Security Council be held in Geneva, where Arafat, spared the embarrassment of having to apply for a visa to the United States, was able to vilify Israel hysterically to an audience of millions. At a press conference after his speech, Arafat showed television viewers an Israeli coin that he claimed held a map of Israel on it with borders extending from the Nile to the Euphrates. Although there is no such coin, some viewers may have been taken in.

Baker announced that the United States was prepared to consider the possibility of sending UN observers to the territories, a proposal that he knew would be unacceptable to Israel. The French announced that they were sending a fact-finding mission headed by a member of the French government but, in an unprecedented insult to the Israeli government, refused to coordinate the visit with us. President Bush chose to link the tragedy to the political crisis in Israel. In a statement issued by his press secretary, he pointedly called upon "the Israeli security forces, as well as others, to act with maximum restraint," informing all concerned that, "based on experience, we believe that violence in the Middle East will continue and possibly grow so long as there is an absence of a promising peace process . . . we look forward to the quick emergence of an Israeli government that is capable of making decisions on issues of peace and is committed, just as we are, to moving ahead on the peace process."

I assumed that Bush had not forgotten that it was Shamir's government which had launched the peace initiative, and that he was aware that by Israeli law the present government, even in this caretaker role, had full governmental authority and prerogatives in all matters, including the peace process, but that he preferred to ignore these facts.

On May 24, I called a press conference to express our concern over the two international meetings that were being convened at that time. The first was the meeting of the UN Security Council in Geneva. The second was the Arab summit, to be held under Saddam Hussein's auspices in Baghdad, which would work toward an all-Arab strategy against Israel.

As so often happens in the Middle East, the march of events suddenly brought about a change of perspective. On May 30, the Jewish holiday of Shavuot, an attempt was made, in two assaults three hours apart, by the Palestine Liberation Front (PLF), a faction of the PLO, to land terrorists on packed Israeli beaches. Intercepted by the Navy and Border Police before any damage could be done—four terrorists were killed, several were captured, and their boats were destroyed—the raid demonstrated the PLO's continuing commitment to terror, despite Arafat's periodic statements to the contrary, and provided proof of our claim that the U.S. dialogue with the PLO was based on a patently false assumption.

Abul Abbas, whose pro-Iraqi group had also carried out the 1985 hijacking of the cruise ship *Achille Lauro* and the murder of Leon Klinghoffer, announced that he took full responsibility for the action on Israel's beaches. Washington demanded that Arafat expel the PLF leader from the PLO's executive committee, but Arafat, safe in Baghdad, refused. No one, he said, who had been "democratically elected" to the executive committee could possibly be expelled. Three weeks later, President Bush finally suspended the eighteen-month-old U.S. dialogue with the PLO, emphasizing his eagerness to resume it as soon as the PLO disassociated itself from Abul Abbas and communicated its abhorrence of "this terrorist act which sticks in our throat."

On June 1, with Shamir's mandate, which had already been renewed

by President Herzog, due to expire on June 8, Shamir was still struggling to assemble a coalition. Endless haggling with potential partners
had so far not produced a government. I suggested to him that, despite
the unpleasantness we had experienced recently, he go back to forming
a government of National Unity with Labor. But by June 7 Shamir was
on the point of putting together a narrow-based coalition government.
While I was sitting in my office with the German ambassador asking
him to pass on to Bonn our request that, after the latest PLO act of
terror, they cease their contacts with the PLO, a call from Shamir was
put through to me. Without any preliminaries, he asked me if I was
prepared to be minister of defense in the new government. He became
a little impatient when I replied that that was really not a subject for the
telephone. "You know I have to present a government, there is no time
to lose," he pressed me. "You're not going to get an answer from
me on the phone. I'll be happy to come and discuss it with you," I
replied.

I met with him that afternoon. He said he was close to completing
the negotiations: he had surrendered to Levy's demands to appoint him
foreign minister but was not prepared to make Sharon defense minister.
Now everything hinged on my agreement to move from the Foreign
Ministry to the Defense Ministry. I told him that I thought this would
be a bad government—bad for the country and bad for the Likud. If it
failed, Peres would form an alternate government on the ruins of this
one, and if we went to elections we would not go to the voters from a
position of strength and were likely to fail. But his mind was made up,
and he pleaded with me to agree, saying that this was his last chance.
Under the circumstances I felt that I had little choice but to agree.

On Friday, June 8, at 3:00 P.M., the day on which Shamir's mandate
was to run out, the coalition members signed the coalition agreement in
the prime minister's office and raised a toast to the new government.
My lack of enthusiasm for this government, no secret, became apparent
to all when I absented myself from the signing ceremony. On Monday,
June 11, the Knesset approved Shamir's new government by a vote of
62 to 57. Israel finally had a new government. David Levy was named
foreign minister; Yitzhak Moda'i would be minister of finance; and
Shamir made Ariel Sharon—now returned to government—minister of
construction and housing, also appointing him head of the ministerial
committee on the absorption of immigration. I thought those gentlemen would probably go on doing whatever they wanted and that they

were unlikely to be effective in furthering Israel's interests, and I told Shamir so.

"If this government fails," I wrote in my diary that week, "as I fear it will, we will have an alternate government formed by the Labor Party on the ruins of this one. Even if we then go to elections, the Likud will not go from a position of strength after having demonstrated success. It does not look to me as a positive development. . . ."

Defense Minister

On June 12, 1990, I drove into the Defense Ministry compound in Tel Aviv. The chief of staff, Lieutenant General Dan Shomron; the director general of the ministry, David Ivry; and troops representing the air force, navy, and the ground forces were lined up to salute Israel's new defense minister. I had gone through the same ritual over seven years ago when I took over the post from Ariel Sharon. Being Israel's defense minister is, in my view, one of the toughest jobs in the world. Other defense ministers may control larger military establishments, but none face the daunting task of preparing their forces to meet a threat to their country's existence from forces far larger, which may come at any moment, while dealing with daily acts of terror and violence that threaten the lives of soldiers and civilians alike. Although Israel's prime minister has a wider and all-encompassing responsibility, it is the defense minister who has to deal directly and immediately with all security problems, and who is subsequently seen by Israel's citizens as the man responsible for their safety and the well-being of their sons and daughters serving in the army.

When I became defense minister in February 1983, the Israeli Defense Forces were deployed in much of Lebanon, including the eastern sections of Beirut. I had withdrawn our forces to the Awali River, establishing a security zone that was designed to protect Israel's civilian population living in the northern part of the country from attack by terrorist groups operating from South Lebanon. I had enlisted General Antoine Lahad, a former Lebanese Army general, as commander of the South Lebanese Army (SLA), a force composed of inhabitants of the security zone that we hoped would take some of the burden of policing that zone from the IDF. Under Rabin there had been a further withdrawal, narrowing the security zone. Lahad's SLA had developed into a reasonably effective fighting force, composed of Christian, Druze, and Shiite Lebanese, which permitted a significant reduction in the size of Israeli forces that needed to be deployed north of Israel's international border with Lebanon.

The situation in Judea, Samaria, and Gaza had been relatively quiet during that period, giving me the opportunity to carry out the first major reorganization of the IDF. The IDF's organizational structure had not changed since its establishment in 1948. The four chief components of the ground forces—the armored corps, artillery, infantry, and engineers—had no unifying superstructure and their heads reported individually to the general staff, as did the heads of the air force, the navy, and the commanders of the three regional commands. I believed that changes in weapons technology necessitated close integration of these forces and a unified direction for training, development of tactics, and weapons system acquisition. This was to be accomplished by setting up a Ground Forces Command. Although this organizational change had seemed to me both obvious and urgent, it had been resisted over the years by those generals who felt that their authority would be curtailed in the process. Initially the move was accompanied by some criticism, but it was quickly accepted, and within a few years it was difficult to imagine how the IDF had operated without it.

I had also emphasized the development of weapons systems to give the IDF the quality edge it needed to overcome the numerical superiority of its adversaries. Many of the IDF's weapons were acquired in the United States, but their advantage was rapidly disappearing as the United States began to sell these same weapons to Arab countries. Israel now had to rely on its own defense industry, which in a number of areas had succeeded in developing technology not available anywhere else. Many of our defense industry products were, for obvious reasons, highly classified; but four items that have received publicity give a clear indication of our industry's potential: the Merkava main battle tank, the most advanced in the Israeli Armored Corps; the Lavi fighter aircraft, which was intended to be the backbone of the Israeli Air Force; the Ofek satellite, first launched in 1989; and the Arrow ballistic missile interceptor, the most advanced system of its kind.

I felt confident in my ability to envisage the battlefield of the future and to predict the technologies that would have a major impact on future warfare. The accuracy of such predictions is crucial since it takes about ten years for a weapons system to go from conception to operational usage, and thereafter it may have a lifetime of another ten to twenty years. In my view, technological developments would influence the future battlefield primarily in four areas: precision guided munitions (PGM), capable of pinpoint accuracy regardless of target range; night-vision devices, which provide the ability to fight around the clock; helicopters, which add a third dimension to ground warfare; and Command Control Communication and Intelligence (C^3I) systems, which give commanders at all levels information about the disposition of their own and enemy troops and the appropriate means of control to deploy and engage their forces. A number of locally developed systems were already part of the IDF's inventory and others were in development.

The chief of staff, Lieutenant General Dan Shomron, was the archetypical Sabra. Born and raised in Kibbutz Ashdod Yaakov, he had spent his life in the army, eventually becoming Israel's most senior military officer, with an impressive combat record. He was the silent type, always calm and composed. Like many of his generation, he had not had an opportunity to obtain a university education and did not speak English. During my first tenure as defense minister I had appointed Moshe Levi as chief of staff, passing over Shomron, who had also been a candidate at the time. I had dissuaded him from retiring by convincing him that his chances were good to make it the next time around, and he had agreed to remain and become the first commander of the newly constituted Ground Forces Command. And in fact, when Levi completed his tour of duty as chief of staff in April 1987, Rabin appointed Shomron. We knew each other well and I was quite confident that we would work well together, even though when he called for the cancelation of the Lavi fighter program we found ourselves on opposite sides of the fence.

I had brought with me my personal staff from the Foreign Ministry: Salai Meridor; the ministry spokesman, Danny Naveh; and Ilana Biennenshtock to run my office staff. Afterward, as we assembled in the defense minister's office, I told them that now it was really going to be serious business, where people's lives would depend on my decisions in a most immediate and direct sense.

My first challenge was the Intifada, now in its nineteenth month, with no sign of abating. On the Palestinian side, there were hundreds dead and many thousands injured, and tens of thousands imprisoned. On the Israeli side, there were tens killed and hundreds injured. Rabin had used severe measures—all of the schools and universities in Judea, Samaria, and Gaza had been closed. But to little avail. The Palestinians had suffered grievously, while more than a hundred thousand Israelis in the territories traveled on the roads at considerable risk to their lives. I knew that bringing about an improvement in the security of the Israeli settlers while trying to establish a dialogue with the Palestinians was not going to be easy.

Although Israelis living on the Israeli side of the "green line" read about the Intifada in the newspaper or saw it on television, the settlers faced it daily on the roads of Judea, Samaria, and Gaza; men and women going to work, and children being bused to school. I was eager to demonstrate that the lot of the settlers was going to receive top priority from now on. On my second day in office, I scheduled a visit to the two largest Israeli settlements in the territories: Maaleh Adumim, in the Judean desert, a five-minute ride from Jerusalem, with a population of close to 10,000; and Ariel, a half hour ride from Tel Aviv, in central Samaria, with a population of 7,000.

I arrived by helicopter with Dan Shomron. We were greeted by Major General Yitzhak Mordechai, head of the Central Command, and his aides, as well as by the local mayors. I was amazed to learn that Rabin throughout his five-year tenure as defense minister had never visited these towns, and that it was Shomron's first visit as well. In the eyes of the settlers there could be no clearer indication of the level of priority that had been assigned to maintaining their security. "Provide safety for those traveling on the roads," I instructed the army. "Do whatever is necessary, whether it means stationing soldiers along the road, increasing the number of patrols, or even seizing buildings alongside that provide control over stretches of road." Although providing safety for the tens of thousands of Israeli vehicles traveling on thousands of kilometers of roads, many of them running through Arab villages, was no simple matter, a significant reduction in rock throwing at passing cars was achieved shortly. The army command had looked on the policing duties in Judea, Samaria, and Gaza as a headache that interfered with its primary mission of preparing for full-scale war. Only after I made it clear to the chief of staff and the other senior officers that dealing with the Intifada was their foremost mission were the army's priorities set accordingly.

I quickly began establishing contact with Palestinians in the territories. During my first two weeks in office I met with Elias Freij, the mayor of Bethlehem, who was an old friend from my previous tenure as defense minister; the mayors of Bet Sahur and Bet Jalla; Fayez Abu Rahme, the well-known Gaza lawyer; Dr. Akram Matar, who ran the Gaza eye clinic, and his brother, who was head of the Gaza architects' association. I explained to them that although Israelis and Palestinians differed strongly on the terms of the settlement to the conflict, it was not a "zero-sum game" and therefore we should identify those steps that would be of mutual benefit. I urged them to help stop the violence and thereby make it possible for me to reopen the schools and universities, withdraw the army from populated areas, and set the stage for the holding of elections and subsequent negotiations between us.

The reception to my plea was generally positive, but the fear of terrorism was always in the air. When I asked Palestinians if they would be prepared to be candidates once elections were held, they usually answered that their families would not agree out of fear for their lives. I knew that they were telling the truth, because while we were bringing about a significant reduction in acts of violence against Israelis, and as a result in casualties among Palestinians from Israeli fire, every day brought news of Palestinians being killed by Palestinians. I could see that the natural leaders of the Palestinian population—the professionals, academics, and business people—were too frightened by the gangs that terrorized the streets of towns and refugee camps to exercise leadership. Those like the PLO who opposed the holding of democratic elections were using terror to prevent elections from being held.

I was convinced that elections were a key step in any significant progress toward an accommodation between Israel and the Palestinians. We needed to negotiate not with self-appointed leaders or men held hostage by terrorist guns, but with men and women who had been elected, had received a mandate from their constituency, and felt responsible to the population that elected them. I also hoped that the democratic process would bring with it the values associated with Western democracy—tolerance, respect for human rights, and rejection of violence as a means of settling differences of opinion.

The IDF was facing a difficult and unpleasant task in carrying out policing operations in Judea, Samaria, and Gaza, operations that brought eighteen- and nineteen-year-old soldiers into direct contact with the Palestinian population in towns, villages, and refugee camps. In Israel, there was much concern that these encounters would have a corrupting influence on the army and lead to an abandonment of the high standards that had become a tradition of the IDF. Actually, I found that even though there had been individual cases of brutal and immoral behavior by some soldiers and officers, on the whole the way the men of the IDF handled this extremely difficult task was impressive. Youngsters who had just finished high school showed an amazing sense of maturity, handling their unpleasant duties in a responsible manner. All of them preferred to serve on the Lebanese border, where they faced far greater danger, but they accepted their assignment in the territories calmly.

Before becoming completely immersed in the challenges facing me at the Defense Ministry, I decided to send off a parting letter to Secretary Baker so as to set the record straight. On June 18, I wrote:

Dear Jim:
Now that we have finally formed a government, and in the process I have moved to the Defense Ministry, I have the opportunity to review our cooperative efforts during the past year and a half and also to do a little stocktaking. Unburdened by diplomatic restraints, I can write to you freely.

I have always believed that a mutual understanding of the concerns and motivations of the parties is a prerequisite for an agreement. My impression is that there has not been that understanding between us this past year. As for us, the fall of the government and the ensuing crisis were only a reflection of the deep fears and anxieties that beset the majority of Israel's population—a feeling of being embattled and beleaguered by the hostile Arab world.

When you visit Israel, as I am sure you will sooner or later, you must visit some of our military cemeteries. They are a stark reminder that we are a bereaved nation that has to pay the highest price of all for its very existence. It is only based on an understanding of our very real concerns that agreements leading to an accommodation will be reached.

Last September when I saw you in New York I thought we had an agreement that would be acceptable in Israel; namely, that the US, Egypt and Israel would determine the composition of the Palestinian delegation to discuss the election procedures with us. But the Egyptians backtracked and you decided to go along with them. Since then the Egyptians have

145

been avoiding us. It almost seems that rather than building on the foundations of the Israeli-Egyptian peace treaty, as envisaged in the first point of our peace initiative, we are facing a deterioration in the relationship. This deterioration seemingly stems from disagreements between Israel and Egypt and also between Israel and the US on how best to promote Israel's peace initiative. Strange as it may seem our combined efforts to make progress seem to be producing counter-productive results.

I think that the new government provides a new opportunity to move forward. It is committed to Israel's peace initiative and its positions will no doubt be more coherent than was the case in the Likud-Labor coalition.

Jim, I want to take this opportunity to thank you for your cooperation during my tenure as Foreign Minister and for the efforts you have invested in the Middle East peace process. I know that we shall continue to work together even though my ministerial position has changed.

A month later, on July 18, Baker sent me his reply:

Dear Misha:

Thank you for your letter of June 28 [sic] and your reflections on the peace process over the past eighteen months. We did come close, with your active help, to an Israeli-Palestinian dialogue, leading to elections and negotiations. I think we can still get there, and working with the Israeli Government, I'm hopeful we will. I will continue to press at the same time for Arab states to signal their commitment to reconciliation and peace with Israel. That is essential, particularly given the weapons of mass destruction proliferating in the area.

On the modality of forming the Palestinian Delegation, this remains a key question. Misha, I don't agree that Egypt backtracked on understandings reached on this issue; and you know very well how hard I worked with you to reach a formula that met the needs of the Palestinians in the territories without at the same time, violating the Prime Minister's principles. Throughout the process, I tried to ensure common understandings and to avoid surprises. I continue to believe, as the President spelled out in his letter to the Prime Minister, that a credible delegation can be formed. I look forward to launching this process.

I wish you well with your heavy responsibilities as Defense Minister. I know that you will tackle the challenges with professionalism. And I also know that we will surely have occasion to communicate in the future, not only on the peace process, but also on many other issues which fall within your new portfolio.

146

To this Baker appended a handwritten note.

> Misha—I very much appreciate your personal efforts (of which I'm well aware)—just before the prior government fell. All the best, Jim.

Since Saddam Hussein's April 2 speech, we had learned that the Iraqis were actively engaged in ballistic missile development and had constructed a number of fixed missile launchers in western Iraq aimed at Israel. Remembering Mubarak's conversations with me in which he told me that the Iraqis seemed to fear an Israeli attack, I thought that if this concern really existed in Baghdad, it could bring about an unintentional outbreak of hostilities. Since we had no contact with the Iraqis, there was no way of putting into place a direct telephone line or some other means of communication between us that would prevent a misunderstanding from escalating.

Knowing that of all the Western nations France, which had made massive sales of advanced weaponry to Iraq, had the closest relations with Baghdad, I called in the French ambassador, Alain Pierret, on July 6, hoping to establish contact with the Iraqis through the French. I explained to him how France might be able to prevent an accidental outbreak of hostilities by establishing indirect contact between Israel and Iraq. He seemed impressed with the mission that I had entrusted to him and promised to convey the message to Paris immediately. Pierret was at the time close to completing his posting in Israel. I sensed that he had become uncomfortable with the consistent anti-Israel positions he had had to represent during the past three years and welcomed the opportunity to participate in a diplomatic move that might turn out to be of some importance. He returned in a few days to inform me that the French ambassador to Baghdad was in Paris and the Iraqi deputy foreign minister was expected to visit Paris shortly, so the matter would be raised with him then.

I had expected that the French would take the matter seriously enough to send a special envoy to Baghdad to meet with Saddam Hussein, but clearly the danger of an Iraqi missile attack on Israel was not of major concern to them. The next time I was to see the French ambassador was at the height of the Gulf crisis. The French had been making a big show of their aircraft carrier, the *Clemenceau*, steaming into the Persian Gulf. "Wouldn't it be ironic if the *Clemenceau* were to be torpedoed by Iraqi-piloted French Mirage aircraft firing French Exocet missiles?" I asked him. He was obviously embarrassed; the *Clemenceau* disappeared from the Persian Gulf a few days later, not to reappear for the duration of the Gulf crisis.

The government had been receiving frequent reports from the Israeli intelligence community about Iraqi efforts to establish nuclear weapons capability for some time. The danger that Saddam Hussein might come into possession of atomic weapons had been of great concern to successive Israeli governments, ever since he began his program of nuclear armament in the 1970s. There was no way of knowing how he would use such a weapon. That he would threaten Israel seemed almost certain. It was far from certain that he could be deterred from using atomic weapons by the threat of a response in kind. These considerations led Begin to the conclusion in 1981 that the nuclear reactor built for the Iraqis by the French nuclear industry had to be destroyed. But the destruction of the Iraqi nuclear reactor near Baghdad by the Israeli Air Force on June 7, 1981, had not put an end to Saddam Hussein's ambition to make Iraq a nuclear power, although it had succeeded in setting the Iraqi nuclear effort back by a good number of years.

When UN inspectors visited Iraq after the war, they discovered that the Iraqis had organized a massive effort, reminiscent of the American Manhattan Project of World War II, that pursued three different paths for the manufacture of weapons-grade material: a centrifuge plant to produce U^{235}; production of U^{235} by electromagnetic separation using calutrons; and production of plutonium in a nuclear reactor. Now their nuclear effort was dispersed in many locations in Iraq and could not be destroyed by a single attack. In their program to build a uranium centrifuge facility they were being assisted by a number of West German and Swiss industries as well as individual scientists and engineers from Western Europe. The program was designed to transfer blueprints, critical parts, and the necessary specialized machine tools from Europe, so the Iraqis could carry on the program independently at the earliest possible moment.

On July 18, 1990, Shamir, David Levy, now serving as foreign minister, and I met with the heads of the intelligence community in the prime minister's office for a briefing on the status of the Iraqi nuclear program. The report we received was alarming: the Iraqis were on the verge of being able to proceed with their centrifuge project without further outside help. Unless steps were taken to derail their centrifuge program during the coming months, they would be in a position to manufacture weapons-grade uranium very soon. The program could not be arrested by a single military strike; international intervention would be needed to stop European industries from cooperating with the Iraqis, and the Iraqis would have to be warned to cease and desist from their nuclear armament program. If help could be obtained, it would have to be from the United States. Washington, we hoped, would realize the extent of the danger. That day I called Dick Cheney in Washington and set up a meeting for us at the Pentagon two days later, July 20.

The following day, accompanied by Major General Amnon Shahak, the head of IDF Intelligence, and by the head of the Mossad, whose name, like that of the head of the General Security Service, is never made public during his term of office, I took the El Al "midnight express" to Kennedy. Cheney had sent a U.S. Air Force Grumman Gulfstream to New York to fly me and my entourage to Andrews Air Force Base outside Washington. By midday, a limousine deposited me at the steps to the Pentagon entrance where Cheney awaited my arrival. He had organized a grand military reception that included a nineteen-gun salute and a large honor guard on the lawn facing the Pentagon.

After lunch we sat down in the conference room adjacent to Cheney's office: Cheney, Undersecretary of Defense Paul Wolfowitz, Defense Intelligence Agency (DIA) head Lieutenant General Harry Soyster, and their assistants on one side of the table, and we on the other side. Before asking Shahak and the head of the Mossad to give their presentation, I described the current situation in the Middle East. Whereas in Eastern Europe there was *glasnost* and the beginnings of democracy, the Middle East, except for Israel, continued to be ruled by dictators, and Muslim fundamentalism was running rampant. The Soviet Union and the Eastern European countries were disarming while the arms race in the Middle East was intensifying. Saddam Hussein had built a large army and an advanced defense industry; he already had the ability to conduct chemical warfare and was working frantically to attain nuclear weapons. He had repeatedly threatened Israel with destruction by chemical weapons. There was a rapidly developing military cooperation between Iraq and Jordan. A combined Iraqi-Jordanian fighter squadron had been established and Iraqi aircraft were flying over Jordan. Should Iraqi ground forces enter Jordan, Israel's strategic position would be radically affected. Arab armies were being equipped with ground-to-ground missiles with sufficient range to reach Israel.

I also stressed the need for continued U.S. support for the Arrow ballistic missile interceptor program. This development by the Israel Aircraft Industries was being carried out within the framework of President Reagan's Strategic Defense Initiative, and funded in large part by the United States. At the time of my talk with Cheney, the Arrow was the most advanced system anywhere in the Western world for the interception of ballistic missiles.

Then I asked Shahak and the head of the Mossad to give our evaluation of the status of the Iraqi nuclear program. For close to an hour they presented detailed information on the assistance the Iraqis were getting from Europe for their centrifuge program, concluding with their estimate of the date by which a nuclear device would be within Saddam Hussein's reach. Cheney and the other Americans listened but asked almost no questions. Then Cheney thanked me for the presentation, indicating that they would give it consideration.

I did not know what to make of this low-key response. Did he doubt the veracity of the information? Was he too shocked to enter into a discussion about it? It was only after the Gulf War that we learned that the message we brought to Washington that day had evidently not surprised our hosts—it seems the administration had been aware of the Iraqi nuclear effort for some time. Less than two weeks later, Saddam Hussein occupied Kuwait and the Gulf crisis was on.

On the night of August 2, 1990, the Iraqi Army marched into Kuwait. For days they had concentrated large forces on the Iraqi-Kuwait border, and once they decided to move, it was a walk-over. Saddam Hussein's rhetoric was reminiscent of Hitler. He claimed that Kuwait was historically an integral part of Iraq, the nineteenth province, and that he had been invited to enter Kuwait by a new government that had replaced the one that fled to Saudi Arabia as the Iraqi Army moved in. On August 3, I called Cheney to tell him that if we could be of any help, I would be happy to discuss it with him. He was reticent. I had the feeling that he was afraid of being trapped into collusion with Israel, so I let it go at that.

My primary concern was that the Iraqi Army might enter Jordan and that we could find them one morning deployed in the Jordan Valley within mortar range of local Israeli towns and villages and within artillery range of Jerusalem. Iraqi-Jordanian cooperation and coordination seemed to be getting closer from day to day, especially in the military field. Jordan's King Hussein was a frequent visitor in Baghdad. A good highway links Baghdad to Amman, five hundred miles away, and the move could be carried out in twenty-four hours. Early on the morning of August 7, I called in Shomron, Barak, and other senior officers to discuss the danger of an Iraqi entry into Jordan.

The next morning, Bill Brown came to my home in Savyon at seven o'clock with a message from Washington. Sitting beside me on the couch in our living room, he pulled the cable out of his briefcase, and informed me that the United States was deploying military forces in Saudi Arabia. Israel was requested not to take any preemptive action. I told him that we understood that President Bush was attempting to obtain the cooperation of Saudi Arabia, Egypt, and other Arab countries, and therefore did not want to be perceived as being in collusion with Israel. We were, of course, prepared to help if our help was required. In any case the present situation required close operational coordination between the United States and Israel; we had a common enemy in Iraq. But Israel urgently needed intelligence information from United States satellite photos of the deployment of the Iraqi Army, so that we would have sufficient warning if the Iraqi Army began moving toward Jordan. We also needed to be apprised of the operational plans of U.S. forces, especially in the air, to prevent any accidental conflict between our forces.

That evening an Iraqi spokesman announced that Israel had painted its air force aircraft with U.S. markings and provided its pilots with U.S. identification papers and was now preparing an attack on Iraq. He went on to threaten Israel with severe retribution if such an attack were to be carried out. These lies were a transparent attempt by the Iraqis to mobilize the Arab world in their support, but could also be a prelude to an Iraqi attack on Israel.

Tension grew in Israel. The newspapers headlined the Iraqi threats. Much space was devoted to explaining the potential effects of chemical warfare. Except for the Kurds in the mountainous villages of Iraq, no civilian population had ever faced the danger of attack with chemical weapons. Almost overnight the civilian population of Israel, which had enjoyed a feeling of security for as long as most of them could remember, was faced with the possibility of attack from a country with which Israel had no common border and which in the past had been only a peripheral participant in Arab aggression against Israel. Iraq had become the largest producer of chemical agents in the world. Mustard gas and nerve agents were being produced at the facilities in Samarra, Falluja, and Salman Pak that had been built using German and other Western European technology.

Years earlier, the Israeli government had begun a program of acquiring gas masks to be kept in storage for distribution to the population if the need arose. Now calls were being made for the gas masks to be distributed immediately. I tried to weigh the problem as rationally as I could under the circumstances. It was not known whether the Iraqis had chemical warheads for their missiles; in any case, their missile warhead was relatively small and the number of missiles they could launch at any one time was probably no more than ten. Although fairly large chemical bombs could be delivered by their Soviet-supplied long-range bombers, I was confident of our air force's ability to intercept those before they reached Israel. Also, irrational as he might seem, Saddam Hussein would have to take into consideration the Israeli response to such an attack. The distribution of the gas masks to the general public might be taken as a signal that the government expected the Iraqis to launch chemical warfare against Israel's civilian population, and cause panic. I decided against it.

On August 9, I attended the graduation ceremonies of the National Security College, a one-year course run by the IDF for officers at the level of lieutenant colonel and colonel scheduled for promotion to higher rank. On the campuslike grounds of one of the army bases not far from Tel Aviv the graduates assembled with their families, the senior echelons of the IDF, and hundreds of reporters who had come to hear Shamir speak and to press me for my reaction to the fast-developing situation. Shamir in his speech branded the Iraq accusations against Israel as fabrications and announced that Israel would know how to defend itself if attacked. In my comments to reporters, I did my best to allay the anxiety that had spread among Israel's population: Israel was prepared for all eventualities. I assigned a very low probability to an Iraqi attack with chemical weapons.

But I was worried; there was no knowing what the Iraqi dictator was up to. In his mind, attacking Israel might seem like a good response to the confrontation he had gotten himself into with America and the Arab alliance Bush was putting together against him. He might believe that such an attack would bring the Arab world to his side. Although I estimated that his ability to inflict physical damage on Israel's population centers was limited, I knew that the psychological damage would be great, and that it would not be easy to respond in such a way as to put an end to the danger. I repeated my desire for a coordinated effort with the United States in another meeting with Brown, and then called

Deputy Secretary of State Larry Eagleburger, whom I trusted to be absolutely straight with me. I asked him to pay close attention to the message that Ambassador Brown would be forwarding to the White House, the State Department, and the Pentagon. He promised me that the message would be given appropriate attention.

There was disturbing news from Jordan: large demonstrations for Saddam Hussein in the streets of Jordan's cities, which King Hussein was either unwilling or unable to control. After having chosen to join Egypt and Syria in their war against Israel in 1967, and having decided to stay out of the Yom Kippur War in 1973, King Hussein was now making his third fateful choice: supporting the Iraqi dictator in the Gulf crisis. We received an intelligence report that King Hussein had changed his stance and was about to invite the Iraqi Army into Jordan, and asked Washington to warn him against such a move.

On August 7, speaking in the Knesset, I had warned Jordan against the entry of Iraqi troops. Replying to a motion on the agenda regarding Iraq's takeover of Kuwait, I said: "The Iraqi invasion of Kuwait provides clear proof of the potential threat we face from the East. It should be emphasized that the Iraqi invasion of Kuwait does not constitute a geo-strategic change for Israel. But the moment we see that we are facing such a change, such as the entry of the Iraqi Army into Jordan, we shall act. This was and continues to be the policy of Israeli governments. Israel will watch closely the moves of the Iraqi dictator and will know how to defend its interests and security." I hoped that this message would be duly registered in Amman as well as in Baghdad and would deter the Iraqis from opening an additional front with Israel. A few days later, King Hussein announced that Jordan was not about to open its borders to "tourist visits" by foreign armies from either East or West. I assumed this was his reply to my warning.

Had we followed the advice of the Israeli left and abandoned control of the West Bank, we would have faced the danger of Iraqi troops deploying a few miles from Tel Aviv and in the center of Jerusalem.

The inner cabinet met to discuss the situation on August 15. The danger we were facing—I told my colleagues—was either of an Iraqi missile and air attack against Israel's cities or the entry of Iraqi troops into Jordan, possibly both. We were well prepared to intercept the enemy's aircraft; the damage his missiles could inflict was limited; and we had made it clear that the entry of Iraqi troops into Jordan would mean a full-scale war. What I did not say was that I was concerned about the possibility of a change of government or a coup in Jordan by the PLO or some other Iraqi-backed group. Ariel Sharon wanted to see a presentation of detailed operational plans for all eventualities. I was concerned that elements of such a presentation might leak out and cause inestimable damage. During the meeting, Sharon passed me a note asking that he be called up for active duty.

It was a time of considerable tension. Israel was on the verge of another war. A confrontation between the United States and the allies Bush had managed to mobilize and Iraq that might lead to the destruction of Iraq's military capability and put an end to its nuclear program was in the best interests of Israel. It behooved us therefore to do nothing that might interfere with Bush's Iraqi strategy, even if he was keeping Israel at arm's length. It was best for us to prepare for the dangers that might develop while maintaining a low profile and not assisting Saddam Hussein's attempt to portray the conflict as an Arab-Israeli one. Although other suggestions were heard at the meeting, the consensus was to stay out as long as we could.

On August 17, we received information that the Jordanian Army alert had been raised to the highest state of readiness. I do not know if this was in expectation of an attack by us, in anticipation of the entry of Iraqi forces into Jordan, or maybe just King Hussein's way of gaining support for himself from the mobs demonstrating in Amman. The United States was continuing to pour troops into Saudi Arabia. By now Saddam Hussein had probably missed his opportunity to overcome the Americans with numerical superiority. Although he still had superiority on the ground, U.S. airpower in the area would have been sufficient to even the odds. He evidently did not believe that Bush was ready to commit his forces. It was one of a number of mistakes he was going to make in this crisis. Given various opportunities for graceful compromise, he missed every one of them. Had Saddam understood American politics, he would have realized that once Bush had deployed 500,000 troops and much of the U.S. Navy and Air Force in the Gulf, and had said publicly that Saddam Hussein was worse than Hitler, there was no turning back without at least some minimal concession from Iraq.

In the meantime I continued my efforts to establish operational coordination between the United States and Israeli military and to obtain real-time satellite photo intelligence data from Washington; but to no avail. I considered the option of sending our reconnaissance aircraft over Iraq to obtain updated aerial photos of Iraqi troop deployment and of the areas in western Iraq from which missiles could be launched against Israel, but decided against it since such overflights would surely be noticed by the Iraqis and would serve as grist for their propaganda mills at a crucial juncture of the developing crisis. The week of August 19 I started holding daily meetings with Shomron, Ehud Barak, and Shahak, so as to be continuously updated on the unfolding events. By this time the Israeli Air Force was on alert, interceptor aircraft ready to take off on a minute's notice, and surface-to-air missile batteries deployed, their radars scanning the skies for enemy aircraft.

At the weekly government meeting on Sunday, August 19, without any prior warning, Foreign Minister David Levy astounded Shamir and the rest of the members of the government by accusing me of taking too lightly the mortal danger facing Israel's population from an impending Iraqi chemical attack, and demanding that gas masks be issued immediately to the public. Shamir tried to placate him by saying that he could raise the subject at the next meeting of the inner cabinet, but that it was not a suitable subject for discussion in the full government. Immediately after the meeting, Levy personally briefed reporters; the following day he appeared on television, repeating his accusations and calling for the immediate distribution of gas masks. It was not clear to me whether Levy had simply lost his nerve, or was trying to score points with the public even at the risk of increasing their anxiety, or possibly both, but I found his behavior unpardonable.

At the very beginning of the crisis I had ordered the Defense Ministry to take stock of the gas masks in storage. It turned out that there was a considerable shortage of the special kits required for babies and of masks for small children. No gas masks had been acquired for the Palestinian population in Judea, Samaria, and Gaza. This situation alone was enough to keep us from issuing the masks to the public. I would have gladly made this information available to Levy had he bothered to check with me. The Gaza Strip was out of range of the Iraqi missiles, but the rest of Judea and Samaria could theoretically be hit by missiles launched from western Iraq, although the likelihood that Saddam Hussein would target the Palestinian population seemed to me negligible. Nevertheless, I knew there would be an outcry—probably from Israelis and not from Palestinians—if gas masks were distributed in Israel and the Palestinians in the territories were left out. To cover this eventuality, we started scouring Europe for gas masks.

An Israeli official returning from a trip to Cairo reported to me on a conversation he had had with a senior Egyptian Intelligence officer, who had told him that Israel should not worry about the possibility of an Iraqi missile attack. "Saddam Hussein knows that you have atomic bombs, and that your leadership is totally reckless when it comes to Israel's defense and will not hesitate to retaliate with these weapons if attacked by Iraqi missiles. He knows that even the Americans will not be able to restrain you if you are hit by missiles. So don't worry!" He was wrong.

By the beginning of September, a good part of the IDF had already been in a state of alert for a month. That, in addition to preparing the civilian population for the possibility of an Iraqi missile attack, was adding significant expense to the already strained defense budget. Although the United States was actively raising funds among its richer allies to assist those hurt economically by the Gulf crisis, Israel so far had received no indication that we would be on the list of recipients, among them, Egypt, Turkey, and Syria. At the same time a steadily increasing share of Israel's own resources was being allocated for the absorption of Jews from the Soviet Union, who, undeterred by Arab threats, had begun streaming into Israel in large numbers. I knew we could not expect any help from Saudi Arabia or the other oil-rich Gulf sheikdoms, so I turned to what was then still West Germany for assistance.

On Monday, September 3, I walked into Helmut Kohl's office in Bonn, accompanied by David Ivry and Amnon Shahak. Kohl, a large, expansive man, was in an exuberant mood that day. He was in his ninth year as leader of what had become, after the United States and Japan, the third most powerful country in the world (the Soviet Union had already lost its superpower status), and was congratulating himself on having saved Gorbachev by extending German economic assistance to him, and on leading Germany to reunification. Now he wanted to hear about the Gulf crisis. West Germany could not get involved because the postwar German constitution prohibited the sending of armed forces outside West Germany's borders, but he was curious to hear how George Bush was going to extricate himself from this mess. "Aren't we all lucky that the guy from Boston [meaning Dukakis] didn't win the election?" he joked. "Is the allied blockade of Iraq going to work?" he asked, and immediately ventured his own opinion that it was not.

"What is King Hussein's situation in Jordan? Is he going to survive this crisis?" Kohl was expecting King Hussein that afternoon at 3:00 P.M. The streets of Bonn were bedecked with Jordanian flags, and Kohl was using me to prep himself for his meeting. He also wanted to know whether Mubarak was seriously threatened by Muslim fundamentalism in Egypt, and just how stable the Saudi regime was. I was glad to have brought Amnon Shahak along. He gave an extended intelligence briefing on the Middle East in general, and the Gulf crisis in particular. Then I explained everything Israel was doing to prepare and how it was becoming a heavy economic burden for us while the Saudis raked in profits as the price of oil rose. Kohl well understood why we could not expect to get any help from that direction.

Kohl listened attentively and he seemed sympathetic. Then he said: "Ich will mir das überlegen" (I want to think about it). And that was it. I was not to hear from him again until Scuds started falling on Israel.

While I was in Bonn, David Levy was being wined and dined in Washington. Baker had evidently received detailed briefings from his staff on the internal politics of the Likud, on Levy's constant attempts to undermine anybody he perceived as a potential rival for the future leadership of the Likud, and his animosity toward me. He had concluded that Levy's alliance with the other superhawks in the Likud—Sharon and Moda'i—was no more than a marriage of convenience, and that Levy's opposition to the Israeli government's peace initiative should not be taken too seriously now that he had become foreign minister. If Baker played up to Levy's ego, he could probably get him to agree to moves that Shamir would oppose. The famous Baker "questions" that had caused the downfall of the National Unity government, which Levy had opposed adamantly, seemed to have been consigned to oblivion. In addition, Baker brought Levy into an eight-minute photo opportunity with President Bush. It seemed to work. A few days later in New York, Baker succeeded in getting Levy to agree that the Israeli government would report to Washington on any future construction in the territories, including East Jerusalem. This was without precedent in the longstanding debate between Jerusalem and Washington on settlements in the territories.

Ten days later, I visited Washington. I had been invited to speak at a seminar of the Washington Institute for Near East Policy, and thought I would take the opportunity to impress upon Cheney our need for intelligence and economic assistance. Since the administration was urging its allies and Japan to help defray the expenses of the Middle Eastern countries involved (although Israel for some reason did not appear on the list), and was proposing to Congress to cancel Egypt's $7 billion debt incurred over the years in acquiring weapons from the United States through foreign military sales, I thought that there was a chance that my request would be considered seriously in Washington.

I reminded the audience at the seminar of the perception gap that had characterized much of Israel's relationship with the United States over the years. Our apprehension of Arab dictators who were acquiring vast quantities of arms was considered paranoia by official Washington. When we took their frequent threats against Israel seriously, we were considered alarmists. Arab demands for territorial concessions by Israel, which we found outrageous, were given some legitimacy in Washington. That perception gap, I said, seemed to have collapsed on August 2, the night the Iraqi Army marched into Kuwait. Now the Middle East as viewed by Israel was pretty much the Middle East as viewed by the United States. There was nothing like U.S. armed forces facing Saddam Hussein's military machine at close range, or as Dick Cheney put it, being "in harm's way," to concentrate the minds of official Washington. And yet it turned out that I was being somewhat optimistic. At the time I was not yet fully aware of the extensive support the Bush administration and Baker in particular had been giving to Iraq right up to the eve of Iraq's annexation of Kuwait.

When I met Dick Cheney in the Pentagon on the afternoon of September 17, I told him that I was operating on the assumption that once the United States initiated military action against Iraq, there was a significant probability of Israel being attacked by Iraq in an attempt to demonstrate to the Arab world that this was really a war against Israel. We were likely to be hit by Iraqi missiles, possibly with chemical warheads. We had to take into consideration that the Iraqis might even strike out at Israel prior to any U.S. military action, if the blockade made them desperate. On the other hand, if the crisis was not resolved by U.S. military action, then we in Israel could count on a confrontation with Iraq at some future date. Of all the countries involved in this crisis, Israel was the most exposed. Under the circumstances, I could see no reason for not supplying us with intelligence information and creating a framework for operational coordination between our armed forces if the need were to arise. Cheney was reticent on both issues. He was not prepared, or maybe not authorized, to pass on to us real-time satellite photos of Iraq, and the very talk of operational coordination between the United States and Israel seemed to cause him considerable unease.

I moved on to detail the economic assistance that we required to deal with the ongoing emergency. I explained that simultaneously with the allied deployment of forces in Saudi Arabia, we had had to deploy Israel's armed forces in preparation for situations that might occur as the crisis unfolded. This had involved a substantial increase in flying hours for our aircraft, with a subsequent increase in utilization of spare parts and maintenance costs. There were similar costs for our ground forces. Added to this was the burden of preparing our civilian population. I estimated that the total cost would be about $1 billion by the end of the year. In addition, if the administration intended to go through with the $20 billion arms deal for Saudi Arabia that was being prepared for congressional approval, Israel would need a further $700 million dollars in annual military assistance so as to balance the strengthening of the Saudi armed forces.

Cheney was completely taken aback by my requests. I could see that the administration had not given a moment's thought to Israel's situation and the needs that situation created, except insofar as they might affect the strategy that Bush was pursuing at the moment. Cheney's response was limited to suggesting that there might be a possibility of additional pre-positioning of U.S. materiel in Israel and the supply of Patriot surface-to-air missile batteries. He obviously knew that this was a far cry from what I considered our real needs to be.

From the Pentagon I went to see Brent Scowcroft, the president's adviser on national security. Gaunt as a scarecrow, this former air force general seemed to have no feeling, certainly no sympathy, for Israel. His only concerns at our meeting seemed to be that Israel by some preemptive act might change the script of the scenario that the White House had written for what they referred to as "Desert Shield," and that Israel's opposition to the $20 billion arms deal for Saudi Arabia might block congressional approval. Scowcroft bluntly suggested that if Israel were attacked by Iraqi missiles, it should not hit back but rely on the United States for an appropriate response. I told him that if we were attacked we would hit back, but saw no purpose in arguing the point with him.

That evening I had dinner with some of Israel's best friends in Washington: Jeane Kirkpatrick; Senators Howard Metzenbaum, Carl Levin, Frank Lautenberg, and Joe Lieberman; and Congressman Larry Smith. I gave them a rundown of the Gulf crisis from Israel's vantage point, and detailed our needs at this time. Here there was complete understanding and sympathy for Israel's precarious situation. Metzenbaum, probably still suffering pangs of conscience over his optimistic report of his visit to Saddam Hussein the previous April, suggested that my $1 billion request was probably insufficient, and said he would call Baker the next morning to ask him to delay presenting the $20 billion Saudi arms deal for approval to Congress.

The following morning Senator Daniel Inouye came to my hotel for breakfast. According to Jewish tradition, the world continues to exist because of thirty-six saintly men who walk the face of the earth. I was sure that the senator from Hawaii was one of the thirty-six to whom we owed our existence. He had supported Israel through thick and thin ever since he entered the U.S. Senate, always demonstrating his deep understanding of the history of the Jewish people, of the tragedy of the Holocaust, and of the dangers that faced Israel. As always in time of need, now too he promised to do all he could. There followed meetings with Senator Bob Kasten and Vermont's Senator Patrick Leahy. While I was in Leahy's office, I received a call from the Pentagon informing me that the Secretary of Defense wanted to see me again.

Cheney must have consulted with other members of the administration and concluded that to ensure Israel's cooperation, a price would have to be paid. After telling me again how important it was that Israel not take any military action, and expressing his hope that Israel would not oppose the Saudi arms deal, he suggested that the United States would be prepared to pre-position artillery and tank munitions in Israel above the current plans, as well as to provide Israel with two Patriot anti-aircraft batteries and twelve to fifteen U.S. Air Force surplus F-15 aircraft. I replied that I appreciated the offer but that it did not come close to meeting our needs. As for the Saudi arms deal, which involved advanced U.S. weapons, it was going to erode Israel's quality edge, which was essential for us because of Arab numerical superiority, and would therefore require us to allocate funds to Israeli weapons development.

Although Baker was, of course, aware of my meetings with Cheney, Scowcroft, and the others, he made no move to contact me. I assumed that this was part of his hug-Levy strategy. He probably thought that Levy would not be happy with such a meeting. I was not to hear from him until Scuds started falling on Tel Aviv.

In September, a few days apart, the Fatah faction of the PLO and the Hamas each celebrated its version of the one thousandth day of the Intifada. Actually, they had little to celebrate. A thousand days of physical suffering and economic deprivation had not achieved much for the

Palestinian population in Judea, Samaria, and Gaza. And the Intifada seemed to be fading. It was becoming more and more difficult to get people out into the streets for demonstrations. I had reopened all the schools and community colleges in the territories, and in September, after meeting with the heads of Bethlehem University, I reopened that institution as well. I announced that if there was no renewal of violence, it was my intention to open the other universities. In the past three months no Palestinian had been killed by Israeli fire in Gaza, and only two or three in Judea and Samaria. Television and other media coverage of events there was dropping to zero. I had no doubt that the leaders of the PLO and Hamas were frustrated in seeing what had been a most effective instrument in the fight against Israel being blunted.

But sporadic acts of violence continued. On September 20, the second day of Rosh Hashanah, an Israeli reservist was murdered in the Gaza Strip. Amnon Pomerantz, an electronic engineer from the agricultural village of Havatzelet Hasharon, had been assigned reserve duty in the Gaza Strip. He had not reported with his unit, having taken his two-month-old son for an examination to the hospital. From there he drove to Gaza in his own car, lost his way, and by mistake drove into the El Burej Palestinian refugee camp. A mob threw rocks at his car. One hit Pomerantz and he lost consciousness. Gasoline was thrown into the car, a match lit, and he was burned alive while the mob cheered. No one had stepped forward to aid him. I waited, hoping that some Palestinians would denounce this brutal murder, but no such voice was heard.

Eighteen days later, on October 8, during the Succoth holidays, a major conflagration occurred on the Temple Mount in Jerusalem. As is traditional during the Succoth holidays, thousands of Jewish worshippers had congregated at the Western Wall, the only remnant of the ancient Jewish Temple. Above them, on the Temple Mount, there were thousands of Arabs, who had come to worship at the two mosques, Omar (the Dome of the Rock) and El Aksa, which had been built centuries ago where the Temple once stood. The Arabs began throwing rocks at the Jews below, causing injuries and panic. Unable to respond in kind, the crowd, including many women and children, fled. Armed Israeli police units quickly appeared on the scene and were also met by a hail of rocks from the Muslim worshippers. Some policemen opened fire, and in the confusion nineteen Arabs were killed and more than a hundred wounded.

News quickly spread throughout the world of this bloody event on the site considered holy by Jews, Muslims, and Christians. It was followed by riots in Judea, Samaria, and Gaza. Five days later, the United Nations Security Council unanimously adopted a resolution, proposed by the United States, that ignored the causes of the riot, condemned Israel, denied Israeli sovereignty in Jerusalem, and called on the UN Secretary General to send a team to examine the situation in the territories and report back. Among those voting for the resolution were such traditional supporters of human rights as Yemen, Ethiopia, Cuba, Romania, Malaysia, China, and the Soviet Union. The Bush administration evidently decided to use Israel as a sacrificial lamb in its efforts to bolster its anti-Iraq alliance with the other Arab countries. At Shamir's initiative, the Israeli government, at its meeting on October 14, rejected the Security Council resolution.

I decided to implement a curfew in the territories, which put an end to the rioting. Bush's coalition with the Arabs survived the incident intact. But the administration's posture toward Israel became increasingly confrontational. Bush announced that he expected Israel to accept the UN resolution, and Baker issued a number of strongly worded statements against Israel. They seemed to have forgotten that Israel was their ally in the confrontation with Iraq, or, more likely, they had concluded that Israel's loyalty to the alliance was in any case assured.

On October 21, an Arab from the Bethlehem area entered the Baka neighborhood of Jerusalem early in the morning, armed with a knife and intent on murder. His first victim was an eighteen-year-old girl, whose path he accidentally crossed in the street. Next, he murdered a middle-aged gardener. Then he turned his weapon on a thirteen-year-old boy, who managed to escape after being injured. An off-duty policeman, who rushed to the scene, shot the Arab but was careful not to kill him; he was knifed to death.

In light of these bloody attacks, I decided to prohibit the entry of Palestinians from the territories into Israel temporarily. This was no simple matter. Most of the Palestinians in the territories were dependent on work in Israel for their livelihood. Parts of the Israeli economy had become dependent on cheap Palestinian labor. An extended closure of the territories would bring great deprivation to the Palestinians, as well as dislocation to some branches of the Israeli economy. The economy would adjust in due course, with Israelis, and especially new immigrants from the Soviet Union, taking the place of Palestinian workers; but there was no quick or easy solution for the plight of the Palestinians.

After a few days I decided to lift the closure, though much of the Israeli public, unaware of the full implications, would have preferred its continuation. My decision came under violent attack from two ministers, Ariel Sharon and Rafael Eitan, a former IDF chief of staff, now a leader of the right-wing Tsomet party. They claimed that they knew how to "deal" with Arabs. Grab anyone who steps out of line, transport him to the Jordanian border, give him a good whack on the head that he will remember for the rest of his life, and boot him across the border. This kind of advice I felt I could do without.

The Americans continued to build up their forces in Saudi Arabia, keeping everybody guessing as to when they would actually begin the assault on Kuwait. It was clear that they wanted to attain overwhelming numerical superiority before they initiated hostilities. The extended period of buildup encouraged Saddam Hussein to believe that Bush was afraid to take the offensive. As the allied blockade began to tighten, the Iraqis announced that they considered it a declaration of war against them, and that the United States and its ally Israel would not go unpunished. We had to be prepared for the possibility of an Iraqi missile attack on Israel's cities. Shamir and I had a number of meetings in which we discussed the options for Israel's response if it came to a long-range exchange of blows. We were certain that their missiles could reach Israel with conventional warheads. Based on the information at our disposal, we could not exclude the possibility that they had chemical warheads as well. There was even some information that they had been working on bacteriological weapons.

An intensive procurement effort had by now succeeded in eliminating most of the early shortages in gas masks, and some of the tension among the Israeli public that accompanied the beginning of the crisis had subsided. I felt that the time had come to begin the distribution of gas masks. It was essential to do this in gradual and orderly manner so as not to cause panic. On October 1, we issued an announcement that a trial distribution would begin on October 7 in three small localities: Ofakim, Kfar Yonah, and Yokneam. We hoped that this would provide a clear signal that there were no indications of an impending attack, and therefore no need for an emergency distribution to the entire population. The public took the announcement in stride; no demands for gas masks were heard from other areas and there was no panic. On October 7, the gas masks were distributed at the three localities. All was calm.

Dick Cheney had called me the previous week to inform me that the president had approved the grant of two Patriot anti-aircraft batteries for Israel. The F-15 aircraft and additional pre-positioning of American equipment, he said, was still under discussion. Washington evidently thought that in anticipation of the additional assistance we needed, we would refrain from taking any preemptive action or opposing the Saudi arms deal.

Syrian dictator Hafez al-Assad decided to take advantage of the situation created by the Gulf crisis to complete the Syrian takeover of Lebanon. He was being wooed by the United States to join the coalition against Saddam Hussein, and could feel confident that it would not interfere. Similarly, he counted on Israel refraining from taking any preventive action that might fracture the U.S.-led coalition. He was unwittingly assisted by General Michel Aoun, the Lebanese Christian general who had refused to recognize the legitimacy of Lebanon's Syrian-backed President Harawi, and who, backed by Christian units of the Lebanese Army, had installed himself in the presidential palace at Baabda. From there, Aoun called on the Syrians to remove their armed forces from Lebanon and restore sovereignty to that long-suffering country. Many Lebanese probably sympathized with these views, but Aoun did not bother to build a united home front to back him. He antagonized the Muslim and Druze community in Lebanon, and split the Christians. As usual in Lebanon, this internecine strife resulted in almost daily killings of Lebanese by Lebanese. Aoun, losing contact with reality, seemed incapable of compromise with friend and foe alike.

Assad had been biding his time, waiting for the appropriate moment to dislodge Aoun. Now it had come. Ever since the Lebanese War, the Israel Air Force had controlled the skies over Lebanon. Any Syrian aircraft that ventured into Lebanese airspace were chased back into Syria. On October 12, our chief of staff informed me that there were indications that the Syrians were preparing to use their air force to subdue Aoun. I decided that this was not the time to get into a war with the Syrians, and ordered our air force not to engage Syrian aircraft. The following day the Syrians attacked, using Syrian aircraft and artillery as well as Lebanese forces loyal to Harawi. Hundreds were killed in the fighting, but it was all over in a few hours. Aoun ordered his troops to surrender, while he took refuge in the French Embassy in Beirut. There was no condemnation of the Syrians at the United Nations; their brutal interference in Lebanon was not even debated in the Security Council.

By the middle of October the Middle East had become a favorite location for important visitors. Baker and Cheney had visited the area; so had the Japanese foreign minister, Taro Nakayama. But all of them avoided Israel like the plague—they did not want to offend their Arab allies. Finally, Britain's foreign secretary, Douglas Hurd, who was visiting the area, came to Israel as his last stop. I thought him a great improvement over John Major. In the Defense Ministry conference room, sitting across from each other, we carried on an easy, pleasant conversation that ranged over the problems we were currently facing. He seemed quite understanding of our difficulties, although he urged us to accept the UN team that the Security Council had decided to dispatch to Israel in the wake of the Temple Mount incident. I reminded Hurd that he was in Israel at a time when we were beginning the distribution of gas masks to our civilian population—a reminder that we faced the danger of chemical warfare, a danger not faced by any of the other countries affected by the crisis. And now the UN Security Council, rather than condemning the Muslim fanatics who started the riot on the Temple Mount, was blaming Israel. Adding insult to injury, the United Nations decision also denied Israeli sovereignty in Jerusalem, Israel's capital. Hurd seemed to be at a loss for words, but we parted friends.

On October 29, Washington broke its embargo on official visits to Israel. Donald Rice, the secretary of the air force, was given permission to come to Israel. A former president of the Rand Corporation, himself an aeronautical scientist, he was easy for me to talk to. I explained to him how dangerous the absence of coordination between the IDF and the U.S. armed forces was in the present circumstances. If the Iraqis were to attack Israel, we would have to respond. Our choices were either to overfly Jordan or to seek alternate routes. If our air force were to overfly Jordan on the way to Iraqi targets, it would inevitably require the destruction of the Jordanian Air Force and their ground-to-air capability. That would have far-reaching consequences for the entire region. Alternative routes would require coordination with the U.S. Air Force and would avoid the dangerous complications of the first alternative. If the United States were to open hostilities, we could run into a situation in which Israeli and U.S. aircraft were operating in the same airspace, and unless we had adequate coordination there was the danger that our aircraft would fire on each other. He had no argument with me, but evidently did not have the authority to approve the coordination I had called for. U.S. policy was to keep Israel at arm's length regardless of the dangers that involved.

In the beginning of November 1990, the U.S. Congress passed budgetary legislation for the next fiscal year that included large-scale benefits for Israel. The annual military assistance was going to be disbursed from now on at the beginning of the fiscal year, which would save significant interest costs. The quantity of U.S. materiel to be pre-positioned in Israel was going to be increased. Large stocks of weapons and other materiel were to be "drawn down" from U.S. stocks and shipped to Israel at no cost, while other "surplus" weapons and materiel would be made available free of charge. Most of these generous benefits, whose monetary value was estimated at close to $2 billion, had been made contingent on the administration's approval. But Senator Robert Kasten, who had played a key role in getting this legislation passed, told me that Dick Cheney had assured him that the administration would implement the aid package to Israel. I was gratified, feeling that I had succeeded in imparting to congressional leaders during my recent visit to Washington the extent of Israel's security needs at this time of crisis. As it turned out, the Bush administration was to prevent implementation of the major part of the package.

The Gulf crisis had been going on for three months with no end in sight. President Bush announced a further buildup of American forces in Saudi Arabia, which would double the present size of the ground forces deployed there and significantly strengthen the air and naval forces in order to ensure "an adequate offensive military option." I had no way of knowing whether this was a feint intended to screen an early initiation of hostilities by the United States, or whether the additional deployment was truly intended to be carried out, in which case we would be facing at least another few weeks of tense waiting.

Baker visited Saudi Arabia around this time but did not visit Israel. Bush followed, to be with the troops for Thanksgiving. He met with the Syrian dictator Assad in Geneva, and also bypassed Israel. I wondered if they realized it was no accident that Saddam Hussein, who had been a sworn enemy of Israel for years, had also turned out to be an enemy of the United States. As I watched the massive buildup of American and allied forces and as I heard President Bush explain to the American people that Iraq had the fourth largest army in the world, I assumed that he understood that had it not been for the Iraqi invasion of Kuwait, Israel would eventually have had to face the Iraqi forces, most likely joined by armies of other Arab countries, alone.

. . .

In early December, Bill Brown asked to see me urgently. Always friendly and smiling, this time he looked somewhat crestfallen. He told me that he was taking his life into his hands to pass information to me without having received authorization to do so, but he felt that it might be of vital importance to us. American Intelligence had learned that the Iraqis had test-fired three medium-range ballistic missiles from eastern Iraq into western Iraq. I was moved by Brown's readiness to take the initiative out of concern for Israel's safety; few diplomats I knew could meet that moral standard.

Within a few hours the news of the Iraqi missile test was reported by the Reuters news agency, still before we had received official notification from Washington. It was clear that they had decided to withhold this important information from us. For this kind of duplicity I thought there was no excuse. When I saw Brown again the following day at Ben-Gurion Airport at the farewell ceremony for Shamir, who was leaving for Washington, I reminded him of our longstanding request for satellite photos of the Iraqi missile-launching sites in western Iraq; he countered by asking if I could give the United States a guarantee that we would take no action against these sites. I assumed that he had either been instructed to obtain such a guarantee, or else felt that that would be Washington's condition for providing the satellite photos to Israel. I replied that we had no plans to attack these sites at present, but that I could not give him an open-ended guarantee, since we would do whatever we felt was essential to protect our civilian population. If we concluded that the missile-launching sites had to be hit, we would do so regardless of whether the United States did or did not supply us with the photos.

On my instructions, the IDF had continued planning and training for the operations we envisaged might be necessary against Iraqi missile-launching sites if we were attacked. These would be complex and dangerous operations carried out at considerable distance from our home bases.

Two weeks had passed since the United Nations Security Council, on November 29, had passed a resolution authorizing the use of force if Iraq did not evacuate Kuwait by January 15, 1991. The countdown to war had started, yet I was convinced that the slightest conciliatory gesture by Saddam Hussein would bring about a stay of execution by Bush. But if Hussein continued on his bellicose course, Bush would have no choice but to give General Norman Schwarzkopf, commanding the allied forces in the area, marching orders.

On December 19, the cabinet met to discuss the changed deployment of the Jordanian Army. Jordanian units were now taking up positions on the east bank of the Jordan River, in immediate proximity to our towns and agricultural settlements on the West Bank. I was puzzled. Why was King Hussein doing this? Why was he not being as careful as I had expected him to be under the circumstances so as not to create a situation that might call for an Israeli response? Maybe he was really afraid of an Israeli attack. Or maybe he was coordinating his moves with his ally in Baghdad. In any case, it was another cause of concern.

If I still entertained any illusions that facing a common enemy would strengthen the bonds of friendship between Jerusalem and Washington, they were shattered on December 24. Bill Brown came to see me to hand me a message he had just received from the State Department. The message demanded that Israel stop immediately all defensive ties with South Africa; and called for the cessation of cooperation with South Africa in the area of nuclear, chemical, and biological weapons technology. Israel had never had any contact with South Africa, or for that matter wth any other country, regarding nonconventional technology of any kind. I had made this clear to Cheney in past meetings, as had my predecessor, Yitzhak Rabin.

Our assistance to South Africa had started many years ago, at a time when South Africa was the only country on the African continent that maintained diplomatic and trade relations with Israel. At the time, Israel was looking for funding for some of its programs. South Africa, in pursuit of its own interests, stepped into the breach. All this had been explained by Rabin and myself to Cheney. At Washington's urging, Israel had committed itself to not signing any new contracts with South Africa and to renegotiating the present contracts so as to cease all activity by December 31, 1992. This had been done, and I had informed Cheney of it during my last meeting with him.

My response to the American ambassador was anything but diplomatic: I let out all my frustrations on him, even though I knew that he was no more than an unwilling messsenger. The fact that Bush and Baker would send Israel this kind of message at this time was to me an indication of utter distrust. The purpose—if there was a purpose to this exercise—was probably to put us on notice that the administration had the power to publicly embarrass Israel, and that we better behave ourselves. It was a crude move, characteristic of much of the Bush administration's diplomacy toward Israel.

By the end of 1990 gas masks had been distributed to the entire urban population of Israel, including the Arabs of East Jerusalem. The Iraqis were conducting a number of test launches of ballistic missiles, and Saddam Hussein's rhetoric toward Israel was becoming daily more antagonistic, invariably concluding with the threat to launch attacks against us. Even though I did not know whether this man could be deterred, I decided to state publicly for his benefit that if Israel were attacked, the Iraqis should expect a response. Shamir made similar statements.

In informal meetings with Shamir and a select group of ministers, the subject of what kind of response this was going to be was discussed a number of times. At meetings of the Knesset's Foreign Affairs and Defense Committee, the matter was referred to indirectly. Yitzhak Rabin, on a number of occasions, publicly stated his opinion that Israel's response if attacked should not be "automatic." I was surprised that he would make remarks that could only weaken whatever deterrent image we possessed, and I said so to Rabin when I invited him for a private briefing at the Defense Ministry on December 31. He said that his remarks had been taken out of context by the newspapers, but I think he realized that he had made a mistake. He never referred to the subject again publicly.

Early in January 1991 we had the first sign that Washington was willing to cooperate, at least a little. In great secrecy, a secure telephone line had been set up between Cheney and myself. Our end of it was located in a hut in the Defense Ministry compound, which from this point on was staffed by a small team of American technicians and Israel Air Force officers. In order to use it I had a two-minute walk—or one-minute run if it seemed urgent—from my office on the second floor of the ministry, so the call required some coordination. It took getting used to since, unlike a regular telephone, only one of us could speak at a time. The Americans had code-named the line with the improbable appellation of "Hammer Rick." On Friday, January 4, I picked up the open phone to Cheney and scheduled the inauguration of the secure line for the following Monday, January 7, at 3:00 P.M. Israel time, 8:00 A.M. in Washington.

On that Monday, I walked down to the hut where "Hammer Rick" had been installed, wondering where Cheney's end of the line was located. Cheney sounded very determined. He held out little hope for the meeting between Baker and Iraqi Foreign Minister Tariq Aziz, scheduled for January 9 in Geneva, and referred to January 15 as a date of great significance. He asked me for reconfirmation of Shamir's promise to Bush that we would not take preemptive action, and I gave it to him. He knew that I was concerned about the Iraqi missile-launching sites in western Iraq, some of them located near the air bases H-2 and H-3 built by the British in the thirties along the now-defunct Iraqi oil pipeline to Haifa, and informed me that they had plans to hit targets in those areas. But when I said to him that it was high time for us to begin operational coordination, he said he would have to check with his boss.

On January 9, the eyes of the world were on Geneva, where James Baker and Tariq Aziz were meeting in a last-minute attempt to defuse the crisis. The meeting lasted for several hours, with a break for lunch, giving rise to speculation that an agreement was being reached. But when at the conclusion of their discussions Baker and Aziz faced the television cameras, it became clear that no progress had been made in breaking the impasse. Baker reiterated the U.S. position that Iraq would have to leave Kuwait by January 15 or else face the use of force. Aziz, in turn, announced that Iraq would not submit to this ultimatum and that Kuwait was an integral part of Iraq. In answer to a question about whether Iraq would attack Israel, Aziz replied, "Absolutely, yes."

The following day, Thursday, January 10, I called Cheney on the secure link. "Now that the Baker-Aziz talks have ended in failure," I said, "it looks like the countdown to the initiation of hostilities has really begun. We have taken notice of Aziz's declaration that Iraq would attack Israel, and have now to consider the possibility of an Iraqi strike against Israel even before you initiate hostilities. This state of affairs makes it essential that we set up operational coordination between us immediately. In the absence of such coordination we would probably have to fly over Jordan in responding to an Iraqi attack on Israel, which might have serious consequences. I assume this is well understood by you in Washington."

Cheney at first evaded the issue by telling me that Larry Eagleburger and Paul Wolfowitz would be arriving in Israel on Saturday and that they would discuss this matter with the prime minister. Then he asked me what the alternative was to us flying over Jordan, to which I replied that the alternatives would involve coordination with the United States.

"We cannot make such arrangements," he countered. I felt that he was just trying to stall me but decided to push on in this one-at-a-time conversation that did not enable me to interrupt him. "What I am saying is that it is essential that we establish a mechanism for operational coordination between our air forces. For this to be done, the appropriate military people on both sides would have to get together."

Cheney stalled again, referring to the upcoming Eagleburger visit, saying that Eagleburger would be ready to discuss contact on a real-time basis with us. Then, in an apparent attempt to calm my apprehensions, he continued: "I want to emphasize that the targets in western Iraq will be dealt with by the U.S. Air Force, including all targets that could be a threat to Israel."

"If you succeed in eliminating the threat in your initial strike, there will be no problem," I replied, "but we have to be prepared for the possibility that Iraqi capability to hit us might continue to exist and that then we would have to attack them."

Cheney acted as if he did not understand what I was talking about. He said that they could not talk to the Saudi government about this and that it could be discussed with Eagleburger and Wolfowitz when they came to Israel. "From a military point of view there will be no need for you to respond; there will be no targets in western Iraq that will not be taken care of. Possibly, you might want to respond for political reasons," he argued.

"You know," I said, "that the Iraqi mobile launchers will be difficult to destroy, and even the stationary launchers might escape destruction by the U.S. Air Force. We have to be prepared to respond to an Iraqi attack on Israel." I repeated that we should arrive at an arrangement for "deconflicting" U.S. and Israeli aircraft that might be in action in the same airspace over Iraq.

"Talk to Eagleburger and Wolfowitz about that," he said again. "I continue to hope that the whole thing will be over without Israel being attacked. We are going to allocate a great part of our resources to deal with the threat against Israel. An attack on Israel will be considered a provocation that will call for a move by us." I joined him in his hopes, and told him that we would not push ourselves into the conflict. Then I asked him for the satellite photos that we had been requesting. I was amazed to hear him say that he had not been aware of our request, and that he would discuss the subject with me in our next conversation.

The night of the Baker-Aziz meeting, we decided to call up some

171

reserve units of civil defense personnel, including special teams to deal with areas subjected to chemical warfare. We also released information broadcasts on civil defense for radio and television in Hebrew, Arabic, as well as in Russian and Amharic for the recent immigrants from the Soviet Union and Ethiopia. War fever had started and it was essential to provide the population with information on what to do in case of attack. Our primary concern was the danger of chemical weapons. Everyone had been asked to prepare one room in their home with windows and doors sealed with plastic sheeting. People were told to carry their gas masks with them wherever they went; the following day you could see men and women on their way to work, women out shopping, and children going to school, all carrying a small brown cardboard box. In case of an alarm, the population was instructed to put on their gas masks and the special protective gear on the smaller children and remain in the sealed room until the all-clear was heard. Protective kits had been distributed to all the urban areas of Israel. We still did not have sufficient kits, especially for the smaller children, to supply the Palestinian population in Judea and Samaria. Since I did not want them to be the only ones to whom the equipment was not issued, I instructed the army not to issue the kits in Israel's rural areas. In my opinion, neither Israel's rural areas nor Judea and Samaria faced danger of chemical attack by the Iraqis.

While the urban population to whom gas masks had been distributed seemed to take the gathering stormclouds in stride, those to whom the gas masks had not been issued began to show increasing alarm as January 15 approached. My office was besieged by chairmen of local village councils all over Israel who demanded that we issue gas masks in their areas. My explanations that their villages were in no danger of chemical attack fell on deaf ears. There were threats to break into the warehouses where the equipment was stored. Wanting to avoid incidents of panic at this time, I decided to go ahead and distribute gas masks to the rural areas, as well as to the Israeli settlements in Judea and Samaria.

What followed was an uproar in the Knesset's Foreign Affairs and Defense Committee that I had not anticipated. Led by Yossi Sarid from the left and Benny Begin, the former prime minister's son, from the right, I was accused of discriminating against the Palestinian population in Judea and Samaria. Since I felt confident that neither Israelis nor Palestinians in these areas were in any danger, I reversed course and announced that there would be no distribution of gas masks in Judea and Samaria at all. But now it was the settlers' representatives who bombarded me with telegrams and petitions demanding the same protection as was being provided to all Israelis. At this point I was getting sick and tired of this absurd situation. Busy with what I considered to be my real concerns, I decided to take the path of least resistance and issue gas masks to all residents of Israel as well as to the Israeli citizens residing in Judea and Samaria. But now I had to contend with Israel's High Court of Justice. Some well-meaning Israelis prompted a resident of Bethlehem to appeal to the court asking for a judgment ordering me to issue gas masks to the Palestinian residents of Judea and Samaria. To my surprise, the court issued such a judgment and left me in the unenviable position of not being able to obey it.

An additional problem, bordering on the absurd, was the demand of the ultra-Orthodox parties for gas masks that could be fitted over beards. Several weeks would be required to manufacture the necessary contraptions. If we were going to be hit by chemical warheads, the beards would have to come off. Fortunately, that did not turn out to be necessary.

On Friday, January 11, Cheney called me on the secure link to tell me that Eagleburger, Wolfowitz, and Rear Admiral Merrill Ruck of the National Security Council would be arriving in Israel on Saturday in order to convince us not to get involved, not to retaliate even if we were hit, and to leave everything to the U.S. armed forces. "Let me emphasize the importance of Israel staying out of the conflict," he said. "It is important not only for Israel but also for the interests of the United States. From a military standpoint there will be no targets in Iraq that will not be attacked by us, there will be no targets for you that we will not attack. We are in a situation where if Israel becomes involved, it will influence some members of the coalition to cancel their military participation and it will increase the burden on the United States. We will have to take upon ourselves additional missions, and this will cause us more casualties."

I told him that I understood their considerations, but it was important that they understand ours. "If we are attacked before you begin your operation, we will have to hit back. If they attack us after you have attacked them, we will also have to hit back," I continued. He succeeded in raising my blood pressure when he went on to say, "We will suffer casualties in order to destroy targets that threaten you; it's most important that we avoid Israeli participation widening the conflict." I had no choice but to tell Cheney that we had a long tradition of defending ourselves and never asked anybody to fight for us. "If attacked we will respond; we'll be happy to talk to Eagleburger and Wolfowitz, but they will not succeed in convincing us." When I asked him about the satellite photos, he replied that he could not commit himself yet.

At Cheney's suggestion we had agreed to talk again on the secure link the following day, Saturday, January 12, at 5:00 P.M. Israel time. I went to the office that afternoon, only to be informed at the last minute that Cheney would not be in his office and that our telephone conversation had been canceled. I suspected that he had decided to await the outcome of Eagleburger's conversation with Shamir that evening.

In anticipation of that meeting I had spoken to Shamir urging him to stand fast on our position, that if attacked we would respond. When they met that night, Eagleburger, as we had expected, urged Shamir to keep Israel out of the conflict. When Shamir turned him down, Eagleburger explained that he had brought a "fallback position" from Washington: If Israel were attacked and decided that it had to respond, the United States and Israel would then consult in order for U.S. forces to "stand down," in other words, to clear a mutually agreed area of Iraq of its forces and permit Israeli forces to take action there. Shamir gave his assent to this proposal.

The following day I left the government meeting on the second floor of the prime minister's office to meet with Eagleburger, Wolfowitz, and Ruck in the prime minister's conference room. Eagleburger reported on his meeting with Shamir the previous evening, and the fact that they had agreed to his fallback position. Eagleburger made it clear that the United States was still not prepared for joint operations with Israel, nor to provide us with targeting information or assist us in obtaining overflight rights. However, he assured us that the U.S. armed forces felt completely confident of their ability to eliminate the missile threat against Israel. They intended to attack western Iraq and the potential missile-launching sites in the very early stages of their operation; so there was nothing for us to worry about.

I reminded Eagleburger that the Patriot anti-aircraft missile batteries that we had requested and been promised last September had not as yet been delivered, and as a result Israeli crews for these batteries had not been trained. He replied that they had been needed for supply to U.S. troops, but he offered them now, together with U.S. crews to man them for as long as it would take to train Israeli crews. After consulting with Shamir, I refused the offer, not wanting to set a precedent of foreign troops serving in the defense of Israel.

On January 14, I called Cheney to report on our meetings with the Eagleburger delegation. It was clear Cheney had already been briefed on the talks. I returned again to our need for satellite photos of western Iraq, a subject I had raised with Eagleburger but to which I had received no reply. And again Cheney told me he would check into it. This time he informed me that he would use the secure link to give me a few hours' advance warning of the start of the impending American operation. When I spoke to him again on January 15, I still could not get a positive reply to my request for the satellite imagery.

With every passing day, war became more certain, and the responsibility resting on my shoulders became heavier. I was not at all sure of the American ability to eliminate the Iraqi missile threat against Israel, angry at their lack of readiness to provide us with intelligence that was of utmost importance to us, and frustrated by the distrust that colored their relations with us. They made what was in any case a life-threatening situation that much more difficult.

That afternoon the cabinet met in Jerusalem for an intelligence briefing on the developing situation. Lieutenant Colonel Mike Herzog, President Herzog's son, who served in the IDF's intelligence branch, reviewed the deployment of Jordanian troops and quoted the Jordanian prime minister's recent announcement that Hafez al-Assad had promised to come to Jordan's defense if it were attacked by Israel. The minister of transport, Moshe Katsav, reported that international airlines were suspending their flights to Israel, and that insurance premiums for ships calling at Israeli ports had gone up by a factor of twenty. A lengthy discussion ensued on the advisability of closing the country's schools. After three hours of debate, Shamir announced that crisis decisions would be taken by the cabinet, but should it not be possible to convene the cabinet, urgent decisions would be taken by the prime minister, the defense minister, and the foreign minister. As to the closing of schools, that decision would be taken by the defense minister and the chief of staff, in consultation with the minister of education. Immediately after the meeting we decided to close all of Israel's schools as of the following morning, Wednesday, January 16.

Cheney called me at 7:20 P.M. on January 16 to inform me that they had received information that the Iraqis were developing an unmanned MiG-21 to carry chemical bombs. He considered the information reliable. There was nothing I could do; gas masks had been distributed and our air force was already on alert to intercept enemy aircraft. After I signed off, Cheney added: "We'll be talking to you later," and I knew the war was about to begin. At midnight, Cheney called again to inform me that the operation would begin in two hours. At 2:00 A.M. I was in my office watching Baghdad being bombed on CNN. At 4:00 A.M. I saw President Bush announcing the beginning of hostilities; and at 5:00 A.M. Cheney was on the secure line providing initial information on what had been accomplished thus far, and emphasizing that considerable airpower had been assigned to deal with the ballistic missile threat in western Iraq.

At nine o'clock on Thursday, January 17, the cabinet met in Tel Aviv. Amnon Shahak reported on the air attacks that had been launched against Iraq during the night, singling out the operations over western Iraq. He concluded that the Iraqis still maintained the capability to launch missiles against Israel. He also reported that the Jordanian Army had called up reservists. Dan Shomron reported that our army had imposed a curfew on the Palestinian population in the territories, and I reported that all schools had been closed and that I had ordered a work stoppage in all but essential industries.

War

At 2:00 A.M. on Friday, January 18, air-raid sirens awakened the people of Israel. They were followed by loud explosions in the Tel Aviv and Haifa area, and we realized that Israel was at war. Saddam Hussein had made good on his threat. Following instructions, people rushed out of bed into the sealed rooms they had previously prepared. Babies were put under protective crib covers. Everybody else pulled their gas masks over their faces and waited for the radio to announce when the raid would be over.

I had been fast asleep when the sirens sounded. Within two minutes I had dressed, kissed my wife, who was fumbling with her gas mask, and was out of the house. There was no time to wait for my driver to arrive. With my bodyguard sitting beside me, I drove through empty streets, not stopping for red lights, from my home in suburban Savyon toward Tel Aviv. My anger was too great for me to put on the gas mask, which my bodyguard had been careful to take along. As I drove westward on Aluf Sadeh Road, I heard loud explosions that seemed to come from both sides, and felt the concussion. It sounded as if Tel Aviv was getting a beating.

I made it to the Defense Ministry in ten minutes. By now the explosions had stopped, and the silence was eerie. I headed directly for the underground bunker that served as the command and control center and was frustrated to find that I could not enter. The doors were locked. The guard, whom I could see through a window in the door, was wearing his gas mask, and had evidently gotten instructions not to open the door for fear of gas entering the bunker. I could not tell whether he had recognized me but he could not hear me through the heavy sealed door. I rushed to a different entrance where I was recognized, entered, and ran down the long corridors that led to the central control room.

The chief of staff had not yet arrived. The team on duty was busy receiving reports from around the country. Our most immediate concern was whether the missiles that landed had chemical warheads. Crews with special chemical-detection equipment were already at the sites where the missiles had landed. First reports that poison gas had been detected were quickly corrected. Three missiles had landed in the Tel Aviv area, another on the northern outskirts of Haifa, and two others had fallen into the sea. Only one of the missiles had landed in a densely populated area, in the Shchunat Ezra quarter of South Tel Aviv, where there had been considerable property damage but no fatalities. In all, seven people had been slightly wounded during the raid.

At 4:32 A.M. I received a call from Baker on an open line. I was still in the command post. Baker told me that the president was outraged by the Iraqi attack on Israel, but that he hoped we would restrain ourselves so as to not endanger the coalition. He told me that the president would be calling the prime minister to talk to him as well. Baker was trying to be very friendly. "The next time you are in Washington it is very important that we get together," he concluded.

Thirteen minutes later, Cheney called me on the secure link. After giving him a report on the hits we had taken, I told him that we now had to put the Israel Air Force into action and try to prevent additional attacks. This would require close operational coordination with General Schwarzkopf's Central Command, which was directing the U.S. operation out of Saudi Arabia.

Cheney: Do I understand you want to take military action against Iraq?

I: Yes.

Cheney: In other words you need our people with you to assure proper coordination?

I: Right.

Cheney: You need an immediate answer?

I: If we get an immediate answer, we may be able to delay our action.

He went on to give me details on the type and number of aircraft being used to attack the area, saying that they needed time, and that it was difficult to find a mobile Scud launcher at night. I told him that we had ideas on how to locate the missile launchers, but that operational coordination with the Central Command would be needed to implement them.

Cheney: You want military personnel with the appropriate expertise in Tel Aviv as early as possible.

I: Right.

Cheney: I understand that you are concentrating on western Iraq, and you have no interest in attacking farther east.

I: I wouldn't say we have no such interest, but first things first.

Cheney: I'll check your request and get back to you.

I phoned Shamir during the night to ask that he call a meeting of the cabinet first thing in the morning so that I could present the IDF's plans. I asked that the meeting be held in Tel Aviv, as I did not want to be away from the command post. At 8:30 A.M., we met in the prime minister's office in the Defense Ministry compound. In addition to the cabinet members, the prime minister's and my aides, the meeting was attended by Dan Shomron, Ehud Barak, Amnon Shahak, and air force commander Major General Avihu Bin-Nun. The army had displayed a map of Iraq on the wall, on which the launching sites of the missiles that had been fired against Israel the previous night had been marked, based on information received from the Americans. The United States had a geosynchronous satellite in orbit over the area, whose infrared sensors could detect Iraqi missile launches and the approximate direction of each missile's launch trajectory. The warning of such missile launches against Israel were transmitted to Washington and from there via "Hammer Rick" to the Defense Ministry in Tel Aviv, providing us with a few minutes' warning time before the missiles hit.

I asked Shahak to brief the cabinet, and then Bin-Nun presented the plans for the IDF's response to the Iraqi missile attack. The plan was not without its problems, to put it mildly: the distance to Iraq, the absence of updated intelligence, and the lack of operational coordination with the U.S. Central Command which could lead to dangerous complications for our forces and theirs. The last consideration dominated the other two. Without such coordination, the planned missions looked reckless under the present circumstances.

Nevertheless, Sharon, Moda'i, "Raful" Eitan, now minister of agriculture, and Minister of Energy Yuval Ne'eman argued for the execution of some or all of the missions the IDF had presented.

When everybody had had their say, I presented my position. I stressed that we needed updated intelligence, "the level of information that will be provided to the air force and the other forces to be engaged, so they will be able to locate and identify the targets and deal with them. Most difficult is the problem of the missile launchers, which are small targets, and even more so the mobile missile launchers, which are small moving targets." To send forces out to search for them represented a problem. "We can obtain updated intelligence ourselves or from the U.S. I hope we shall hear from the Americans today. The last hour for time over target is 2:00 P.M. So time is short."

The following exchange ensued:

Sharon: Send the aircraft to photograph!

I: Even without coordinating with the U.S.?

Sharon: Notify them and fly!

I: It's a possibility, but notification is not coordination. We could tell them, Do what you like. If you want to intercept us, go ahead, but we will intercept your aircraft also.

Shamir was calm throughout the tense discussion. There were no objections when at 11:00 A.M. he proposed the following decisions:

1. To approve the Defense Minister's and the General Staff's proposals for attacks against the H-2/H-3 area.
2. To approve the Defense Minister's and the General Staff's proposals

to obtain the updated intelligence for this action, either from U.S. satellite photos or by photo reconnaissance.

3. All of the above, subject to coordination with the U.S.
4. The Prime Minister, Defense Minister, and Foreign Minister are empowered to take urgent decisions if the Cabinet cannot be convened.

Immediately after the cabinet meeting I called Cheney on the secure link, to tell him that we were awaiting his okay for us to obtain updated intelligence for western Iraq, or alternately to receive their aerial photos, as well as the definition of the "deconfliction" mechanism that would permit us to begin operations. Cheney referred to a conversation Baker had had with Shamir during the night, and said he was now prepared to send a team from Central Command. "We'll immediately send Major General Tom Olson, the number-two air force operations officer in the Gulf, to Tel Aviv." When I asked where he was coming from, Cheney replied, from Riyadh.

"He'll be here in two, two and a half hours?" I asked.

"I don't know, we'll do what we can. I thought that if we send a team, it will give us some time." I told him that we might have some patience when it came to a retaliatory mission, but as for a mission with the purpose of preventing further Iraqi missile attacks, it was essential to carry it out that night.

Cheney: We still have a problem with the mode of operation. How will you get there? We hesitate to do anything other than "standing down."

I: I understand. We prefer flying around Jordan. If we can arrange for deconfliction, maybe just "standing down" will be sufficient. We need your assistance: if you leave the area we can photograph.

Cheney: You are asking for aerial photos or else you want to photograph yourselves?

I: Correct.

Cheney: I will check the matter of aerial photos today. We'll see what our situation is. There are weather problems. We'll get the team together so as not to hold things up. What you're asking is to clear an aerial corridor so that you can attack Iraq. This is a problem.

I: As for the corridor, you also prefer that we not fly over Jordan.

Cheney: The corridor, overflight rights, that's a problem. We'll assemble the team and check if we can transfer to you existing photos.

I was getting exasperated. "We're not asking for overflight rights; just so we don't shoot each other down. Do you understand?" Cheney repeated that he would send the team, and that the man who led it would be able to make the arrangements. In a last attempt to make things absolutely clear, I said: "This is most urgent. First, to know about the photos—do we get them or do we go out to photograph ourselves? Second, if we go in today, it has to be coordinated immediately." Cheney signed off, saying, "We'll go to work."

He called back fifteen minutes later; it was now 11:15 A.M. "We're working as fast as we can," he said. "General Olson will bring the imagery for the attack missions. I don't want to deceive you about the quality of the photos; you're getting everything we used. We're checking if we have anything new to give you." "The important thing is that he come as quickly as possible," I said. "As soon as we have an estimated time of arrival I'll let you know." I felt he was stalling again.

By 6:00 P.M. General Olson had still not shown up and I had heard nothing from Cheney. We had no choice but to call off our operation. I called Cheney to tell him that. "We canceled our operation, which we considered very important, because in our opinion it might prevent another launch, since we failed to get an answer from you. Olson is still not here. We assume we will be able to do tomorrow what we didn't do today." Cheney replied that Olson should be arriving, and that he appreciated our decision to cancel the operation. Then he proceeded to report on the anti-Scud flights they were conducting. I asked him about the degree of success they were having against fixed and mobile launchers, recalling Schwarzkopf's comment that day that they had had success against mobile launchers in southern Iraq. Cheney confirmed this, but added that it was not clear what the status of the fixed launchers was and they were going to return and attack them that night.

The Americans had been reporting great success for the Patriots in intercepting Scuds over Saudi Arabia, so I asked Cheney if they could send us some Patriot batteries. Cheney reminded me that we had earlier rejected the idea of Patriot batteries manned by American crews, but promised to check. I said: "I hope your people understand that tomorrow we intend to carry out our planned operation." Night had already fallen in Israel, and I wondered if the Iraqis were preparing more missile launches against Israel that night. At eight-fifteen that evening the sirens sent the people of Israel scurrying for cover, but it turned out to be a false alarm.

Close to midnight, General Olson was ushered into my office. Our expectations were shattered in one stroke. He had brought satellite photos of western Iraq but they had been taken on December 17, over a month ago. When pressed to begin operational coordination between the Central Command in Saudi Arabia and our air force, he informed us he had no authority to do so.

The next morning, Saturday, January 19, the air-raid sirens sounded, and this time it was the real thing. I sprinted from my office to "the hole," as we referred to our subterranean control center. I felt a pressure wave bounce off me as I emerged from the building and knew that a missile must have hit pretty close. Within minutes the reports were in. Four Scuds had landed in the Tel Aviv area; three had exploded, while the fourth had bored its way through two floors of an office building on Allenby Street and stuck there with its warhead undetonated. One had landed at the Tel Aviv Fairgrounds without causing any damage to speak of, and another had exploded in the sand dunes of Rishon Lezion. The one that had done considerable damage had fallen into the densely populated Hatikva quarter. Fortunately, although there was great property damage, only twenty people were lightly injured. It seemed that luck was on our side, but how long could I expect it to hold if Saddam Hussein continued sending Scuds our way?

In the hope that we would succeed in arranging the necessary coordination with the Americans, I called Shamir in Jerusalem, asking him to convene the cabinet again so that the army could present its plans for approval. He was reluctant, but he finally agreed to set the meeting for 1:00 P.M. in Tel Aviv. He told me that Bush had called him during the night, as Cheney told me he would, asking that Israel not take any military action. I got the impression that he was inclined to go along with Bush's request.

At 11:00 A.M., Cheney called me wanting to know if I knew of the president's conversation with the prime minister. He went on to inform me that a corridor could not be arranged and that the president considered flying over Jordan a dangerous alternative. He asked when we intended to carry out the operation, and I suggested that our people sit with General Olson and pass that information on to him. "Okay, the president is waiting for a call from the prime minister," Cheney said.

At the cabinet meeting that afternoon, Shahak reported on the morning's missile attack and on Jordan's latest announcement that Jordan would fight any intrusion into its airspace. I reported on my conversations with Cheney and on General Olson's arrival with the outdated photos of western Iraq. Shamir told us that Bush had called him twice; once the previous evening and then again this morning after the Scud attack. Bush had talked about the U.S.-Israeli relationship, referred to the troubles of the past, but said that things were improving and he hoped would continue to improve. He pleaded with Shamir that Israel take into consideration America's concerns and not take military action, which in his view would not affect the outcome of the war. Shamir told him that what he was asking was impossible, and that a mechanism for operational coordination had to be set up between us. Bush concluded by asking for our suggestions and promising to discuss them. When Bush called back in the morning, he said he had been informed of our plans and demanded that Israel not carry them out.

I asked Avihu Bin-Nun to present our plans for a photo reconnaissance mission and for attacking the H-2 and H-3 areas in order to hunt down Scud launchers. He said that the pilots were already in their cockpits, awaiting the order to take off, but that we still did not have coordination with the United States. Sharon, Moda'i, Eitan, and Ne'eman argued for an immediate go-ahead. The eyes of all the cabinet members turned to me. "With great regret," I said, "I cannot recommend the implementation of this plan today. Tomorrow, or the day after, things may change." Shamir closed the meeting by saying that he opposed any action without coordination with the United States.

The sun was setting as I walked from the cabinet meeting through the Defense Ministry compound to the shed that housed the "Hammer Rick" communication equipment, to call Cheney. The young air force technician on duty approached me apologetically to remind me that the secure link over which I was going to speak to Cheney was also the link over which the early warning that a Scud had been launched against Israel would be transmitted, so would I please keep the conversation as short as possible. When Cheney got on the line, I informed him of the cabinet's decision not to authorize the plan to attack the Iraqi missile launchers at this point. Although we had complied with the president's request this time, I told him, it would be a different story if we were to be subjected to further Scud attacks. Cheney was pleased with the news, and promised that they would do everything possible to prevent such attacks. "This is a great example of strategic cooperation, in the opinion of the U.S. government you are deserving of admiration," he said. I could not get an adequate explanation from him as to how the Iraqis had been able to get off four launches in daylight that morning, even though he assured me that the area had been under continuous surveillance. "Hope we get through this night okay," I signed off.

Actually the Scud, the code name assigned to the missile by NATO, was an antiquated Russian weapon—a 300-kilometer-range liquid-propellant ballistic missile with a primitive guidance system—based on World War II German V-2 technology. The Iraqis, with outside help, had lengthened the propellant tanks in order to extend the range to 600 kilometers, while reducing the warhead to a relatively small 250 kilograms. The missile was launched from pre-surveyed sites off a mobile transporter, the erection and countdown to launch taking only a few minutes. The impact accuracy was low, on the order of two to three kilometers, but when the missile was fired against large population centers, that was sufficient. The structural engineering involved in extending the missile's range had been poor and resulted in the missile usually breaking into pieces as it encountered high pressure on reentry into the atmosphere. This made it almost impossible for the Patriot ground-to-air missiles to intercept the Scud, not being able to discriminate between the Scud's warhead and the other "junk" that followed in its wake. On some occasions it seemed that a Patriot had intercepted a piece of the Scud's disintegrating structure, while the warhead, as well as other parts, impacted the ground undisturbed. Detecting the launcher from the air at night, either just before or immediately after the launch, when the rocket exhaust had clearly signaled the launch point, turned out to be even more difficult. The launchers were well hidden during the day, came out of hiding during the night, completed the launch procedure in a matter of minutes, and again disappeared into hiding. This is why we were convinced that it would take commando units operating on the ground to seriously impair the Iraqis' ability to launch Scuds against Israel.

The Scud's flight time from western Iraq to Israel was about seven minutes. When its launch was detected by the American geosynchronous satellite hovering over the area, the information was relayed to Washington, and then via Hammer Rick to Tel Aviv. The sirens sounding in Israel provided about four minutes of advance warning before the missile hit.

The Americans had underestimated the problem of neutralizing the Scuds. As it turned out, there was no basis for their promise that they would eliminate the threat against Israel in twenty-four hours. Wishing to get a better understanding of how they were going after the Scud launchers, I asked to meet with General Olson. He was brought to my office late in the evening by Amir Nahumi, a boyish-looking brigadier general who was serving as chief of operations of the Israel Air Force. Nahumi had a great deal of operational experience under his belt, including participation in the 1981 raid on the Iraqi nuclear reactor. Olson explained the mode of operation of the U.S. Air Force over western Iraq, and detailed the mission schedule for the next twenty-four hours. I could see that the Americans were in fact not keeping the area under continuous surveillance and were not planning to attack some areas that we considered potential launching sites. Their plans did not provide for real-time damage assessment and immediate reaction to that assessment, nor for immediate reaction to the discovery of a Scud launch that would destroy the launcher. As became clear later, during the six-week Desert Storm operation not a single mobile Scud launcher would be destroyed, despite statements to the contrary. I called Cheney at midnight and received a promise that corrective steps would be taken.

Olson's arrival in Israel was only part of Washington's strategy to keep Israel from responding to the Scud attacks. Bush informed Shamir that Eagleburger and Wolfowitz were returning to Israel for an indefinite stay as his special envoys. They had evidently been chosen because they were supposed to have established special relationships with Israelis now in leading positions. Although always the loyal State Department official, Larry Eagleburger was an outspoken friend of Israel. Paul Wolfowitz, the number-three man at the Pentagon, was Jewish, and had a sister who had immigrated to Israel. Over the past few years he had developed a close relationship with David Ivry, the director general of the Ministry of Defense. Now Bush had dispatched them to Israel to "hold our hand" while Scuds were coming down and persuade us that it was in our best interest to stay put.

They wasted no time, arriving the day after the second Scud attack, on January 20. When I met with Eagleburger, I took the opportunity to emphasize our three requirements: real-time satellite imagery; a U.S. Air Force team that would work with our air force people in dealing with the Scud threat; and direct contact with the Central Command.

The more we are being kept in the picture, I told him, and the more confident we are that the missile threat is being handled adequately, the less pressure there will be for Israel to take action. Eagleburger informed me that he and Wolfowitz would be staying in Tel Aviv rather than Jerusalem, to demonstrate that they would be sharing the dangers with the population that had come under attack in the last few days, and I appreciated the gesture.

That afternoon Cheney called me to tell me that they were now applying 30 percent of their aerial assets to western Iraq. I asked him again whether they were keeping the area under continuous surveillance and he assured me they were. He informed me that the U.S. Air Force was prepared to share its photo intelligence data with us. But when I returned to the need for real-time contact with Schwarzkopf's Central Command, I could sense his hesitation as he said that he would have to check on that. I had become aware that there was now an ongoing contest between the people in Washington and Schwarzkopf about how much airpower to allocate to western Iraq. Schwarzkopf, who had already publicly belittled the effect of the Scud attacks on Tel Aviv, referring to them as nothing worse than a thunderstorm over Atlanta, was arguing for decreasing to a minimum the number of aircraft assigned to missions over western Iraq while allocating a maximum to the Kuwait theater of operations. Cheney, concerned about Israel's reaction to further missile attacks, was taking the contrary position. I was doing my best to reinforce Cheney's concerns.

I invited Eagleburger to have lunch with me at one of Tel Aviv's now almost empty hotels. I thought this might be an opportunity to find out what lay behind the Bush administration's antagonism toward Israel, and the behavior of the State Department these past two years. Why was it that even now when we were facing a common enemy, the United States was still not treating us as an ally? Why had there been such a radical departure in U.S. policy toward Israel since Bush became president and Baker secretary of state? Eagleburger, ever the civil servant, did not answer my questions. Instead, he appealed to me not to involve Israel in the fighting. "There's great appreciation for the restraint you have shown. You now have a lot of money in the bank in Washington; don't waste it," he said. I think even he, the old Washington hand, did not realize how quickly the Bush administration was going to depreciate the currency of our "deposit" in Washington.

On Tuesday, January 22, Shamir, Levy, and I met with our two guests from Washington. I told our American guests that we had been misled: during their previous visit, they not only had assured us that the U.S. Air Force would eliminate the Iraqi missile threat in the first twenty-four hours, but also agreed, as their fallback position, that if Israel was attacked, there would be a "stand down" of American forces in the area in which Israel intended to operate, so that we could take the necessary action. It must have been clear to them that such action required an aerial corridor; but now that the time had come, they told us they could not clear such a corridor. "You must make good on your commitment and clear the corridor for us," I told them. Levy spoke at great length. While Eli Rubinstein, the government secretary, was valiantly translating from Hebrew to English, our guests seemed to be dozing off, probably suffering from jet lag. That was the end of the meeting.

That evening the Iraqis launched a single Scud against Israel. It landed at 8:37 P.M. at an intersection on Abba Hillel Street in downtown Ramat Gan, causing severe damage to neighboring apartment buildings; over fifty people were wounded, and three elderly people died of heart attacks. I was in the Defense Ministry when the sirens sounded, and received the initial report on the Scud's point of impact in the control center. The hit was only a few minutes' drive from the ministry, and I decided to go out there and see for myself. The scene reminded me of pictures I had seen of London during the Blitz: fire engines, stretcher bearers, ambulances, police, and special army evacuation units attempting to save people trapped in the rubble.

When I got back to the office, I called Cheney. After reporting to him on the Scud hit, I asked him to arrange for an aerial corridor that would enable us to go into action. He inquired about some of the details of our plan, and then informed me that he was at the White House and that he would have to consult with the president. I told him the cabinet would be meeting in the morning and that I expected support for the planned operation. "If you will operate there, we will simply leave the area west of 42 degrees longitude," he said. I took that as a sign that he had reconciled himself to an Israeli operation against the launching sites.

Three hours later, at 2:40 A.M., a message was passed to me via Hammer Rick which indicated that my conclusion was premature. The message, given to Salai Meridor by Rear Admiral T. Joseph Lopez, Cheney's executive assistant, was: "Lopez requests to transmit to Arens from Cheney, that Eagleburger will transmit a message from the president to the prime minister. Till contact between the president and the prime minister is established, action on the matter raised by Arens in his conversation with Cheney is held up."

In anticipation of the next day's cabinet meeting, I tried to analyze the quandary we were in. In three of the past five days, Israel had been hit by Scuds. The entire population of Israel was anxiously awaiting the next attack. According to my estimate, the Americans had succeeded in making it more difficult for the Iraqis to launch Scuds against us, but had certainly not eliminated that capability. There was the additional danger that the next time we might be attacked by Scuds carrying chemical warheads. These were powerful arguments in favor of a decision to order the IDF into action in western Iraq in an attempt to neutralize the continuing Iraqi missile threat against our civilian population. On the down side, this would be a dangerous mission, to be carried out in enemy territory over 600 kilometers from home. I believed that the level of intelligence available to us was not fully adequate, thus significantly raising the operational risks.

But the most serious risk stemmed from the likelihood that the Jordanian Air Force would attempt to intercept our aircraft over Jordan on the way to, or returning from the target area, which would necessitate a forceful response on our part. The inevitable result would be a full-scale war with Jordan, in itself no great challenge to the IDF, but possibly changing the whole nature of the Gulf conflict. If the United States refused to establish operational coordination, we would run the additional risk of accidental encounters with their forces. And yet, beyond the rational calculations, to the extent that I was able to make them, there was my overriding feeling that Israel could not just sit back and take the pounding of Iraqi missiles without responding. The whole discussion was sidelined, however, when Bin-Nun informed me on the day of the cabinet meeting that anticipated weather conditions over western Iraq for the next two or three days would make it impossible to carry out our mission during that period. Shamir seemed relieved.

The cabinet met at nine o'clock on Wednesday, January 23, in an atmosphere of considerable tension. By now, the position of most of the ministers was predictable. Sharon, Moda'i, Eitan, and Ne'eman demanded action almost regardless of the circumstances. Minister of Justice Dan Meridor, Minister of Trade and Industry Moshe Nissim, Minister of the Interior Aryeh Deri, and Minister of Religious Affairs Zevulun Hammer would weigh the alternatives and come down on the side of caution. Minister of Transportation Moshe Katsav and Minister of Police Ronni Milo were less predictable, while David Levy was primarily concerned about our relations with the United States.

The plan I was going to bring to the cabinet that day was the result of an intensive effort that had been going on for the past few months, ever since I had ordered the IDF to prepare for the destruction of Iraqi missile launchers and launching sites in western Iraq. From the start it was clear that this was going to be a difficult and dangerous operation, the likes of which the IDF had never had to perform before. Nevertheless, the IDF had thrown itself into the preparations without reservations and with great enthusiasm. The plan, in its successively more refined versions, had been presented to me numerous times. When its various elements were described in the safety of my office, it seemed relatively straightforward. But as I tried to recount to myself all the things that could go wrong, the casualties we were likely to suffer, the danger of men being taken prisoner, I felt the full weight of responsibility. I had met the commanders charged with the mission and been impressed by the confidence they had in their ability to carry out this daring action. Now they were waiting for the order to go ahead—an order that would have to come from the cabinet.

After Shamir opened the meeting, and before I asked Bin-Nun to present the IDF's plan, Bin-Nun emphasized the complications to be expected as a result of overflying Jordan. "We will have to shoot down any Jordanian aircraft that attempt to intercept us. Should they persist, we will have to take appropriate measures." The tension eased when Bin-Nun mentioned that weather conditions over western Iraq would preclude carrying out the operation during the next two to three days.

I summarized the problems involved: "We are concerned over the possibility of a significant reaction from Jordan. There is the additional danger of a possible Syrian involvement, or that the Jordanians will ask the Iraqis to come to their assistance. If we decide to proceed, it must be clear that we are taking these risks upon ourselves. There are two difficulties with this operation: one is determined by nature, the other by man. Nature's difficulty is the weather. The man-made difficulty is that the Americans agree to clear the area for the required period of time. We would not ask them to arrange for a corridor, but rather to leave the area for three days in order to allow us to act."

Ariel Sharon interrupted me at this point: "Let me understand: if Israel today wants to carry out an action, we have to notify the Americans. And what happens then? Let us assume for the moment that we decide, a decision that should have been taken already a few days ago, to take action. Does that mean that while our forces are in action the Americans know that they cannot bomb the area, that we are carrying out an operation there, and that for the following three days the area is under Israel's responsibility?"

Trying to keep my temper, I replied: "The operation that will be presented today is contingent on the Americans clearing the area for the duration of the operation. If your question is whether we today have an American commitment to clear the area so we can operate there, the answer at the present time is no."

Amnon Shahak added his estimate that flying over Jordan was likely to result in an escalation that could eventually spread to Syria. Then Shamir reported that Bush had called him at seven o'clock that morning and had asked him not to do what Saddam Hussein wanted him to do, namely, to get involved in the conflict. Eagleburger had brought Shamir a letter in the same spirit. The president wrote that while he could "imagine" the pressures on Shamir, he again asked that the prime minister "show restraint in the face of aggression," and that nothing be done to release the pressure against Saddam Hussein—something which, in Bush's view, Israeli military retaliation ("be it most justified") would certainly do. The Israeli plan to attack the Scud launchers had been examined by General Colin Powell and his senior aides and found to be, typically, "full of imagination and daring." But, the president continued, Powell and his aides did not feel that it had a "significant chance" of improving the existing U.S. effort, i.e., allied air attacks and defense by Patriot missiles. The letter closed with another appeal to Shamir that he stand firm, despite the provocation, "for the greater good of Israel and the U.S."

Although Sharon, Moda'i, and Eitan urged the approval of the plan regardless of whether the Americans agreed to clear the area, it was obvious to the majority of the cabinet that coordination with the United States had to be a precondition. Shamir concluded: "The Americans are a very important political and military factor. It is most important, and we have to assure it, that they will help us and not hurt us. In every move of ours, we have to take this into consideration, their position and attitude toward us. . . . We don't have to make a decision today."

The following afternoon, January 24, I went up to Jerusalem to talk to Shamir about his reply to Bush's letter. I was under the impression that he was intent on pleasing Bush and was going to indicate too much flexibility on our part. It was curious to see Shamir, so stubborn in past confrontations with the United States, inclined to accommodate them now. It seemed as though he had set aside certain issues on which he was not going to give an inch, and in compensation was prepared to concede the rest. If he hoped that compliance with Bush's pleas at this stage would earn him greater understanding in the future for Israel's positions in its conflict with the Palestinians and the rest of the Arab world, I thought he was likely to be disappointed. I convinced him to modify the draft of the letter to Bush, so as to put the emphasis on our expectation that the United States would live up to the agreement concluded with Eagleburger during his previous visit.

After the first week of Scud attacks, visitors began arriving in Israel to see the destruction and express their sympathy and support. One of the first to arrive, on January 24, was Hans Dietrich Genscher. He, and much of the German leadership, must have been experiencing pangs of conscience. Though not directly under the aegis of the government, German industry and German scientists had contributed significantly to Iraq's chemical warfare capability, to its nuclear projects, and to improving the Scud missile and its launchers. Now, suddenly and unexpectedly, they faced the danger that the long and difficult process of German rehabilitation they had been promoting, assiduously and successfully, ever since the end of World War II might come crashing down as a result of Saddam Hussein's missile attacks against Israel, and the growing perception that it was German assistance that had enabled him to attain this offensive capability.

On Friday, January 25, Genscher and his aides came to see me in the Defense Ministry. They had visited the sites in Tel Aviv that had been hit by Scuds, and the impression of the destruction they had seen was still visible in their faces. It was 2:00 P.M., three hours before sunset, the time when all Israel began awaiting the Scud attack that might come once darkness had fallen in western Iraq. I reminded Genscher of my trip a year before, when as Israel's foreign minister to Bonn I asked him and Chancellor Kohl to intervene on behalf of Israel in the councils of the European Community to prevent the imposition of sanctions against Israel. I was sure he remembered that despite their assurances to me, the sanctions were imposed, to be lifted only now, in the wake of the Iraqi missile attacks. "Why do people in Israel have to be killed before the decision to revoke the sanctions is taken?" I asked.

I mentioned the meeting with Kohl last September, when I had recounted Israel's pressing economic problems resulting from the Gulf crisis, and suggested that West Germany should assist Israel at this time; we had never received a reply to our first request. Genscher was very apologetic and promised to deal with the matter immediately upon his return to Bonn. "You know," I said to him, "there are some similarities between Saddam Hussein and Hitler; with him, as with Hitler, the question arose as to whether he should be appeased or confronted, and for a number of years the Western world chose the path of appeasement. But one thing the appeasers of the 1930s did not do was to help arm Hitler, whereas the Western world not only appeased Saddam Hussein, it also helped to arm him." Genscher, seemingly embarrassed, countered that the West German government had not entered into any government-to-government agreements with Iraq for the sale of arms, and he was not about to make excuses for those Western governments that had done so. He concluded by inviting a Defense Ministry mission to West Germany to discuss aid.

A few days later, we sent a team to Bonn. The team was headed by Hanan Alon, the head of international affairs at the Defense Ministry, and Major General Danny Yatom, head of the planning branch of the IDF. In Bonn, they got the royal treatment. Kohl insisted on chairing the meetings, making it clear that he had decided to provide Israel with extensive assistance. On my instructions, Alon suggested that Bonn take upon itself the cost of construction of two submarines for the Israeli Navy. I had canceled our program only a few months earlier, over the protests of our navy, as I could not find sufficient funds for it in the defense budget. Since the submarines would be built in Germany, I thought it would be relatively simple for the German government to fund their construction. But that was not the way Kohl saw it. He explained to Alon that Germany could not assist Israel in the purchase of offensive weapons, but was eager to help it to acquire defensive equipment. Alon's reply was that if on his return to Israel he were to report that Germany's help at this time would be limited to providing Israel with gas masks that could be used as protection against poison gas produced in Iraq with the help of German scientists and industries, the news would probably not be well received. That seemed to convince Kohl. "You'll have your submarines," he said. When Alon reported to me on his return that he had succeeded in saving the navy's submarine program, I remarked jokingly that the two submarines should be named after the men who enabled us to acquire them, Saddam Hussein and Helmut Kohl; and if there was going to be a third one, it should be named Hanan Alon.

All these last few days, General Olson and his aides were having regular meetings with Israel Air Force officers to exchange views and information on how best to eliminate the Iraqi missile launchers. Our people, who had a wealth of experience behind them, were quick to propose solutions that had not been considered by the Americans.

On Friday afternoon, January 25, with two quiet nights behind us, I decided to go home for the first time since the Iraqi attacks began. No sooner had I stretched out for what I considered a well-deserved nap than the sirens woke me. The Iraqis had launched five Scuds toward Tel Aviv and three toward Haifa. Only one had landed in a populated area, this time in the Ramat Hen quarter of Ramat Gan, a suburban neighborhood of single- and two-story dwellings. One man was killed, many injured, and lots of property damaged. We received conflicting reports about the degree of success the Patriot batteries were having in intercepting the Scuds, but there was no question that the Patriots were causing considerable secondary damage, as the spent missiles returned to the ground, often landing in residential areas. The American attacks on western Iraq had obviously not diminished the Iraqi ability to launch missiles against Israel.

Olson had by now been replaced by U.S. Air Force Major General Malcolm Armstrong. I had appointed Brigadier General Giora Rom, an experienced Israel Air Force officer, to head the Israeli side of the team that was meeting daily. The improved coordination was providing us with considerable information on the western Iraqi theater of operations and the tactics the U.S. Air Force was using against the missile launchers. It also strengthened our conviction that we could make an effective contribution to neutralizing the missile threat directed against us, and as a result increased our level of frustration.

On Saturday night, January 26, I called Cheney on Hammer Rick to fill him in on the latest missile attack. The following conversation ensued.

I: Yesterday we had five hits in the Tel Aviv area. Much property damage, tens wounded, one dead. This is very difficult, people expected that the ability to attack us would be eliminated. We fired twenty-nine Patriots; they were not effective.

Cheney: In Saudi Arabia we fire about two Patriots against every Scud and obtain better results. I've asked that our Saudi experience be transferred to you.

I: What is your estimate of the remaining Iraqi capability to launch missiles against us, and your ability to eliminate that capability?

Cheney: We have invested a great deal . . . we're doing the best we can.

I: In my opinion not enough is being done. We believe they still have significant capability. What is your opinion?

Cheney: We don't know how many launchers they have left. The fact that they launched seven missiles yesterday proves that they still have significant capability.

I: The question here is, When will we participate in order to put an end to it?

Cheney: I hear you. I'm limited by the president's instructions.

I: In addition, we are concerned that they may start to use chemical warheads. We have to coordinate between us what the response will be; it could happen any day.

Cheney: We have to assume that he has chemical warheads. We are not speaking publicly about how we are likely to respond if he starts with chemical warfare. Do you have any thoughts on this?

I: We can't talk about this on the phone. This we have to discuss face to face. It may happen suddenly and require an immediate reaction.

By ten o'clock that night we had another attack. It looked like four or five Scuds in the Tel Aviv area and two in the Haifa area. They had fallen into unpopulated regions, so there was no damage to speak of, but I used the opportunity to call Cheney again. "Look, we've had another attack; where do we go from here?" He suggested that Ivry and Barak come to Washington to discuss with Powell and other military people how best to handle the Scuds. I agreed to send them the following morning. Eagleburger and Wolfowitz had by this time returned to Washington and presumably reported on the mood in Israel, and I hoped that the Ivry-Barak visit would result in the Americans now being convinced that the time had come for us to intervene.

At the cabinet meeting in Jerusalem on January 29, Sharon again demanded immediate Israeli action, warning of an Iraqi chemical attack, insisting that there was not a moment to lose. I recommended not taking a decision that day, and Shamir closed the meeting.

On the way back to Tel Aviv, I saw a long line of cars moving in the opposite direction. The inhabitants of Tel Aviv had surmised that they were Saddam Hussein's primary target, that Jerusalem was not going to be attacked, and that the southern part of Israel was evidently out of range of his missiles. Many of them had moved in with friends or relatives outside the area, coming to work in Tel Aviv in the morning and leaving as the sun set. The resulting traffic jams became one of the signs of the strange war Israel was experiencing. Tel Aviv's mayor, Shlomo Lahat, a former army general, caused a public furor by castigating those of his constituents who had "deserted" the city, but I saw nothing wrong with people moving their families out of the endangered areas for the duration.

The Iraqis were getting a daily pounding from the air. Their surface-to-air missile batteries had by now been destroyed, and their air force was not capable of dealing with the allied attacks. To save their air force from total destruction, the Iraqis flew about a hundred of their best fighter aircraft, including their French Mirage F-1's, to Iran, where they took refuge, or were taken hostage by the Iranians. Western technology had turned out to be preponderant, and the daily aerial attacks against Iraq could hardly be considered a contest, except for the glaring failure to subdue the launching of Scud missiles. They continued against Israel, as well as Saudi Arabia. In the duel between a primitive ballistic missile and the latest in Western aeronautic and electronic technology, the Scud was the winner. It can only be assumed that the men operating the Scud launchers were more enterprising and innovative than the men charged with their destruction.

The Iraqi reaction to the mounting destruction inflicted on them was to escalate their rhetoric. They were now threatening "to use weapons that they had not as yet used." Since they had made good on their threats in the past, the possibility of chemical warfare had to be taken into consideration, especially as they seemed to be getting more desperate as the allied attacks continued. So far, Saddam Hussein had proven undeterrable. Although he probably assumed that Israel possessed nuclear weapons, that did not prevent him from launching his Scuds. It was little comfort to us that America's military prowess was also not sufficient to deter him from challenging the United States and its allies to battle. If anything might deter Saddam Hussein from the use of chemical warfare, it would be the fear of an allied nonconventional response. Unfortunately, that threat was taken away when John Sununu, the White House chief of staff, announced that even if the Iraqis were to use chemical warfare, the United States would not respond with nuclear weapons. I called Cheney at eight o'clock that evening to draw his attention to Sununu's remarks and he promised to check with the White House.

An hour later, we had a Scud alarm. After forty-five minutes, one of our teams discovered a single missile crater near the Arab village of Dir Balut in Samaria; no damage was done. This was the first indication that the continuous pressure of allied air attacks was possibly interfering with the Scud launch procedure and affecting their accuracy. A few hours later a shower of Katyusha rockets, fired from southern Lebanon, landed on Israel's northern border. This was the PLO's "contribution" to Saddam Hussein's war against Israel. It was meant to emphasize Yasser Arafat's declarations of support for Iraq. His position seemed to reflect the popular feeling among Palestinians in Jordan, as well as in Judea, Samaria, and Gaza. Throughout the territories, Palestinians could be seen on the roofs of their houses at night, watching for the fiery trails of Scuds landing in Israel. Each Scud was accompanied by cheers and dancing. It did not seem to matter that Saddam Hussein had invaded another Arab country; he had promised to destroy Israel.

Sharon began calling publicly for military intervention, claiming that the Israel Air Force could put a stop to the Iraqi missile attacks. But most Israelis seemed to support the government's policy of restraint. At the January 30 cabinet meeting, there were the usual Sharon polemics, followed by a long and tense discussion. At the end of the meeting, I summed up the situation:

"The question we face is whether to take action that is coordinated with the Americans, or to act even without such coordination. . . . We have presented an operational plan aimed at eliminating, as far as possible, the Iraqi missile threat. We can begin the operation tomorrow. . . . The plan exists, the capability exists, but the capability will be significantly greater if the plan is carried out in coordination with the U.S. . . . Since the war started, certainly since the first attack on us on January

18, we are in contact with the Americans in an attempt to achieve the coordination that will enable us to act. I think we are doing what needs to be done to convince them . . . and also to increase, day by day, night by night, their incentive to act as massively and as effectively as possible in the area."

I did not preclude the possibility that we would act even without coordination with them. The question was when? ". . . Since the initial attack on us," I went on, "when we began discussing this question, there have been a number of changes for the better in the military sphere. First, the level of our intelligence on the area in question has improved tremendously. . . . Another change for the better, over these past few days, is the heavy destruction resulting from the American air attacks in the area. That will make it easier for our forces when they enter the area. Eight days ago H-2 and H-3 were active air bases with their complex of aircraft and SAM batteries intact. Had we entered the area then, we would have had to deal with them. . . . The task we face today is considerably easier than the one we would have faced a week ago. Ivry is now on his way back from Washington, where he had talks aimed at achieving coordination with the Americans. At the moment I don't know what message he is bringing back from Washington; I suggest we wait."

That evening Ivry and Barak returned from Washington and immediately came to my office. They had met with Cheney, Powell, and other senior military officers, and had been provided with detailed reports on allied military operations in Iraq and the damage that had been inflicted on the Iraqi Army and its installations. Their opinion on how to deal with the Scud threat to Israel was listened to attentively by the Americans, and they even got the impression that their advice might be followed. But the Americans were still adamant that there should be no Israeli intervention. Although I had wanted them to make it clear to their hosts in Washington that we were determined to take military action even if the Americans refused to arrive at the necessary coordination with us, I had the impression upon hearing their report that they had not made that point with sufficient emphasis, and had left Cheney with the idea that now that he had let us blow off some steam things could continue as before.

The following day, January 31, I went up to Jerusalem to meet with Shamir. I told him that it was my feeling that the people in Washington had the impression they could continue to rely on us to practice restraint, and that we must make every effort to change that impression. I suggested that he call Bush to tell him that he was sending me to Washington with a special message for the president. I would put forward our demand for the operational coordination that would enable us to take military action that was linked with the allied forces in the area, while making it clear that we were prepared in any case to act unilaterally. Shamir hesitated. He was not going to place the call to the president that day; possibly tomorrow. All my arguments were of no avail, and without Shamir I could not move. I could only hope that continued pressure would get Shamir to agree. The Iraqis launched a Scud against Israel that evening, though it fell wide of the mark, not far from the Arab village of Kibya in Samaria.

On Friday, February 1, the IDF gave me a detailed presentation of the updated plan for military intervention in western Iraq, with the aim of suppressing Iraqi capability to launch missiles against Israel. It would involve the air force as well as special forces in the area. It had by now been planned in every conceivable detail, and the units involved had practiced their missions endlessly. And yet everybody around the table, from Dan Shomron down, realized that this was going to be a daring and dangerous operation. At the end of the presentation, the chief of staff recommended that I approve the plan. There were no dissenting opinions. I turned to the man who had been designated to command the operation, Brigadier General Nehemia Tamari, and asked him whether he felt confident in his ability to carry out the plan. The veteran paratrooper, whose combat experience included the rescue action at Entebbe, gave his positive answer without hesitation. I approved the plan.

Now I was eager to get going. I had no doubt that our forces would be considerably more successful than the Americans in dealing with the Scud threat. It was clear that aerial attacks alone were not sufficient to do the job; but, in addition, that forces on the ground appearing in the launch areas would make it difficult and maybe impossible for the missile launchers to be taken out of hiding, for the crews to go through the aiming and launch procedure, and then go into hiding again. The daily pounding the Iraqis were taking from the air, and the failure of their attempted incursion at Al Khafji, had made it clear to all members of the coalition what the eventual outcome of this war was going to be, and had therefore decreased considerably the danger that Israeli intervention would lead to a breakup of the coalition. In my opinion, every day that went by would make it less likely that an Israeli military action would harm the coalition President Bush had put together, or ignite a full-scale war with Jordan. I suggested to the IDF that we should undertake an action in order to obtain an indication of the reaction of the parties concerned, but Shahak was skeptical that the potential gains of such a mission were balanced by the attendant risks, and so I dropped it. Nevertheless, I was determined to return to this mission soon, feeling that the time available for Israeli intervention was limited.

When I called Shamir after the meeting, he still had no intention of calling Bush. Instead, he was busy bringing the two-man Moledet (Motherland) party into the coalition. This party was headed by Rechavam Ze'evi, a former army general with an illustrious record, and appealed to those Israelis who, after long years of conflict, had concluded that Jews and Arabs would never be able to live together, and that therefore the only "solution" was the transfer of the Arab population to the surrounding Arab countries.

I was strongly opposed to this extreme party joining the coalition. Their platform was in total contradiction to the Likud's policy of dealing with the Israeli-Palestinian conflict, and was abhorrent to me personally. When I remonstrated with Shamir, telling him that I and many others in the Likud were opposed, he threatened to resign if we did not support him on this issue. I would have resigned, were it not for the war. Under the circumstances, I had no choice. Four days later, the Knesset confirmed the new addition to the government coalition. It was supposed to be strengthened by the two additional votes. Actually, it was weakened by the inclusion of a discordant element that was beyond the consensus of Israeli popular opinion.

Two Scuds were launched against Israel during the night of February 2. Both landed short, in unpopulated areas of Samaria. This was the third time in a week that Scuds that must have been aimed at Tel Aviv landed about 20 kilometers to the east. The Iraqis must have moved their launchers to new sites that had not been pre-surveyed, or else were launching from sites farther east without having made the necessary adjustments for the increased range requirement.

Despite my repeated requests, Shamir would not call Bush to arrange my visit to Washington, so I decided to take matters into my own hands. Cheney and Powell were going to visit Saudi Arabia on February 8, so I called Cheney the day before his departure, told him that I thought it was important that we meet, and suggested either that he come to Israel, or that we meet in Europe at his refueling stop on his way home. He told me that his instructions from the president were to go directly to Saudi Arabia and return from there to Washington without any intermediate stops, but that he would be glad to meet me in Washington the following week. Here at last was an opportunity for me to put our case to the Americans, but it was essential that Shamir and I present a united front. The impression in Washington had been that Shamir, unlike myself, was inclined to go along with their insistence that Israel refrain from attack. The only thing that could change that impression would be if Shamir called Bush to tell him that I would be carrying a message from him personally. Before I had a chance to make a last-minute appeal to Shamir, another Iraqi Scud landed in a populated area of Ramat Gan.

When I saw Shamir in Jerusalem the next day, he agreed to call Bush. Half an hour before I took off for Washington on Sunday evening, February 10, with Ivry, Barak, and Salai Meridor, Shamir called. He had spoken to Bush, and the president had told him that he would be "delighted" to meet me and receive the message from Shamir.

At 11:30 A.M. I walked into the Oval Office accompanied by David Ivry, Ehud Barak, and Zalman Shoval, Israel's smart and articulate ambassador to Washington. The president, Dan Quayle, Dick Cheney, Jim Baker, Brent Scowcroft, John Sununu, CIA Director Robert Gates, and Richard Haas of the NSC were there. Bush rose to greet me and we shook hands all around. In presenting Ivry, I mentioned that he had been the commander of the Israeli Air Force at the time of the raid that destroyed the Iraqi nuclear reactor. This did not elicit the slightest sign of acknowledgment on Bush's face. He motioned me to the chair at his right, in front of the familiar fireplace, and we sat down, the Israeli contingent facing the Americans.

I started by telling Bush that Israel was at war, even though it was not a member of the coalition, and that in many ways it was more exposed, its civilian population under attack by missiles, than any of the members of the coalition. Thirty-one Scuds had been fired against Israel so far, causing 13 fatalities, 237 injured, and 6,500 domiciles damaged. The Patriots had shown themselves to be of doubtful effectiveness against the Scuds. If these attacks continued, Israel would have no choice but to take military measures designed to put an end to the missile threat. We understood the problems of the coalition, and the complications that might result from our flying over Jordan, but we were close to the point where we would have no other choice. It was therefore essential that we make the arrangements for coordination between our forces now.

Bush replied by describing the punishment that was being meted out to the Iraqis. He seemed satisfied with the progress of the war. When I told him that the kind of destruction caused by Scuds in Israel's urban centers had not been seen anywhere in the Western world since World War II, Cheney handed him a chart, which showed the decrease in the number of Scuds fired against Israel during the past weeks. Bush pointed to the chart and said: "This is really a dramatic improvement." "Yes," I said, "but the impression created by this improvement and the reports of successful Patriot intercepts have aroused expectations among the population that the missile threat has been eliminated, and now that we have just had another Scud causing great destruction, people feel disappointed and frustrated." Cheney interrupted to assert that based on his information, the Patriots had been doing very well.

"Mr. President," I said, "the probability of Patriots intercepting Scuds has been about twenty percent in Israel." Bush wanted to know what I meant by that, and so I spelled it out: "out of every ten Scuds launched against Israel, we would expect that two would be successfully intercepted by Patriots." Bush looked at me in disbelief, obviously accepting his defense secretary's version. Actually, I thought my report somewhat on the optimistic side. As became clear later, it is doubtful that we had a single successful Patriot intercept throughout the war. The Patriot, the best of all anti-aircraft missiles, had not been designed to intercept ballistic missiles, especially the kind that broke up on entering the atmosphere.

"Well, what can your air force do that the U.S. Air Force can't do?" Bush asked me. I was convinced that the IDF would be considerably more effective in hunting down the Scuds, but saw little point in getting into an argument. "I don't want to be presumptuous and tell you that the Israel Air Force can do things that the U.S. Air Force can't do, but it is our intention to send our entire air force on this mission, and as you know that would mean considerably more aircraft over the target area than you have been able to spare from other missions. We do not intend to limit ourselves to an aerial action, and we would introduce additional dimensions to the attack on the launch sites." I was trying to counter his question without providing details of our plan.

At this point Bush took a sheet of paper from his breast pocket and began reading from an opinion poll that had been taken in Israel showing that Shamir had reached a peak of popularity and that the majority of the population supported the policy of restraint. Why, then, was I suggesting that there was pressure for an Israeli action? I replied that this support was fragile, and would disappear overnight if there were further Iraqi attacks on our urban centers, or if the Iraqis were to begin using chemical weapons. Bush suggested I look at the "big picture": the allies were destroying the Iraqi military potential, and Israel's entry into the war would make things much more difficult by threatening the existence of the coalition. He was responsible for the lives of American soldiers and could not countenance anything that would increase the danger to them.

I knew I would be meeting Cheney and Powell later on and could continue the discussion with them. There seemed no point in pursuing the argument and reminding the U.S. president of the responsibility we had for the safety of our own civilian population.

As I was about to leave, a message was passed to me that there had been a Scud alarm in Israel while we had been talking. Bush, somewhat taken aback, asked me if many alarms turned out to be false, and I replied that in most cases the alarms were followed within a few minutes by Scuds. To my surprise, Baker approached me as I was leaving and asked that I meet him that afternoon, and I agreed to come to the State Department after my meeting with Dick Cheney.

We met with Cheney and Powell at the Pentagon in the afternoon. Cheney had assembled a number of generals and admirals to give us an extensive briefing, using slides and movies, of the aerial campaign being waged against the Iraqis. It was modern technology at work—precision guided munitions with pinpoint accuracy, night-vision devices permitting operations in the dark as if it were daylight, stealth technology masking attacking aircraft from enemy radar. In preparation for the opening of the coalition's ground offensive, they claimed to have already destroyed 20 percent of the Iraqi tanks, armored personnel carriers, and artillery. Cheney, turning to Ivry, said that they had learned from Israel Air Force operations and were now doing it in spades. I was impressed, even though the allied aircraft were operating over Iraq with essentially no opposition and I suspected that their estimates of the damage incurred by the Iraqis were inflated.

After the briefing, I returned to the need for establishing closer coordination. Cheney suggested that we discuss this in a smaller forum, and Ivry, Barak, Cheney, Wolfowitz, and I then moved to Cheney's office. We gave him a list of targets in western Iraq that should be attacked, and explained our need for reconnaissance photos to supplement the information we were getting from satellite photos. The battle damage assessments (BDAs) we were getting, I pointed out, were sent to us after considerable delays, thus not giving us access to the situation in the area on a real-time basis. In addition, since we had not been allowed direct contact with Central Command, there was another time delay before our input reached the people in charge of operations at Centcom. "Let's establish a level of coordination so that we will have a real-time picture of the situation, so that we contribute our suggestions how to operate against the Scud threat, and so that we shall be able to go into action, when we so decide, in coordination with you," I told Cheney.

"If you intervene, we will break off contact and get out of the area; then we won't need coordination," Cheney said.

"I don't see it that way," I insisted. "If we get involved, both of us will be operating against a common enemy, even though it may be in different theaters of operation. I don't think it will be good to carry out such an operation in an uncoordinated fashion; many problems will arise that will require coordination."

Cheney referred me to higher authority: "I'm sure you understand that if you decide to intervene, the prime minister will have to speak to the president, and they will decide, yes or no, and under what circumstances." I assumed they were counting on Shamir to veto my plans to intervene, or at the very least, on Bush persuading Shamir that Israel should stay out of the fighting.

As we walked to the door, I tried to draw Cheney out on the coalition's plans for launching ground operations. He led me to believe that they did not intend to start during the next few days. They were comfortable with the present situation where round-the-clock aerial attacks, meeting no opposition, were softening up the Iraqi Army.

The meeting with Baker had been set for six o'clock, and as the meeting at the Pentagon had dragged on, I asked Shoval to notify Baker's office that I would not be able to meet him. I thought that this was just as well, as I had nothing in particular to discuss with him and was all too aware of David Levy's sensitivity about my stepping on his turf. Baker replied that he would be waiting in his office to meet with me whenever I finished at the Pentagon. I tried to call Levy in Jerusalem to advise him of the Baker meeting, but I assumed that he did not want to talk to me. He must have been miffed at my meeting with Bush, and here I was going to meet the secretary of state. The following day, Levy announced that he was canceling his scheduled forthcoming visit to Washington.

It was after seven when I got to Baker's office with Ivry, Shoval, and Meridor. Baker, Eagleburger, Dennis Ross, and State Department spokesperson Margaret Tutweiler were there. This was the first time since I had changed places with Levy at the Foreign Ministry that Baker had been willing to meet with me. In recent months he had chosen to snub me in the hopes that this would please Levy. I was curious to see what he wanted to discuss with me, but instead, he asked me what was on my mind. "You were in the president's office this morning and you heard what I had to say—we may now have to act," I told him. Baker remarked that "our boys are doing the job for you." I felt anger beginning to cloud my vision, but before I had a chance to respond in undiplomatic language, a secretary entered and gave me a message that a Scud had just landed in Savyon, not far from my home. I left the room to call my wife, managed to get her on the line in a minute, and was relieved to hear that she was all right.

When I went back to the meeting, I told Baker and company what had happened. After polite inquiries about my wife's safety, Baker continued as if nothing had occurred. He switched the subject to our economic concerns, asking what aid I felt we required. I was eager to leave and get on the airplane that was waiting at Andrews Air Force Base to take me back to Israel, and so I answered curtly that the estimate I had given Cheney in September, about $1 billion, had proven to be approximately correct.

"Where are you going to get this money?" Baker asked, explaining that it could not be included in the supplementary budget to be submitted to Congress for Desert Storm. "I am the only ally you have for including this money in the supplemental, because I don't want it to come out of the FMS [foreign military sales] budget, since that would impact on moneys allocated to countries like Egypt and Turkey," he added. "Well, if you're our ally on this, then we're bound to win," I said.

Baker was visibly upset by my remark, probably thinking ahead as to what was likely to be leaked to the press after the meeting. "Don't misunderstand me," he said, "I do not support the inclusion of this money in the Desert Storm supplemental."

On the flight back to Israel I could not sleep. I had failed to convince Bush to approve establishing operational liaison with us. A military action that was not coordinated with Schwarzkopf's command would involve risks beyond those inherently connected with the dangerous action we had planned. Would I be able to convince Shamir that we must take action even under these circumstances? And how much more damage from the Scuds would Israel have to take before this war was over? I wrestled with these thoughts throughout the night until the Israeli coastline came into view.

After stopping off at home, I went to see the area of Savyon where the Scud had landed. A number of houses were totally destroyed, only the rubble indicating where houses had stood. Many people had been injured; fortunately, there were no fatalities. Our own house, only a few hundred yards from the impact point, had some cracked walls to serve as a reminder of a close call.

When I read Thomas Friedman's report of my meeting with Bush in the following day's *New York Times*, I began to suspect the real reason for the odd meeting in the State Department:

> . . . Administration officials said Mr. Arens' visit to the White House seemed intended both to prepare Washington for any possible Israeli retaliation and to try to impress Mr. Bush with the sacrifices Israel has made in not retaliating so the Bush Administration might deal more favorably with Israel's financial needs. . . . An Administration official said the Israeli official seemed to be "laying the groundwork, if the Israelis decide to retaliate" and "softening us up" for a new Israeli aid request—something that some Americans in the meeting resented. . . . While officials did not say so explicitly, they left the impression that the Arens-Bush meeting did not enhance Israeli-American relations. . . . An Administration official said he got the feeling that Mr. Arens was sent to emphasize to Mr. Bush how big a sacrifice it is for Israel to continue not responding to the Iraqi missile strikes in the hope that this will prompt the Administration to respond more favorably to Israel's increased economic aid needs.

The subject of economic aid to Israel was not even mentioned in my meeting with Bush; it had only been raised by Baker in the State Department meeting, but the manipulative leak to the *New York Times* by an unnamed "Administration official" had succeeded in distorting the nature of my mission to Washington to the readers of this newspaper. There was more to come. Three days later, Baker summoned Zalman Shoval to give him a dressing down about a remark Shoval had made in an interview with Reuters. Referring to the $400 million loan guarantee Congress had approved to help in the absorption of newly arrived emigrants from the Soviet Union in Israel ten months earlier, but that had still not been extended by the administration, Shoval said: "We sometimes feel we are being given the runaround, although to the best of my understanding Israel has fully complied with the requests that were raised in this connection."

Shoval had been absolutely right, but Baker had taken offense. So much so that he asked the president to issue a statement on the subject, which said that Shoval's Reuters interview had been "outrageous and outside the bounds of acceptable behavior by the ambassador of a friendly country." It continued: "The secretary of state made this clear to the ambassador yesterday, and the president protested to Prime Minister Shamir by cable this morning. We deserve better from Israel's ambassador." This Bush-Baker move against Israel's ambassador had, to the best of my knowledge, no precedent in modern diplomatic history. Never had an ambassador of a friendly country been publicly castigated in such manner in Washington, and this during a war in which we were supposed to be allies. Bush and Baker had set the stage for Shoval's recall, but Shamir took the insults in stride, and Shoval stayed in Washington.

On February 13, I reported on my trip to the cabinet. There were the usual polemics from Sharon, now joined by Ze'evi. During the intelligence briefing, General Shahak reported that the latest Scuds had been launched from Al Qaim, in northwestern Iraq. The Iraqis, because of the aerial attacks, had evidently moved their launchers into a new area.

Almost exactly a month after the beginning of allied aerial attacks against targets in Iraq, the world received the first indication that Saddam Hussein was prepared for compromise. He authorized Baghdad Radio to announce on February 15 that the Revolutionary Council had decided it was ready to consider the UN resolution on Kuwait, including the possibility of withdrawal. The list of conditions included Israeli withdrawal from the territories, cessation of all attacks against Iraq, and restitution for damages incurred by Iraq as a result of the allied attacks.

Although the conditions were quickly rejected by Bush, as well as by spokesmen of other allied governments, the Baghdad announcement seemed to indicate that Saddam Hussein realized he was in trouble and was looking for a way out. His ultimate surrender was probably delayed by Gorbachev's attempts to stake out a position of his own with a futile attempt to mediate the conflict. Tariq Aziz was rushed from Baghdad to Moscow via Teheran twice, but as should have been expected, with no substantial result.

On the night of February 16, four Scuds landed in Israel without causing damage; one directed at Haifa landed in the sea, while three landed in unpopulated areas of the south. Baghdad announced that they had attacked the atomic reactor at Dimona; if that had really been their target, the missiles were way off, in range as well as in azimuth. The next attack came three days later, during the evening, just as four U.S. senators were meeting with me in the Defense Ministry's conference room. Senators Daniel Inouye, Sam Nunn, Ted Stevens of Alaska, and John Warner of Virginia had come to Israel after visiting the troops in Saudi Arabia. They sat opposite me with the brown cardboard boxes containing the gas masks they had been issued on arrival next to them, as I briefed them.

Suddenly the air-raid sirens started wailing. I had no gas mask to put on, and the senators did not put on theirs. The control center informed me that one Scud was headed in the direction of Tel Aviv. We sat silently waiting for the missile to land. When it came after a few minutes, there was a dull thud, indicating that the Scud had landed some distance away. Shortly afterward the control center notified me that the impact point had been north of Petah Tikva and that no damage had been done. But it was a dramatic demonstration for the senators of the average Israeli's experience during the past month. It was reinforced the following day when the senators visited the sites in Ramat Gan that had been hit by Scuds. I was gratified when Sam Nunn told a reporter that he hoped that Israel would continue to practice restraint, but would understand if it decided to take military action.

Since my return from Washington, in almost daily meetings with Shomron, Barak, Shahak, and Bin-Nun, I urged them to present me with a plan for measures that would provide us with an indication of what the Jordanian response to our use of their airspace for military action in Iraq would be. Shahak thought that the Jordanians would try to intercept us. None of them seemed enthusiastic about testing the

Jordanian reaction by sending an aircraft or helicopter over Jordan. I was convinced that whatever King Hussein's intentions had been initially, he must by now have lost most of his enthusiasm for the Iraqi adventure. Our generals argued that a short incursion into Jordanian airspace would not provide the necessary evidence, while an extensive incursion might set off a full-scale conflagration. "Find a way," I told them.

After a meeting of the cabinet on February 20, I flew by helicopter to Gaza to take stock of the situation there. We had begun to relax the curfew that had been imposed after the first Scuds fell on Israel. Now, after four weeks, half of the Gaza population was still under curfew, and a small trickle of Palestinian workers had resumed the daily trek to Israel. The population, which lived in squalid misery in the best of times, had experienced great suffering since the war started. Residents were cooped up in their homes, except for a few hours every few days for shopping, their children stuck at home, and their regular source of income from work in Israel cut off. I was not surprised to hear that during the previous night's Scud alarm there had been great exultation throughout Gaza.

Now we were attempting to return Gaza gradually to what used to be called normalcy. I suggested to Major General Danny Rothschild, whom I had recently appointed to the post of coordinator for the territories, to organize parent-teacher associations which would assume responsibility for preventing the schools from becoming centers of agitation and rock throwing, and thus assure their continued functioning. I also instructed him to try to put together local councils which could begin running the municipal affairs of Gaza and the other cities in the area. If that could not be done, we would have to hold municipal elections, regardless of who was likely to be elected. But I knew that too presented a problem, since terrorist gangs would try to terrorize candidates and voters alike in an attempt to prevent the elections from taking place.

For some time now I had concluded that there was nothing to be gained by continued Israeli control of the Gaza Strip. Unlike Judea and Samaria, which bordered Israel's population centers, and whose mountains overlooked most of Israel, Gaza was not of ultimate strategic importance to Israel. I had no illusions about who would rule Gaza after an Israeli withdrawal, and that we would have to contend with acts of terror against Israel originating from there, but I was convinced that it would be easier to handle such terrorism from positions in Israel surrounding the thin, elongated strip than from inside the densely populated area. The continued burden of ruling Gaza was weighing heavily on Israel's society and economy, to the point where I thought it might in time prejudice our ability to maintain control of Judea and Samaria. Most Israelis had become sick and tired of Gaza and wished to be rid of it.

I had shared these thoughts with Shamir on a number of occasions, but had been rebuffed by him every time. "Gaza is part of the Land of Israel," he said. To me, the borders of the League of Nations Mandate, which had included Gaza in the area allocated to the future Jewish State, were not sacrosanct. I had opposed total withdrawal from the Sinai, continued to oppose withdrawal from the Golan Heights overlooking northern Israel, even though they were not part of the Palestine Mandate, and I supported withdrawing from Gaza, which was part of the original Mandate. But as long as I could not obtain Shamir's support, I knew that bringing it to the government would be futile, and I had decided not to make a public issue of it. Instead, I looked for ways of advancing local self-government in Gaza, in the hope that this would permit me to substantially reduce our military presence there.

I had been invited to a concert at the Jerusalem Theater of the Israel Philharmonic, featuring Zubin Mehta as conductor and Isaac Stern as violin soloist, on Saturday evening, February 23. Mehta and Stern were well-known supporters of Israel, who had made invaluable contributions to the Israeli cultural scene. Both had made a point of performing in Israel in times of crisis. The auditorium was packed when Muriel and I arrived at six-thirty. It seemed almost natural that the members of the audience held brown cardboard boxes in their laps in addition to the evening's program. The orchestra had just begun when the air-raid sirens went off. I rushed to the nearest telephone. When I returned to my seat, Isaac Stern was playing violin to an enchanted audience wearing gas masks, a sight that I shall never forget. The Scud had fallen just east of the Israel Aircraft Industries complex, near Ben-Gurion Airport. Its warhead had not exploded.

Bush had presented Saddam Hussein with an ultimatum that expired at 7:00 P.M. that very evening, requiring him to evacuate Kuwait unconditionally or else face a ground assault by allied forces. Although the Iraqi had made some seemingly conciliatory speeches during the last few days, as well as sending his foreign minister, Tariq Aziz, to Moscow twice to assess the Soviet Union's readiness to mediate, Bush was not ready to let go for anything less than the conditions he had announced publicly. This was evidently too much of a humiliation for Saddam Hussein, and as the hours passed a ground war became inevitable.

I had decided to spend the night after the concert at the King David Hotel in Jerusalem, since I would be attending the next morning's government meeting there. I was awakened at two A.M. to be told that Dick Cheney was trying to reach me. In half an hour I was at the Ministry of Defense in Tel Aviv and had Cheney on the line. Keeping a promise he had made during my visit to Washington, he notified me that within a few hours Bush would announce on television that since Saddam Hussein had not accepted the terms of the ultimatum, the ground campaign would begin. By the time the government met the next morning, the ground offensive was in full swing.

That night two Scuds landed in Israel, the first at three-thirty, the second two hours later. Both must have been aimed at the Dimona atomic reactor, but they fell wide of the target, smashing to the ground somewhere in the Negev Desert. We were astonished to find that one of the missiles had a block of reinforced concrete in place of the warhead. They must have fired one of their test missiles by mistake, or else they had run out of live missiles in the launch area that night.

I called Cheney in the afternoon to say the Scuds were still falling. "Maybe the time has come for a division of labor between us," I said. "You take care of the eastern front, and let us handle western Iraq." Cheney replied that he had not given that any thought.

That night a Scud missile launched from southern Iraq against Dhahran in Saudi Arabia hit a warehouse that had been converted into a barracks for U.S. military personnel. Twenty-eight American soldiers were killed and ninety-eight wounded.

I was frustrated by the slowness of our army's response to my request for testing the Jordanian reaction. Repeatedly the generals argued that the mission would be either non-productive or else overly provocative. Each time I sent them back to prepare a plan that would attain my objective. When the army finally presented me with a mission profile for an aerial incursion into Jordanian airspace, I considered it unsatisfactory, did not approve it, and asked for a revised plan. At last, on Tuesday, February 26, I was presented with a plan that I felt met our requirements. I hoped that the mission would confirm my expectation that the Jordanians would not react to our overflights in this area. With that proof I hoped to be able to convince Shamir to authorize our operation against the Iraqi missile sites.

The action was scheduled for that day, and I quickly called Shamir to obtain his approval, but he refused. He insisted that the war was almost over, and there was no justification for taking any risks. The argument between us became heated, but he refused to budge. I could see the opening for our carrying out a military operation closing—the war might last only a few more days. It was important for Israel to be an active participant, and not limit its involvement in the war to firing Patriot anti-aircraft missiles that failed to intercept incoming Scuds. In his last days of despair—as the "mother of all battles" was turning into the "mother of all defeats"—Saddam Hussein might attempt to launch Scuds with chemical warheads against us; but it was also important for Israel's image in the world, and in the Arab world in particular, that the unprovoked attacks against us not remain unpunished, and that the coming cease-fire should find Israeli soldiers deployed in western Iraq, so that Israel would become a party to the cease-fire.

I went to Jerusalem early the next morning, February 27, to try to convince Shamir. He listened quietly to my arguments, and after I had assured him that the danger of a Jordanian attempt to intercept our aircraft was minimal, he finally agreed.

We would fly the mission that day. Based on its results, I expected to bring the operation for approval to Shamir and thereafter to the cabinet. In the afternoon I called Cheney, congratulated him on the coalition's successes in the ground offensive, and told him of my concern that Saddam Hussein might decide to initiate chemical warfare against Israel. "Israel must take action to eliminate this threat," I told him. "As long as the missile threat hangs over Israel, our entire economy is in low gear. We must return to normalcy and put away the gas masks. The danger to the coalition has certainly passed, the Jordanians are not likely to interfere; the time has come for Israel to act." Cheney said he thought that an Israeli action at this time would not be appropriate, but in any case he was not authorized to give his agreement; it would have to be discussed by the president and the prime minister.

Toward the evening of the 27th I was informed that changing weather would not permit flying the reconnaissance mission. At the moment I did not realize that we had missed our opportunity. At 4:00 A.M. Israeli time on Thursday, February 28, President Bush announced on television that he had given the order for a cease-fire. This time we had been given no advance notice. I could not imagine what had led to this precipitous decision after only four days of fighting on the ground, with much of the Iraqi Army still intact. The real purpose of Desert Storm—eliminating the danger that Saddam Hussein and his gigantic military machine posed to the Middle East and the world at large—had been only partially accomplished.

Thursday was Purim, the Jewish holiday that commemorates the rescue of the Jewish community of ancient Persia from Haman's plans for their destruction. Ordinarily it is an occasion for celebration, especially for the children, but everyone was still taking the precautionary measures that had been the rule during the past six weeks. There was no certainty that the Iraqis were going to follow the cease-fire instructions announced by the Americans, or whether they would apply the cease-fire to Israel. But I decided to take a chance, and disregarding counsels of caution from some of my advisers, issued instructions canceling all of the orders that had been in force throughout the war. Within minutes Israelis were walking the streets without their little cardboard boxes. It was a sunny day, spring was in the air, and the people of Israel realized that the war was over.

The true origin of the Gulf War was not the invasion of Kuwait on August 2, 1990, but rather the invasion by Iraq of Iran ten years earlier, on September 22, 1980. Saddam Hussein, in violation of a treaty he himself had signed with Iran a few years earlier, decided to exploit the seeming weakness of Iran after the Ayatollah Khomeini came to power. This unprovoked aggression did not arouse opposition from the international community. No sanctions were imposed on Iraq for the blatant contravention of international law. On the contrary, Iraq became the recipient of an increasing stream of economic and military assistance from the Western world. The Iraqi use of chemical warfare against Iranian troops in 1984, and thereafter against Kurdish civilians in Iraq, went unpunished and almost unnoticed, even though it was in violation of the international convention on chemical warfare, to which Iraq was a signatory.

In the years that followed, Iraq's industrial capability to produce chemical weapons was augmented by Western industrial and technological assistance. In November 1984, after Iraq had begun to use chemical warfare, the United States resumed formal diplomatic relations with Iraq, which Iraq had severed after the Six-Day War in 1967. Thereafter, the United States provided Iraq with billions of dollars of loans and loan guarantees, many of them destined for the acquisition of arms and weapons technology, in addition to satellite intelligence to assist them in the war against Iran. Even after Saddam Hussein, on April 2, 1990, boasted that he now was able to produce binary chemical weapons, and publicly threatened that he would burn half of Israel to the ground with them, there was no international response to this outrage. My attempts at the time, as foreign minister, to initiate consultations with the United States on the subject remained unanswered. Saddam Hussein must have been pleasantly surprised when a delegation of U.S. senators led by the Senate Minority Leader Robert Dole visited him in Iraq ten days later. Dole told Saddam Hussein that President Bush had "assured me that he wanted better relations, and that the U.S. government wants better relations with Iraq," while adding his personal assurance that Bush would oppose sanctions legislation in Congress. At the same time Baker sent a message to Saddam Hussein reminding him that when an Israel Air Force raid had destroyed the Iraqi nuclear reactor, "we condemned the 1981 raid. And would do so again today. We are telling Israel so." When the senators arrived in Israel on their way back, they reported that Saddam Hussein was a man you could do business with, and there was no reason to be concerned about his intentions.

I believed then that among nations common ideals and values make for common interests, and I considered the warm relationship that the Reagan and Bush administrations had developed with Saddam Hussein, a cruel despot and an implacable enemy of democratic Israel, as an aberration. It was in my view only a matter of time before the United States and the other democracies of the world realized that he was their enemy as well. It took a long time, but the day finally came when he invaded Kuwait and took over that country's rich oil fields. But it turned out that this time, the enemy of my enemy was not my friend.

It was the first war won by airpower. The largest aerial armada in history had been concentrated against the Iraqis, using the latest in modern technology. American planes pounded away at the Iraqi ground forces and their logistics night and day for five weeks before the ground offensive began. When it finally did, it was a walk-over. The Iraqi Air Force never rose to the challenge. Its best aircraft fled to Iran; the remaining ones evaded challenging their vastly superior adversary. The Iraqi surface-to-air missiles gave no serious account of themselves; they were either blinded by electronic warfare or knocked out from the air.

All in all it was a stunning demonstration of the power of advanced technology on the battlefield. It was also a victory of American weapons over Soviet-manufactured weapons, except for the Scuds. Almost six weeks of around-the-clock Scud hunting, some of the reports to the contrary, did not manage to destroy a single Iraqi mobile missile launcher.

For Israel, it was a war unlike any of the six wars it had experienced since the establishment of the state in 1948. This time Israel was attacked by an enemy that had no common border with it. The Iraqis enjoyed a geographic advantage in that the distance from western Iraq to Israel's population centers is about 500 kilometers, whereas the distance from Israel to Baghdad is 1,000 kilometers. Although the effect of the thirty-nine Scuds that hit Israel was limited, they caused damage to the psyche of Israel's population.

Saddam Hussein had built up a gigantic war machine; Bush correctly referred to the Iraqi Army as the fourth largest army in the world. It took five months to deploy the 500,000 men, and their equipment, before the Americans felt they had sufficient forces in the area to take on the Iraqis. In terms of military equipment, the Israeli Army was about half the size of the Iraqi Army. Had Saddam Hussein decided to attack Israel rather than Kuwait, he probably would have headed an Arab coalition whose military potential would have been double that of the Iraqi Army alone. Although Israeli Intelligence probably had better information on the Iraqi buildup than other intelligence services, the Iraqi potential, once fully revealed, contained many surprises and serves as a warning of the level of armament a distant dictator can achieve as long as he has sufficient economic resources at his disposal. Some years earlier, Israel had taken certain steps in anticipation of the possibility of an attack from a distance. The Arrow ballistic missile interceptor was in the early stages of development when the Gulf crisis began, and two satellite launches were an indication of Israel's ability to put an intelligence satellite into orbit and obtain the kind of information we lacked at the beginning of the war.

Two cardinal questions need to be dealt with in light of the Gulf War. First, what would have been the course of events if Saddam Hussein had displayed more patience and delayed the annexation of Kuwait until such time as he had acquired a nuclear bomb, something that seems to have been within months of his reach when the war began? And second, if Saddam Hussein had attacked Israel rather than

215

Kuwait, would the United States and its allies have rushed to Israel's defense? I posed this question to some of the visiting politicians from abroad during the war, and was invariably told that Israel would have received the same assistance as Kuwait, but I remained unconvinced.

Six weeks of aerial attacks, and four days of action on the ground, finally persuaded Saddam Hussein to agree to the American ultimatum. Prior to that, he seemed undeterrable. The deployment of 500,000 troops and a large armada of ships and aircraft in the area did not convince him to withdraw, although, considering the mixed signals he received from Washington, it seems not unreasonable that he did not expect the United States to deploy military forces in response to the annexation of Kuwait, nor to use these forces if he did not withdraw. The friendly visit of the senatorial delegation and the, at best, ambiguous messages delivered to him by the U.S. ambassador in Baghdad, April Glaspie, must have seriously affected the strength of the U.S. deterrent in his eyes. Considering the Arab code of "honor," withdrawal in the face of the buildup of forces and UN resolutions became difficult for him. But here, too, doubts regarding the readiness of the majority of the U.S. Senate to authorize military action probably influenced his evaluation of the consequences of continued intransigence.

As for Israel, it did not succeed in deterring Saddam Hussein from launching missiles against Israel's cities. During the months of crisis leading up to the war, there was speculation that Saddam Hussein would be deterred from carrying out this act by his expectation of the Israeli response; but that obviously was not the case as long as he was using conventional warheads. Possibly, had Israel been unambiguous in its threatened response, it would have been taken more seriously in Baghdad. The fact that Hussein did not use the chemical warheads in his possession is an indication that he did not want to take the risk of what the Israeli response might be in that case. The unequivocal warning issued by me in the Knesset on August 6, 1990, against the entry of Iraqi troops into Jordan may have been instrumental in preventing the Iraqi Army's entry into that country.

It has been suggested that it was not possible to deter Saddam Hussein, because he was not rational or intelligent. April Glaspie said about Saddam Hussein after he invaded Kuwait: "We didn't realize he was so dumb." But it is not difficult to list a set of seemingly rational arguments for Saddam Hussein's actions, ever since his invasion of Iran. Modern psychology maintains that intelligence is intimately linked to the kinds of knowledge available to it; in other words, rational thought depends on what a thinker knows. If Saddam Hussein's knowledge of the Western world was distorted, it may very well have been the result of the confusing messages he received.

Over a hundred years ago a British diplomat, Robert Burton, referred to Arab governments as "despotism tempered by assassination." Not too much seems to have changed in the Middle East since then. Saddam Hussein is easily rivaled by other Arab dictators like Hafez al-Assad in Syria and Muammar Qaddafi in Libya.

The overriding lesson of the Gulf crisis is that large quantities of modern weapons should not be sold to Middle Eastern dictators. In the hands of a dictator sitting on, or within range of, much of the world's oil supply, and not reticent to use force in the pursuit of his objectives, they are liable to become a serious threat to world stability. Unfortunately, Western weapons industries continue to sell whatever they can to Middle East countries, and the arms race there is in full swing.

For Israel, the war in the Gulf has emphasized the importance of modern technology on the battlefield and should lead to redoubling the ongoing effort to attain a quality edge in weaponry over the numerically larger Arab armies in the surrounding countries. But, more important, the war served as a reminder that if Israel came under sudden attack, it would have to rely solely on itself for its defense.

On the Road to Madrid

On March 11, Secretary Baker arrived in Israel, on the last leg of a nine-day Middle Eastern tour. Five days earlier, in the triumphal speech he delivered to a cheering joint session of Congress marking the end of the Gulf War, Bush had made settlement of the Arab-Israeli conflict a major theme, declaring the time ripe for the U.S. to move with "vigor and determination" toward closing the gap between Israel and the Arab states and between Israelis and Palestinians" and stressing the need for major territorial concessions. "A comprehensive peace must be grounded in UN Security Council Resolutions 242 and 338 and the principle of territory for peace. This principle must be elaborated to provide for Israel's security and recognition, and at the same time for legitimate Palestinian rights. Anything else would fail the twin tests of fairness and security."

The president also announced that he had asked Baker to go to the Middle East to begin this process. "He will go to listen, to probe, to offer suggestions and to advance the search for peace and stability." It was clear that nothing in the administration's stance had changed as far as Israel was concerned. Nonetheless, it seemed to me unlikely that there would be a confrontation with Baker on this initial visit. Although Bush's popularity had reached a new high in light of what was then being viewed by the American people as a tremendous victory, there was also great support and sympathy for Israel, both in Congress and within the American Jewish community. And although I had no doubt that the administration would try to change this situation, I thought it would go about doing so with at least preliminary caution.

As for how we should present Israel's position to Baker, at the cabinet meeting called on March 6, Sharon, Ne'eman, and Ze'evi had spoken heatedly about abandoning the government's peace initiative; but they had no alternative to offer except for creating what they called "facts on the ground," which had been the policy of Israeli governments in the past but was now, I believed, no option at all. Conventional wisdom might have it that old wine is better than new; I didn't think this was necessarily so. The peace initiative was by far the best route available to us if we wanted to make progress. I suggested a return to my original proposal for the peace initiative as formulated before Rabin had insisted on changing it, i.e., adding (or rather, restoring) the fifth point dealing with an embargo on the sale of arms to the Middle East. I also suggested that the elections among the Palestinians be held at the municipal level, not on a single-district basis for all of Judea, Samaria, and Gaza.

There had been a flurry of important visitors: among them, the members of the European Community troika—Jacques Poos of Luxembourg, Hans Van Den Broek of the Netherlands, and Italy's Gianni DeMichaelis. Echoing Bush's demand that Israel yield territory for peace, and like Bush, rapping Arafat and the PLO over the knuckles for "discrediting" themselves in the war, they offered to provide Israel —and the Palestinians—with financial assistance, proposing the assignment to the Palestinians of a special EC representative. I told them the aid was fine, and badly needed by the Palestinians, but that we would agree to nothing that infringed on Israeli control in the territories; that was something to be handled in peace process negotiations. In the meantime, we would work something out so that EC economic assistance could be given there without eroding our position. I also told them that, so far as Israel was concerned, the Gulf War had not begun either in August 1990 when Iraq invaded Kuwait or in January 1991 when the fighting had started, but on April 2, 1990, when Saddam Hussein began threatening us with missiles and chemical warfare; and that his war machine was the direct result of help he had been given by the USSR and the West. They seemed somewhat abashed when I said that, but I didn't think their momentary contrition would lead to any change in the positions to which they adhered.

Baker's visit began inauspiciously. The day before he arrived, four women standing near a Jerusalem bus stop had been stabbed to death by an Arab from the Gaza Strip, who worked as a male nurse in the Arab town of Ramallah just north of Jerusalem. Shot and arrested by a policeman who happened to pass by, the murderer had mumbled that the killings were his message for Baker. They had, in fact, I thought, been a message for everybody involved as to the nature of some of the Arabs with whom we had to deal. This was no less true of the six Arab infiltrators—all of them carrying Korans, all crazed by their hatred of us—who crossed into Israel before dawn on the following day and were killed in the subsequent engagement with the IDF.

Despite its prelude, Baker's sojourn in Israel proceeded along customary lines: he met with Levy, with Shamir, with me, with leaders of the Labor party, and with Israel's president. He briefly toured Jerusalem —not entering the Old City—and Yad Vashem, where he wrote in the visitors' book: "A chilling reminder of a tragedy that must never be repeated. With great respect and affection for the Jewish people." He also met with twelve Palestinians led by Feisal Husseini, an East Jerusalem activist, who had been authorized by the PLO executive committee to meet with the European Community leaders as well. We arranged a helicopter tour over Israel, and Judea, Samaria, and Gaza, so that Baker could at last see for himself precisely what was under discussion—even though he insisted on not landing in the territories or on the Golan Heights.

I sent along Major General Yossi Ben-Hanan, a hero of the fighting on the Heights during the Yom Kippur War, to explain Israel's strategic problems to him, and Ben-Hanan had prepared a map with an overlay showing how far the Syrians would have advanced in 1973 had they started at the 1967 lines. But if the trip made Baker any more sensitive to Israel's security problems, he gave us no such indication.

He had brought no concrete proposals with him, he said, but he wanted us to know that he had detected a shift in attitude toward us on the part of some of the Arab leaders, and that he had asked them "in due course" to develop steps they might be able to take "to signal their commitment to peace and reconciliation with Israel." When we met, I went over Israel's peace initiative with him, saying that I thought a fifth point should be added: the restriction on the sale of conventional weaponry to the area, because this was perhaps the single most destabilizing element in the situation. Baker was not very optimistic; with the huge pending sale of weapons to Saudi Arabia, the Americans were now the major salesmen to the Middle East. "There's the British and there's the French," he said. "If we don't sell, they will." I said, "Yes, but the United States should take the initiative and get all the arms-producing countries to put an end to the trade." I couldn't get a clear answer from Baker, so I turned to the question of the territories. I said that much of the Arab violence in Judea, Samaria, and Gaza was based on playing to the galleries in the hope of increasing the pressure on Israel from the United States or the United Nations, in the light of which his meeting in Jerusalem with the PLO-approved Palestinians was not helpful.

Then I brought up the question of Egypt: only the United States had the leverage necessary to get the Egyptians to live up to the spirit, as well as the letter, of their peace treaty with Israel. Mubarak had still not met with Shamir nor had Abd el-Meguid come to Israel, though we had given the Egyptians everything we could possibly give. "Now only U.S. leverage will help," I said. Baker didn't dispute the point.

I reminded him that we had suggested a program for rehabilitating the refugee camps, and asked him to look into the matter of our prisoners and MIAs when he went to Syria to meet with Assad next May, and he promised to do that.

In my diary, I wrote:

> The meeting was held in a very cordial atmosphere . . . the Americans seem to have adopted what they call a two-track approach which is really an adoption of the second and fourth points of our initiative . . . maybe, just maybe, they will have some success in getting the other Arab countries to the peace table, although I gathered from what Baker said that the Arab condition for the beginning of any normalization with Israel was our agreement to territories for peace—something which he himself, however, had not explicitly referred to during his visit.

On March 27, Cheney called to inform me that he wanted to pull out the Patriot batteries that had been deployed in Israel with American personnel. I told him there was no problem about that, although we had hoped that we might get one battery within the framework of the drawdown of equipment provided for by Congress, but he didn't volunteer to leave a battery here. They would be gone in a few days. We had Israeli batteries and were to get another one for which the Germans were to pay, so I wasn't too upset about that.

The upsurge of local violence continued and the number of knifing incidents increased. As we neared the week of Passover, I gave instructions for all possible precautions to be taken, reinforcing the troops in Judea, Samaria, and Gaza, and putting elite troops in there since attempts might be made to create disturbances, ambush cars, and kill people.

On March 31, Shamir called a special meeting of the cabinet to discuss internal security. I didn't see any point to such meetings except providing a forum for people like Sharon, who immediately afterward talked to the press about the positions they had taken. But Shamir, probably under Sharon's pressure, went ahead; the results were not very good. Due to the attendant publicity and leaks, the impression was created that we had decided to take new and severer measures, and the government was subjected to another barrage of criticism, including from Washington. I had come to that meeting with a series of recommendations for reinforcing internal security, not much different from what we were already doing, but Sharon lashed into me, charging that essential measures were being omitted and insisting that the government adopt a decision that the Intifada had to be quelled. I tried to explain that the important thing was not a declaration but dealing with it properly. The government should start thinking very seriously why it was that the Intifada had begun after twenty years of Israeli control over Judea, Samaria, and Gaza—a period during which successive Israeli governments had presumably tried hard to bring about Palestinian acceptance of Israeli rule. As for the present, I said, what mattered most was making sure that the Intifada did not yield the Palestinians any political gains. We had to conduct ourselves in full knowledge of the fact that this was being played to an international audience.

During these weeks, I was also concerned with the recommendation to the government of a new chief of staff. Dan Shomron was now due to retire. There were at least three candidates to succeed him, any one of whom would have been an excellent choice. Yossi Peled, born in Belgium and turned over as a baby by his parents to a Christian family for safekeeping during the German occupation, had headed the Northern Command, handling the difficult problems on the Lebanese border in an exemplary manner. Amnon Shahak and Ehud Barak were both native-born Israelis. On April 1, the changing of the guard took place. Ehud Barak was chosen to replace Dan Shomron as chief of staff.

A short time after Baker's visit, Shamir was asked to send someone to Washington to meet with Dennis Ross so that the Americans could confidentially transmit to Jerusalem some questions they had formulated. Shamir gave the assignment to Dan Meridor, perhaps the minister he trusted most. Meridor, ostensibly in the States to speak to some Jewish assembly, met not only with Ross but also with Baker. The three questions he returned with were: (1) Was the Israeli government ready to negotiate a permanent settlement based on UN Resolutions 242 and 338? (2) Was the Israeli government ready to participate in a regional conference called by the United States and USSR? and (3) Did the Israeli government agree to the names of seven Palestinians (which did not include any resident of Jerusalem or anyone who had been deported) to serve as members of a Palestinian delegation?

Shamir was obviously in good spirits when he told me about Meridor's trip. He felt that we could handle those questions and, I suppose, felt also that we could take our time doing so, something that suited his general strategy of procrastination. But late in the evening of April 4, sounding agitated, Shamir called me to say he had just been notified that Baker was returning to the area the following week. Shamir wanted me to come to Jerusalem and talk to him about this visit.

I went up to Jerusalem the following day, although I couldn't talk any sense into Shamir in terms of the positions we should take. He said something about settlements. I told him that I thought there was no point to setting up any new settlements; we should concentrate our efforts on enlarging the existing Israeli towns and villages in the area, and he said yes but went on insisting that new settlements had to be established, and that Israel could not agree to the principle that no more new settlements would be created. I said that we didn't have to agree to any such principle; however, nothing would be gained by putting up new ones at this time. But Shamir had evidently made a commitment to Tehiyya and some of the extremist groups, and I couldn't budge him.

Nor did it make the slightest impression on him when I said that the most important thing, to my mind, was that we deal with the Palestinian Arabs in the territories by holding municipal elections. He didn't like the idea of elections and didn't understand, or maybe didn't want to realize, that the obvious alternative to elections would be a non-elected Palestinian delegation, raising the issue of PLO representation and representation for East Jerusalem. I told him we were making some progress in the search for potential members of an emergency municipal council in Gaza, and had held similar talks in Nablus, but I couldn't arouse any real interest in him on the subject.

Baker was due back in Israel on April 8. I was pretty sure that American steamrolling had begun. When Baker and I met next day, after he had met with Shamir and Levy—at that stage he chose to see each of us separately—he started talking to me about what he called CBMs (confidence-building measures), suggesting that Israel reduce the number of troops in the territories, stop administrative detentions and deportations, reopen schools and universities, and promote indigenous economic activities. I told him that CBM was a totally inappropriate appellation for what needed to be done in the territories. "When and if the violence is reduced," I said, "we will reduce the level of our troops. The same holds for administrative detentions and deportations. As long as we need protective measures against people engaged in active violence or in inciting it, we won't give those measures up."

"You know," Baker responded, "these deportations violate the fourth Geneva Convention." We had been through all that before, but I told him again that this was not the case: not only had the Israeli Supreme Court declared them legal, but the fourth article of the Geneva Convention was not applicable to Judea, Samaria, and Gaza. It dealt with cases of partial or total occupation of the territory of a "High Contracting Party"; the territories were not occupied by such parties. Gaza did not belong to Egypt nor Judea and Samaria to Jordan; Egypt and Jordan had unlawfully invaded these areas in 1948.

Baker said, "How can you do the same sort of thing that Saddam Hussein does to the Kurds?" He had just come back from visiting the Turkish-Iraqi border, where he had seen tens of thousands of Kurdish refugees living in terrible conditions up in the mountains. I could hardly believe that I had heard him correctly. "We are processing the deportation of four individuals who incited to violence that led to the knifing of people. No comparison can be made," I said hotly. "Your visit here must have given you some insight into the problems we face. The last time you came, four women were knifed to death at a bus stop and this time there were additional tragic events. The two Palestinians killed yesterday, the Palestinian woman who was almost murdered and the

Palestinian man who was kidnapped—all acts committed by Palestinians against Palestinians—didn't make the headlines in the same way but they cannot go unpunished." He wanted to know why those people were being killed, and I tried to explain the unexplainable to him.

About "indigenous economic activity," I said that we were interested in creating employment opportunities in the territories, and were doing whatever could be done within the constraints of our resources. Then I turned to the topic of the regional conference that Baker had been pushing and which Shamir had seemed to favor because—as he had said to Levy and me at our meeting the day before—it was his understanding that this kind of conference would be a onetime event after which direct negotiations would commence. I told Baker that if this was so, then well and good; if not, it was a move in the wrong direction. And I talked to him too about the need for an international effort for refugee rehabilitation, and the urgent need for arms control.

"As for arms control," he said, "there's one little problem, contained in one little word: greed." I suggested a meeting of the supplier nations together with the nations of the Middle East to see if some sort of agreement could be reached. He seemed intrigued by the idea. I had already heard from Les Aspin, the chairman of the House Armed Services Committee, who had visited Israel earlier that month and with whom I had talked about arms control, that the pressure from the aerospace industry for sales in the area was such that he saw little chance of anything being done.

Baker changed the subject. "Let me ask you something, a hypothetical question," he said. "What if I could convince the Arab nations to end their boycott against Israel? Would you be ready to announce a cessation of settlements on the West Bank and Gaza?" I knew it was no random question. I remembered that, speaking to the press after his first visit, Baker had said that he would propose unspecified trade-offs before any negotiations began. "In some cases," he had told the reporters, "we will be addressing maybe one specific issue and saying: 'What do you think about this? How does the following strike you? Suppose we were willing to get X to do Y. Would you then be willing to do Z?' That kind of thing." So now he was trying it out on me. I said that the first thing diplomats learned was never to answer hypothetical questions, and we both laughed, but I said I would answer that one. The answer was no.

On the three-day Muslim holiday of Id-el-Fitr, which began that year on April 15, I authorized a large-scale release of Palestinian prisoners. We were holding some fourteen thousand people in prison camps and I asked the Security Services to come up with a list of about a thousand Palestinians who had not been engaged in violent activity against life and limb, or had been in administrative detention for an extended period, or were awaiting trial for periods commensurate with the kind of sentence they were likely to receive, or who had already served most of their sentence. One thousand two hundred people were released on the holiday—a gesture generally, though erroneously, interpreted as being intimately connected with Baker's arrival, which I suppose did no harm since it probably pleased him, though it elicited the usual demagoguery from Sharon and Ze'evi, as did Shamir's agreement in principle to the idea of a regional meeting. "Some progress has been made but we have a long, long way to go; there are many parties involved and lots of questions to be addressed that have still not been resolved," Baker said to the press as he set off for Cairo, Damascus, and a meeting in Geneva with the Jordanian foreign minister.

Baker's eight-trip shuttle was now well under way. His next visit to Israel—the second in ten days—was scheduled for April 18, Israel's Independence Day and, on all counts, hardly an opportune time, though Shamir wasn't prepared to tell Baker so. Despite the holiday, and the fact that Baker had not asked to see me—perhaps to placate Levy or because he thought I was the most obdurate of the three and he would fare better without me—Shamir asked me to meet with Levy and himself to see where we stood. I told them that I thought Baker was backtracking, pushing us toward the international conference we had rejected and a Palestinian delegation that would not only represent the PLO but be hand-picked by it. Both Shamir and Levy were taken aback. Nobody likes to be told they are wrong.

After their two-hour meeting, Shamir told me, on our scrambler phone, that Baker had presented some "unacceptable" ideas and that he had told the secretary that he would have to discuss these with his colleagues before he could respond. I asked Shamir what those ideas were but he wouldn't say anything more, even on the scrambler. That evening, after Baker's departure, Bill Brown called me to tell me that Baker had asked him to convey to me how sorry he, Baker, had been that we had not met. He wanted me to know that he actually felt "closer" to me than to anyone else in Israel and that, next time around, he would make sure we got together.

On Sunday, April 21, Levy reported to the cabinet that Baker had made the following suggestions: the regional meeting should be called a "conference" and it should not be a onetime event, allowance should be made for reconvening it; the Europeans should be permitted to attend it as participants, not just as observers; there should be a UN observer; and we should allow for the possibility that someone from East Jerusalem appear as part of the Palestinian delegation. These were suggestions to which no response had been given, Levy said, and then went on to add, "Look, we shouldn't kid ourselves. If we turn down these suggestions of Baker's, there will be some kind of alternate U.S. move." Shamir didn't add much to this, except to say that reports of a crisis with the United States were much exaggerated, there was no reason to get excited and the talks were going well.

On April 25, Baker was to come to Israel for the fourth time. In the interim, the secretary had traveled to Egypt, Jordan, Syria, and the Soviet Union, but it still didn't look as if there would be as many participants in the conference as he had expected. Most of the Arab world had declined. He was left with only the United States and the USSR as sponsors, a Jordanian-Palestinian delegation, and us. Not even Saudi Arabia had agreed to take part. An Israeli journalist wrote that it was like Haydn's Farewell Symphony where members of the orchestra walk off the stage, until no one remains. Shamir called another meeting with Levy and me to go over the points Baker had raised one by one; Levy always waiting for Shamir to express his opinion before he himself spoke up, invariably in support of the prime minister's views.

First of all, there was the matter of nomenclature. Shamir said he would agree not to call it a "meeting" but instead a "conference." Levy, of course, agreed. I did not. Names are important, I said. Far better to take a stand now on the principle than to be accused later of nitpicking when we objected, as we would, to the gathering being defined as "international." Whoever else did or did not attend, the one participant of whose presence, however disembodied, we could be sure was public opinion, particularly public opinion in the United States, and it would be wise for us to bear that in mind when staking out our positions. As far as European participation was concerned, I was against it. We knew the opinions of the Europeans and we knew that they carried no weight, but once taken into the conference, they would in effect become partners, regardless of what they were called.

I could see that Shamir and Levy wanted to give Baker a positive

227

answer on this. However, on the presence of a UN observer, or the participation of an East Jerusalem Arab, Shamir gave a definite no. As to the possibility of reconvening the meeting, he said that if this were contingent on Israeli agreement, did not take place until six months after the initial meeting, and provided that the agenda included such regional problems as water and energy, he would not object. Nor would Levy. I objected. Everyone else—the Arabs, the United States, the USSR—would want a continuation of the meeting and we would find ourselves in a corner, applying a veto against reconvening. Why be maneuvered into that position?

I was scheduled to meet with Baker in the early afternoon of April 26, after the secretary's separate meetings with Levy and Shamir. When Baker's first meeting, the one with Levy, ended, Levy's office announced that they had had a good talk and that Levy had agreed that the conference could be reconvened, that the Europeans could participate, and that the gathering would be called, at Shamir's suggestion, a "conference for direct negotiations."

Baker went from there to a meeting with Shamir. During that meeting, he was notified that his ninety-seven-year-old mother had died in Houston, and Baker returned to his hotel to pack and go home. He phoned me from there. He was very sorry he had to "bail out," but wanted me to know that he thought he could bring the Arab partners to the conference table if only we provided positive answers to his suggestions. He was turning to me, he said, as someone who knew the American scene and realized, "maybe better than others," why it was so important for Israel to give the necessary agreements.

"The feeling here is that we're being dragged to an international conference," I said. Baker didn't accept that, but I did not want to argue with him over the phone or while he was rushing to his mother's funeral. Afterwards I heard that the meeting with Shamir had been tough, that Baker hadn't allowed Zalman Shoval to be present, and that he had stood up once or twice, gathered up his papers, and indicated that since Shamir didn't agree with his proposals regarding UN participation and reconvening the conference, there would be no point in going on. It looked as though Shamir's position was stiffening, although I felt reasonably sure that Baker would be back.

On May 15, Baker, who had arrived via Jordan, met with Shamir, Levy, and myself. Shamir had accepted my suggestion that the secretary talk to us all together, which would prevent Levy from rushing off to present the media with his statements. Baker informed us that he thought he could arrange for a Palestinian representation to be part of a Jordanian-Palestinian delegation, and that he had held out various economic incentives to King Hussein, provided that Jordan join the peace process. He wasn't happy about Syria, but was pleased that he had succeeded in persuading the Gulf countries to come to the conference as observers and to take part in the talks that would be held on regional issues.

"All we need now," he said, "is that you agree to the symbolic presence of a UN observer and to the conference being reconvened if everybody thinks that this should be done." He understood that the question of the status of the European Community was something we were discussing with the community itself, referring perhaps to my talk the week before with Hans Van Den Broek, to whom I had explained, in some detail, the importance of direct negotiations and why an international conference would do us no good. It was clear that we weren't about to give in on either the UN observer or the reconvening. But Baker was prepared for these contingencies and instantly whipped out his fallback offers.

"Well, if there isn't going to be a UN observer," Baker said, "how about agreeing that whatever agreements are reached should be deposited at the United Nations? I can't tell you now that the Arabs will go for this, but I am ready to try to sell it to them. As for the reconvening, maybe we can just not mention it at all, either positively or negatively." And he suggested that those positions on which we did agree be put in writing. We got Eli Rubinstein, Yossi Ben-Aharon, Salai Meridor, and some of Levy's people together with Dennis Ross and some of the others on Baker's team, and they went to work. They worked all evening but by the following morning still had not arrived at a common position. In the end, Baker, Shamir, and I came up with a piece of paper that the Americans would present to the Arabs. The issues concerning the UN observer and the reconvening were defined as unresolved and the meeting was called a "conference," with no description or adjective attached. As such statements go, it was acceptable but not very substantial. On the whole, Baker was patient and polite; we were not being as flexible as he felt necessary, but he would go on with the mission. And he added, "I'm not in the business of putting the blame on anyone," though I, for one, suspected that if he did not succeed, he and thereafter Bush, would certainly blame Israel. "I'll keep working," he said, and he was off again, with his piece of paper, to report to the White House.

The president was due to make a speech on arms control in the

Middle East, calling for cessation of production of nuclear material, among other things. I had told Baker that I thought it important for the two of us to talk before Bush delivered that speech in order to make sure that Israel could support the presidential statement without any qualifications. Baker gave my suggestion some thought and may even have checked with Washington. Then he said he would not have time for such a meeting. I asked whether it would be possible for the president to delay his statement until Dick Cheney's scheduled visit to the Middle East at the end of the month, when he and I could discuss the subject. Baker did not want to be drawn in any further. "Speak to Bill Brown," he said.

Although Cheney, as far as I knew, was not directly involved in formulating U.S. arms-control policy, I decided to call him and let him know that we felt it was important for Israel to be able, unreservedly, to back the president's statement, and that for this to be the case, we needed to talk. Could Bush's speech conceivably be delayed until then? Cheney said he would check and get back to me. Meanwhile Shamir, at my request, wrote to the president asking him to postpone his arms-control speech until an in-depth discussion between the United States and Israel could take place.

Within days, a letter arrived for Shamir from Washington: no, the statement could not be delayed. What we knew of the statement was that it would call for a meeting of the representatives of the five permanent members of the UN Security Council to discuss possible limitations on arms sales into the area, and cessation of the development and testing of ballistic missiles and production of fissile materials. We were not happy with that nor with the fact that it had not been discussed with us. Shamir had written—in the letter I had drafted—that the problem was the great asymmetry in conventional weaponry, that the large quantity of conventional weapons in the area made them the equivalent of weapons of mass destruction, and that this was the first and most important question to be dealt with.

We seemed to be engaged on all fronts that spring: Judea, Samaria, and Gaza simmered, always erupting somewhere; and by May, the Syrian hold on Lebanon had tightened. The Lebanese Army, extending its control southward, was constantly pushing the PLO and Hezbollah terrorists closer to Israel's borders, threatening security interests we were determined to protect. Passed on to Washington, this information caused some anxiety: was it a warning of impending Israeli military action, intended perhaps to torpedo Baker's next visit? To a worried Bill Brown, I explained that we had no immediate plans and that we would not do anything to make Baker's mission more difficult. But facts had to be faced: the Lebanese Army was encouraging military groups whose primary objective was to carry out military action against Israel; and the protocol of an agreement between Syria and Lebanon providing for the continued presence of Syrian forces in Lebanon—which might well include areas near the Israeli border—had already been drafted. It was not a situation, I told Brown, that Israel could or would tolerate.

On May 22, the day on which the Syrian-Lebanese draft protocol was signed, I flew to the northern border. General Lahad came to see me, looking ill and dispirited. And little wonder. I asked the army to come up quickly with a menu of scenarios. We had paid the tremendous price of the Peace for Galilee operation only nine years earlier so that the people who lived in Israel's north would be safe from terrorist attacks, and we had to be very sure now that whatever decisions we took would be the right ones. In the meantime, I proposed to the cabinet that Israel allow General Lahad to carry out negotiations with the government of Lebanon, such as it was, although our presence in the security zone area was going to become increasingly difficult. We would have to make it very clear to all concerned that Israel would give Lahad whatever support he required.

But not everything in sight was a source of anxiety; there was also Operation Solomon. For many months, long secret discussions had been held by Uri Lubrani—a man who had made a reputation for himself dealing with Israel's Arab population, as ambassador in Ethiopia and thereafter Iran, and generally as a troubleshooter, with Ethiopia's dictator Mengistu Haile Mariam about the financial payment due in return for permission to bring the Jews of Ethiopia to Israel. Some eighteen thousand Ethiopian Jews, almost all of them concentrated in Addis Ababa, were already waiting to be saved when Ethiopia's civil war overtook them. But as the rebels advanced on Addis Ababa, Mengistu fled his land and the plight of the Jews, whom he had "protected," became acute. We had made the necessary preparations for the Israel Air Force to fly them to Israel as soon as Lubrani gave us the green light. At 5:00 P.M. on May 23, Lubrani phoned Shahak from Addis Ababa to say that the operation must proceed. President Bush, whose goodwill was vital to the rebels, had intervened; the Jews would be allowed to go—if they left at once. Shahak flew to Addis Ababa to set up the command post. By five o'clock next morning, the IAF planes were on their way.

Twelve hours later, the first 707 landed at Ben-Gurion Airport, its passengers some four hundred silent, bedraggled, and exhausted Ethiopian Jews, with nothing but the clothes on their backs. Gathered up helter-skelter by the agencies assigned to care for them, not yet identified or sorted out into families, they were whisked off to absorption centers while the airlift went on and on, with a rapidly increasing number of planes in the air at one time.

By 5:00 P.M. on May 25, Operation Solomon was over: within thirty-three hours fourteen thousand Ethiopian Jews had been transported to Israel, on IAF Hercules aircraft and El Al planes—one El Al 747 probably breaking world records by carrying over a thousand people in a single flight. Planned in minute detail, executed without a single leak to the media, it was a remarkably impressive and moving demonstration of imagination, technological skill, and continuing commitment to Israel's determination to deliver Jews from danger, regardless of where that danger happened to be. Israeli pride in the accomplishment—and in the applause it received from much of the world—served also to raise the dip in national morale occasioned by our enforced nonparticipation in the Gulf War.

On May 29, Dick Cheney arrived with his wife Lynn and two daughters. The next day, following a military parade in his honor, the two of us talked in my office about the problem of arms control. I told Cheney that we had a two-thousand-year history of persecution, and that we couldn't afford to make mistakes on a question that was no less than existential for us. I went through all the points I had touched upon with Bill Brown, dwelling on the need for an arms-control conference and the importance of cooperative weapons development between the United States and Israel. American assistance to us in this area, whether by mutual cooperation or via procurement of some Israeli-developed systems, was the only way, I said, in which the United States could make good its declared aim of guaranteeing Israel a quality edge. Since whatever weapons were sold to us by the United States were also sold to the Arabs, that edge could only be created via Israeli development.

Then I did some relevant "sightseeing" with him: I flew him down to the Negev, where I showed him some Israeli developments (an anti-tank missile, the Sholef 155mm self-propelled gun which was a revolution in artillery, and the Merkava tank); and from there to an air base where I showed him others (some unmanned aerial vehicles and some drones and decoys, all developments unique in their operational capability). I think it was more than he expected, and when he met with Shamir, Cheney repeated some of the things I had said about arms control.

Before he left on May 31, Cheney suggested that we retain "Hammer Rick" on a standby basis, and that a committee be formed that would jointly review security problems—both suggestions that I accepted. It had been a short visit, but I thought a good one.

No sooner had Cheney left than Shamir received another letter from Bush in which the president asked that Israel agree to the presence of a UN observer at the conference, and to the possibility of reconvening it, urging Shamir not to stall the peace process over these two supposedly formal issues. This time Shamir was not about to give way. Apparently he had already given Levy the go-ahead to agree to European participation, but that was as far as he was ready to go. I thought that he had already gone too far, but I told him that since at this stage it was mainly an exercise in public relations, and since his reply would probably be published, it was important to present our position in the best possible light.

That week, I appeared before the Likud's Foreign Affairs and Defense Committee to present the three core questions which faced Israel as the conference neared. In the final analysis, they were not whether we went to an international or to a regional conference, nor whether the conference would be limited to a ceremonial opening. What we had to decide was: had the time really come for us to enter the peace process? With whom? And what should we talk about? Everything else was tactics. I recalled the article written in 1923 by Vladimir Jabotinsky, the founder of the Zionist Revisionist party, in which he said that negotiations must be carried on with the Arabs, leading to an agreement between them and the Jews. But first an "iron wall" must be built: the Jews must not only be strong enough but must also be seen by the Arabs as such.

When I asked myself in 1991, nearly seventy years after that article was written, whether the wall had been built, my answer was yes, we could no longer be driven out. And to whom would we talk? "Aside from the Arab states which insist that they are at war with us," I said, "there are the Palestinians in Judea, Samaria, and Gaza. Past Israeli governments, especially Labor-led ones, have said that they would never talk to the Palestinians; that the ultimate status of the territories should be decided only in negotiations with Jordan. But I believe that we must address the grievances and aspirations of the Palestinians, and we should talk to them about a temporary arrangement along the lines of the Camp David Accords. This was the position taken by Menachem Begin in 1978, and probably correct, since the divergence of views between the Palestinians and ourselves was so large as to make it unlikely that we could agree on a permanent settlement yet."

The Intifada continued to define the present. The level of violence was still unacceptable, although, as I wrote in my diary after an early June visit to the Gaza Strip: "Everybody I talked to in the military says there has been a significant moderation here . . . the population appears tired of the violence and interested in improving economic conditions . . . the municipal council we want to appoint in Gaza hasn't yet been achieved but I am assured that we are making progress." Still, an average of twenty Israeli cars a day were being hit by rocks in Judea and Samaria, and the use of firearms, grenades, and Molotov cocktails had increased.

In June, I visited Washington. Among the meetings awaiting me was a session with Vice President Dan Quayle, an old friend whom I knew to be well disposed toward Israel. Over breakfast on the 24th, Quayle cautioned me not to be lulled into thinking that all was quiet on the diplomatic front. "The State Department people are as busy as bees," he said. And he was right. I was stunned afterward to hear that his spokesman had issued a statement to the effect that the vice president had asked me what my response would be to the U.S. position that if we did not cease all settlement activity, the United States would not approve its $10 billion loan guarantee for the absorption of Soviet immigrants. But the vice president had not raised the question at all. So, as he had warned me, the prewar shenanigans were still going on.

Baker was presumably waiting for the Syrians to reply to his initiative and to the conditions for holding the regional conference (as it was now formally named) that he had put forth, and if this was positive, since ours was not, the United States would doubtless come down hard on us. But so far, there was no word from Damascus. With everyone I talked to during those two days—whether Sam Nunn, chairman of the Senate Armed Services Committee, or Les Aspin, chairman of the House Armed Services Committee, or Dante Fascell, chairman of the

House Foreign Affairs Committee, or Danny Inouye, or Dick Cheney who, once again, gave me a royal reception with a military guard, or Senator Pat Leahy, with whom I developed a friendship—it was mainly about the U.S. commitment to ensuring our quality edge. All in all, the visit had been rewarding; there was stronger backing for Israel on Capitol Hill four months after the end of the Gulf War than I had felt for a very long time. That being the case, it was unlikely, I thought, that the administration would get into a fight with Israel which the Hill might not support.

The Syrian answer to Baker arrived on July 15. The first reports from the United States indicated that it was "very forthcoming"; some of my informants even described it as "astounding." Baker himself was said to be overjoyed and already planning a return to the Middle East, while the Syrians announced that they had asked the United States a number of questions and that their letter had been sent only upon receipt of clarifications from Washington. No one had shown us either the letter or the clarifications.

On July 19, in preparation for Baker's next visit, which was scheduled for July 21, Shamir called a "strategy" meeting in Jerusalem to which he invited Dan Meridor, Moshe Nissim, Salai Meridor, Yossi Ben-Aharon, Eli Rubinstein, and myself. It looked as though the Syrians had agreed to UN participation at the observer level, though we still did not know to what else they had agreed. It was clear to me that we would have done better to have stuck to direct negotiations. Now it was going to be hard not to be dragged in the direction of an international conference. But I kept my thoughts to myself; there was no point to rubbing salt into Shamir's wounds by saying, "I told you so." That morning I had heard Baker on the radio from Damascus, giving us a backhanded compliment: Israel, he declared, was interested in peace no less than Syria; words that indicated the administration's basic position equating Israel with Syria when it came to making peace, notwithstanding the Syrian record in general and that of Assad in particular. I told Shamir that he should have no illusions: there was a great deal of hostility toward Israel out there, and we were heading for difficult times. Either we could stand up and fight it out with whatever means were at our disposal, especially our connections in Congress, or we could avoid confrontation by compromising on our initial positions. He knew, of course, which path I preferred.

On the day of Baker's arrival, I talked to our intelligence people, and one of the experts cited three remarks that might provide insight into Hafez al-Assad's thinking, two of them made publicly. Asked in a press conference whether he was going to be unyielding in the matter of UN involvement in the conference, Assad quoted an Arab saying: " 'Do you want to fight with the guard or do you want to eat the grapes?' " "I want to eat the grapes," Assad said. A second quotation came in his reply when asked how he intended to negotiate his differences with Israel. "Syria will state its position," he said, "Israel will state its position; and the world will judge." His third comment was that he would not be like "Sadat the defeatist," but also "not as stubborn as Saddam Hussein." What lay beyond the realm of conjecture was that he couldn't rely on the Soviet Union anymore and that the only remaining super-power was the United States, which obliged him to act as if he were ready to enter the peace process, even if this were not the case. Anyhow, our turn had come; everyone was waiting for Israel's answers to Baker's proposals.

Because Tisha Be'av, the traditional Jewish commemoration of the destruction of the Temple in Jerusalem, fell on July 21 that year and no official Israeli business was ever conducted on that day, Baker's first meeting was not with us but with the Palestinians in East Jerusalem: Feisal Husseini, Hanan Ashrawi, and Zakaria al-Agha from Gaza. Baker hadn't felt well, he said, and wasn't up to a full-fledged meeting that night with Shamir, Levy, and myself. He would meet only with Shamir and then, in the morning, with the three of us. Levy had received him at the airport and reported that Baker, in a good mood and optimistic, had told him that the Syrians had no preconditions and were ready to negotiate directly with Israel, fully understanding that the conference would be ceremonial in nature, would last only for two or three days at most, and would then subdivide into bilateral talks. Was it possible that Baker had really brought it off? That there was a basic change in the Syrian position? Or, had we been cornered after all?

In Baker's meeting with the Palestinians, Baker was reportedly resolute that the PLO, at least openly, could have nothing to do with the Jordanian-Palestinian delegation and that no one from East Jerusalem nor anyone from "outside" could be on that delegation. There were ways around these strictures, and he seemed to have described various possibilities when it came to actual negotiations about there being delegates from East Jerusalem and from abroad, and that the PLO would have its say. All of this had caused considerable consternation in the

Palestinian ranks, and the meeting broke up without any agreement having been reached.

At seven o'clock the next morning, Baker, Dennis Ross, Bill Brown and Shamir, Levy and I, plus Yossi Ben-Aharon and Eli Rubinstein, sat down to talk. Levy was very sullen; unable to follow the English conversation, he had to read Eli's speed-written translations into Hebrew instead. Baker opened by saying, "I want you to know that your Arab neighbors are ready to negotiate with you directly. This is what you asked me to arrange and this I have done." He went on to say that the Syrians had put forth no conditions and that he was "fully" satisfied with their response. But when I asked if he could let us see Assad's letter to Bush, Baker said no, it was against diplomatic practice; one didn't go around showing letters the president received from heads of state. "I am sure," I said, "that you appreciate the importance of this letter for Israel and that we must see it in order to be fully satisfied that it contains nothing unacceptable to us. Could you ask Assad whether he would agree to have the contents of this letter passed on to us?" Baker said: "Okay. Maybe." But I did not think he intended to follow through.

Then he turned to what he expected from us, which was that we agree to a "passive" UN observer and to the possibility of reconvening the conference—if this was agreed upon by all the parties concerned. He also said that the United States would not participate in the bilateral talks unless invited to do so by the delegations involved. That stated, Baker produced a brand-new and short-lived input, obviously intended to ease our way to making concessions on the Golan Heights: that the United States would guarantee any Israeli-Syrian settlement. No one responded, and the suggestion faded away.

Next, Baker started to detail conference procedures as he saw them: the conference would last, at the most, for two or three days, then the direct bilateral negotiations between Israel and its Arab neighbors would begin; and maybe two or three weeks later, we would have the beginnings of the multinational regional talks. There were two other procedural items: the Lebanese, who did whatever the Syrians told them to do, had pronounced themselves ready to hold bilateral negotiations with us; and as for the date, he hoped that it would be finalized at the Bush-Gorbachev summit, scheduled for the last day of July. Perhaps the conference could open sometime in October. I asked about the Egyptian role in all this, but Baker dodged the question.

We had arrived, if somewhat circuitously, at the key subject: the Palestinian delegation, and the question of an East Jerusalem representative. Baker said he had done what we asked him to do: he had brought about direct negotiations with the Arabs and pulled the PLO out of the process. In exchange, he wanted this. Israel had not wanted anyone from East Jerusalem, "but that is a very difficult question to work out," he said. However, an East Jerusalem representative would be able to take part in negotiations on the permanent settlement, whenever those took place. That was when Jerusalem would be discussed. "No," Shamir said sharply, "we have never agreed to discuss East Jerusalem." To which Baker said, well, if we were going to insist that there could not be an East Jerusalem representative at the conference, "we must at least promise that there will be one at the permanent settlement talks." And as for a representative of the Palestinians from "outside," "that can be one of the representatives on the Jordanian delegation." I reminded Baker that only the other day Mubarak had issued a statement saying that representatives of the Palestinian diaspora must participate. "Yes, I know that," said the Secretary, "but when I was in Egypt now, I told Mubarak we were going to finesse it and he said okay."

On the whole, it had been a fairly good meeting; everyone, including Shamir, was relaxed and affable. I too felt reassured by what appeared to be Baker's firmness with the Palestinians and thought that, under the circumstances, we could answer positively about reconvening the conference—subject of course to our approval—and also on the question of the UN observer, once we had committed the United States to veto any anti-Israel resolutions at the Security Council. But there was no need to share these thoughts right away with Baker. He had asked for our answers at an early date, before Bush and Gorbachev issued the invitations. Shamir said he wanted to see the text of the invitations before they were sent and Baker didn't offer any objections. He was off to Malaysia, then to the Gobi Desert for a rest and on to the Bush-Gorbachev summit. Later that morning, at the cabinet meeting, predictably enough—though Shamir reported that we had not agreed to anything yet or yielded on any points—Sharon accused the government of letting itself be entrapped in these negotiations.

Thus far, it had been agreed that the conference opening would be attended by Israel, Syria, Egypt, a joint Jordanian-Palestinian delegation, plus an observer representing the Gulf Cooperation Council (which included Saudi Arabia and Kuwait), to be followed by parallel talks (referred to by Baker as a "dual track") between Israel and the Arab states, and Israel and the Jordanian-Palestinian delegation. The third set of negotiations would revolve around regional issues and the Gulf states would be among the participants. A representative of the European Community would be invited to participate, and the United States had come out in support of Israel's position that Moscow must fully renew diplomatic ties with Israel before taking a place at the conference table. There would be no Palestinian delegate from East Jerusalem, and all of the Arab delegates would have to be residents of the territories and not members of the PLO.

So far, so good. But by the end of July, Shamir had still not given Baker his reply on three major questions: the matter of a UN observer; reconvening the conference, which Shamir claimed would enable the Arabs to avoid direct talks; and the critical issue of the composition of the Palestinian delegation and Israel's right to veto any proposed Palestinian lists.

On July 27, I went up to Jerusalem to talk with Shamir alone. I wanted to find out why he was procrastinating, and to discuss the American position with him again. There could be no doubt that we were moving toward the conference, however nervous this made Israel's extreme right, and whatever the results might be of our sitting down with the Syrians (if that was going to happen), which would certainly cause the Golan Heights issues to come up. Shamir told me that Shoval had cabled him that Ross had requested him, with some urgency, to obtain Israel's positive answers regarding the presence of a UN observer and the reconvening of the conference. I urged Shamir to nail down Baker's unequivocal commitment on the Jordanian-Palestinian delegation: no PLO, no representative of East Jerusalem, and no "outsider" other than someone on the Jordanian delegation whose family originally came from Jerusalem. Baker would have to defend that proposal, I said to Shamir, rather than turn the spotlight on us by charging us with attempting to "interfere" with the composition of the Palestinian delegation. Shamir said he would notify Shoval accordingly.

A couple of days afterward, Shamir told me that he had had three phone conversations with Baker, who was in Moscow with Bush. Baker was pressing for a positive answer, but the composition of the Palestinian delegation had not yet been approved, and Baker felt that in the second stage of the negotiations, i.e., when the permanent settlement was discussed, there should be "a representative of Jerusalem and of

the Palestinian diaspora." Shamir replied that if the Palestinian delegation was not agreed upon, Israel would not participate. Baker said that
he would return to Jerusalem.

He wanted to be able to announce that—subject to settling the
composition of the Palestinian delegation—Israel would take part in
the conference along the lines suggested by the United States. He had
also told Shamir that Bush and Gorbachev were going to announce that
the conference would be held some time in October which, in effect,
left Shamir no choice but to agree. In return, Shamir requested that the
United Nations repeal the infamous Zionism-equals-racism resolution it
had adopted in 1975, and he asked for a commitment from the United
States that it would block any anti-Israel Security Council resolutions
having to do with the peace process. Baker said he would think about
this. Shamir also told him that he wanted a U.S. commitment that when,
and if, Israel opposed the reconvening of the conference, the United
States would do so as well. Baker said he would think about that as
well.

On August 1, Baker was back in Israel. Shamir, Levy, and I met with
him, Ross, and Bill Brown. Baker went straight to the point, looking at
Shamir. "I would like us to meet the press right after this meeting and
for you to say just what you said to me on the phone: that you have
agreed to attend the conference, subject to government approval, and
to agreement on the Palestinian delegation. As for your request, we are
prepared to make a serious effort to get the Zionism-racism resolution
repealed, but it is something we can't guarantee. I can only promise you
that we will make a serious effort. And we will see to it that there is
no competing process in the Security Council as long as this process
proceeds."

Baker and I argued a bit. I told him that the United States should
commit itself to preventing any unilateral resolutions against us at the
United Nations because, as the peace process unfolded, there were
bound to be terrorist acts aimed at undermining it, and we would then
have to take preventive measures, and the next thing would be the
Security Council jumping down our backs. Baker didn't much like that.
The United States, he said, was not ready to "turn its seat at the Security
Council" over to Israel. If we were going to deport people, we couldn't
expect the United States to guarantee that there would be no Security
Council resolutions against it. No purpose could be served by pro-
longing the argument and, anyway, Baker wanted the meeting to be

short. He was very anxious to get out to the newspeople and the cameras and make his announcement. Next day, headlines throughout the world proclaimed that "Shamir Said Yes," though I doubted that many readers had followed the convoluted developments or knew what those words were really about.

After our meeting, Baker spent four hours with the Palestinians—who now had to be reconciled to the fact that the PLO was not going to be represented at the conference and that there would also be no Palestinian from East Jerusalem—and from there he flew to Jordan, then on to Morocco, Tunisia, and Algeria. Perhaps he could get the Maghreb involved in the conference, he said. In my diary, I wrote: "One has to hand it to Baker. Putting this conference together is an accomplishment. He has gone about it very systematically: making a list of points that he knew were unacceptable to Israel; then trying to put together something that did not conflict with our constraints; and finally, aided by the apparent Syrian reappraisal of an altered world, patiently getting his package together." More than anything else, Baker was a dealmaker with something at the ready for everyone: telling the Palestinians that once the process got going, things would start to move in the direction they sought; assuring the Syrians that the United States also hoped that territories for peace would be the conference's end result; telling us he had secured the one thing we wanted, the chance to talk to the Arabs directly, without the PLO. The Jordanians were in need of assistance and wanted to re-legitimize their position in the Western world, so they were easy to bring aboard. It was starting to look as though he had indeed pulled it off.

Although the cabinet, meeting on August 4, approved Shamir's decision by a 16 to 3 majority (Rechavam Ze'evi, Yuval Ne'eman, and, of course, Ariel Sharon voting against), Sharon's attack on Shamir and Levy was violent. "It does not matter what worthless documents will be obtained," Sharon shouted. "This is a conference of war risks. Only the amateurs who are conducting our negotiations don't realize what is happening." He accused Shamir of concealing the real facts from the public, of "giving without getting," and of "having reached an extremely dangerous opening position."

Shamir reacted to the commotion calmly, saying that the personal attack "evidently derived from an uncontrollable desire for power." To the rest of the cabinet he warned against any euphoria, stressing that "many struggles, difficulties and dangers are still in store for Israel," a statement with which I entirely agreed. But, as I said when my turn came to speak, we had been in the throes of political confrontations ever since we had withdrawn from the Sinai in 1982; we had survived the Reagan plan, George Shultz's shuttling back and forth, the opening of a U.S. dialogue with the PLO. Now we had the Bush-Baker offensive, and there would be more of it to cope with as we went along. There could be no doubt about that. We knew with whom we were dealing, and that the United States, the Soviet Union, and the European Community wanted to see Israel return to the borders of 1967. And the Arabs wanted that, at the very least.

"The question before us is whether negotiations are equivalent to withdrawing, or of necessity lead to withdrawal," I went on; "whether refusing to negotiate means that we can hold our ground. . . . I think it is an oversimplification to create the impression that negotiations inevitably lead to withdrawal. When I consider that the traditional position of the Israeli government has been that it will negotiate directly at any time and anywhere with any Arab leader ready to negotiate with us, and the current arrangement with the Palestinians—who are ready to negotiate on the basis of the Camp David Accords—I am convinced that it would be a great mistake for Israel to refuse to enter such negotiations in a framework that permits us to negotiate not only with the Jordanian-Palestinian delegation but also with the Syrians, perhaps also with other Arab countries. We should enter these talks determined to secure our aims, and united—if that is possible."

While the meeting was going on, I was called out to be told that Dick Clarke from the State Department had met in New York with the head of the Defense Ministry's Purchasing Mission, Moshe Kochanovsky, to inform him that the U.S. Department of Commerce was about to issue a register of countries carrying out missile development programs for which any U.S. companies wishing to export items would have to receive special permission. Israel appeared on this list, together with Argentina, Iraq, Libya, Syria, Egypt, and China. Some time in August or September, according to Clarke, the administration might announce that it was imposing sanctions on Israel based on the Missile Technology Control Regime (MTCR) law that had been passed in Congress not long before.

That afternoon I placed a call to Baker, reaching him on an aircraft flying from Morocco to Tunisia. He congratulated me on the cabinet decision, and then told me that we might get some support from what he called the "moderate" Maghreb states, but not from the United Maghreb Association, which included Libya. As soon as I could, I broke in to tell him about the notifications we had just received. Baker said that he had been aware of the impending Commerce Department announcement but not of the possibility of sanctions and that he would look into this right away, although there might not be any flexibility. Two days later he called back, in his most agreeable mode. There might indeed be no flexibility on the question of sanctions, but Dan Kurtzer and Aaron Miller, both of the State Department, were coming to the Middle East to discuss a memorandum of agreement with us and they might have some ideas.

When Kurtzer and Miller appeared, Kurtzer brought along some talking points on the MTCR issue that sounded less friendly than Baker had been on the phone. In fact, my impression was that the administration was using, or hoped to use, these MTCR issues as sticks to beat us over the head, and eliminate Israel's missile capability in the process. I wasn't at all confident, now that we had been grouped with Iraq, Syria, and Libya, among others, that if we adhered to MTCR, we would receive the same treatment as the countries of Western Europe or the Soviet Union which were already members of the MTCR regime. But we prepared a memo, framing talking points for David Ivry to pass on to Kurtzer, and a letter that Shamir would send to Baker; both documents stated Israel's intention of adhering to the MTCR as of January 1, 1992, and expressed regret that the administration apparently had seen fit to place us in the same category as the nation that had sent missiles against us in the recent war.

On August 19, 1991, there was news of a coup d'état in Moscow. For the sixty hours of the upheaval, it seemed that everything had been turned upside down. And then it was over. Gorbachev had survived the coup, though just barely; but it was clear that the USSR would never be the same again. Still, things settled down. The peace process was not delayed; the conference was not postponed; the Soviet Union and the United States were still to act as co-sponsors in October. For the next two weeks, I concentrated on the budget debate scheduled to take place in the cabinet on September 1. Finance Minister Yitzhak Moda'i—who had not consulted with any of the ministers concerned, myself included —had already informed the public that the defense budget had to be cut by 1 billion shekels, which at that time represented about $425 million. Otherwise, he informed the media, appreciably fewer immigrants could be absorbed, unemployment would grow, taxes would have to be raised, and inflation would spiral. I did my best to persuade cabinet members that what was actually needed was an *increase* in the budget of exactly the same amount that Moda'i wanted to slash.

At the debate, I argued that the finance minister's job was not just to decide how money should be spent, but to make sure that adequate resources were available. The lessons of the war had to be applied, quickly and properly. A new dimension had been added to our defense problems: Israel must prepare for the possibility of long-range ground-to-ground missile attacks with conventional or even nonconventional warheads, and we should bear in mind that the Arabs, having seen for themselves the effectiveness of high-tech weapons, were in a race to acquire them. We had to remain one step ahead of them, regardless of the expense.

It was possible, I went on, that we would be able to convince countries throughout the world that this was a time when Israel badly needed help, either on a loan or grant basis. Of course, it would be easier just to make do with existing resources and decide arbitrarily how much to cut the defense budget. But that was no way to deal with the kind of uncertainties Israel faced; we didn't even know how many emigrants from the USSR would be coming to us now or how much assistance we would get toward their absorption. The Gulf crisis had proven to the Arab world, including Iran, that it was possible to hit Israel with long-range ballistic missiles. A major psychological barrier had been broken, and we would have to cope with the resultant perils.

The final result, after some back and forth among Shamir, Moda'i, and me, was that the Defense Ministry would get half of the additional increment I asked for.

CHAPTER 9

The Peace Process Begins

On the morning of September 6, President Bush, meeting with the press in the Oval Office, announced that it was "very, very important . . . to do everything we can to give peace a chance." He was going to ask "every single member of Congress" to defer "just for 120 days" consideration of the $10 billion loan guarantee for immigrant absorption in Israel. This deferral, he said, was in the best interest of the peace process. It was not the time for a "lively" debate over the guarantees (though the President did not actually use the word "guarantees," thus giving the impression that what was under discussion was outright aid), which might "be misunderstood" and "inflame the passions on all sides."

When a reporter asked whether the president would have sought the deferment if Israel had changed its settlement policy, Bush said he didn't want to talk about that; everybody was familiar with U.S. policy on the settlements and it wasn't going to change. "I must do a better job convincing the people here and in Israel that we are correct in this, with our underlying desire for peace." And he repeated that he was going to fight for the delay because "I think this is what the American people want . . . we don't need that ingredient clouding the waters just when the waters are going to clear." Baker, who was sitting next to the president, added: "Give peace a chance; 120 days, that's all the president's asking for, 120 days."

Shamir, rejecting any linkage between the loan guarantees and the peace process, immediately instructed Shoval to submit a formal request for the guarantees which, he stressed, were urgently needed to secure funds for a humanitarian project of historic proportions. Asked by reporters for my reaction, I said that it was "inconceivable that anyone would punish the new immigrants because they didn't like some component of Israeli policy," and that "there is neither justification nor logic in linking financial support to the measure of progress the Arabs will allow in the peace process."

On September 11, I called Senators Inouye and Leahy. Leahy had already been to see the president and sounded somewhat equivocal: a confrontation must be avoided. It was possible to get the resolution through Congress as an amendment to one of the continuing resolutions, and we should work on trying to arrive at a compromise. Inouye was not equivocal at all. He said, "I am putting on my yarmulke; we're going to war." He too had seen Bush and told him that he didn't agree with him, reminding the president of the price Israel had paid during the war when it refrained from retaliating against the Iraqis only because the president had asked it to do so. Nor, he had added, had there been any complaint from Israel when the United States canceled $7 billion of the Egyptian debt. What reason could there be for not giving Israel the assistance for the immigration of Soviet Jews to Israel to which the United States had committed itself? Inouye didn't think that he had made any dent with the president, but he would try again. In the meantime, there were already sixty cosponsors for the amendment, and he expected there would be twenty more.

On September 12, more than a thousand American Jews, representing various organizations and mobilized by AIPAC, went to Capitol Hill to express their support for speedy enactment of the loan guarantees. Bush hastily called a press conference and made an extraordinary televised appeal to the American people. Visibly angry, pounding his fist on the lectern, he made it appear that Israel's insistence on the guarantees was a threat not only to the forthcoming conference but to peace itself. "A debate now could well destroy our ability to bring one or more of the parties to the peace table. . . . If necessary I will use my veto power to keep that from happening."

Then the president took direct aim at the pro-Israel lobby. "We are up against some powerful political forces . . . very strong and effective groups that go up to the Hill," he said. "We've only got one lonely little guy down here doing it . . . [but] I am going to fight for what I believe. It may be popular politically but probably not . . . the question isn't whether it's good 1992 politics. What's important here is that we give this process a chance. And I don't care if I only get one vote . . . I believe the American people will be with me." Then, his voice rising, the president said, ". . . just months ago, American men and women in uniform risked their lives to defend Israelis in the face of Iraqi Scud missiles, and indeed Desert Storm, while winning a war against aggression, also achieved the defeat of Israel's most dangerous adversary." He added that, during the current fiscal year, "despite our own economic worries," the United States had provided Israel with more than $4 billion worth of aid, "nearly one thousand dollars for each Israeli man, woman and child."

Speaking privately, certain officials in Washington described the presidential attack as a "bombshell" and a "declaration of war." But Shamir, who was in Paris, declined any immediate comment, and David Levy's statement merely emphasized that Israel was not looking for a confrontation with the United States and that the request for guarantees was not a hindrance to the advancement of peace.

On September 13, I finally reached Bob Kasten, who advocated trying for a compromise with Bush. He suggested that if we would agree to the loan guarantee delay, maybe the White House would be prepared to make a commitment that we would receive them in 120 days. But when I asked whether he thought the White House was likely to make this sort of commitment, Kasten said: well, everybody up there was ready, except for the president himself, but a lot would depend on what happened when Baker visited Israel in a week's time. I explained to Bob that everything had been made more difficult because if Shamir, in his meetings with Baker, was perceived to make any concessions, people in Israel would say that he had made them because he wanted the loans. And that would create a perception in the Arab world of a link between assistance to the Russian immigrants and the search for peace in the Middle East—something that would inevitably be used as a bargaining chip, although prior to the president's appeal the Arabs had never dared voice to the United States their opposition to this immigration.

When Baker, after visiting the Soviet Union, returned to Jerusalem on September 16, the loan guarantee controversy hung like a dark cloud over our conversations. We were sitting in the prime minister's office, Baker setting forth his plans for the conference he hoped could be convened by the end of October, possibly in Prague as the Soviets had proposed. As for the Palestinians, he said they were still floundering around. "I will have to tell them to fish or cut bait." He had taken his by-now accustomed seat on the couch to Shamir's right. I sat next to him, and Levy took the armchair across from us, while at his side Rubinstein speed-wrote translations of the conversation into Hebrew for him.

Shamir listened without commenting, and then, after a long silence, said: "Mr. Secretary, perhaps we can discuss the guarantees for the loans we want to take to help in the absorption of the immigrants arriving from the Soviet Union?"

"You know, Prime Minister," Baker replied, "all the Arab governments have asked us to produce a freeze on settlements as a precondition for the negotiations. To that, we have said no, but if we push through these guarantees without any conditionality, we will lose the Arabs, while if we apply conditionality, we will link it to the peace process, and that's no good either; we don't want to do that. So the issue should not be discussed at this time."

Baker went on to present a six-point proposal—his own initiative, he said—which was little more than a postponement of the matter to January: the administration would find the appropriate legislative vehicle for the guarantees in January; there would be no further delays after January; the guarantees would be "scored" reasonably; there would be a restatement of the principle of U.S. support for aid to Soviet refugees; any financial loss incurred by the delay would be made up; and the United States would solicit assistance from other governments for the absorption of Soviet refugees in Israel. Casually, he also informed us that it had been suggested that the guarantees be scored at 34 percent; in other words, that the cost of the guarantees to Israel might be $3.4 billion. Although, he said, if we agreed to the postponement, the administration would see to it that the Office of Management and Budget "score" the guarantees more reasonably. "So my suggestion to you is to call off the dogs and strike the subject off the agenda for the next one hundred and twenty days."

There was a stunned silence. For the first time, it was being said that there might be a connection between the loan guarantees and Arab attendance at the conference. Finally Shamir said: "What you are suggesting is good but not good enough; something needs to be added. Maybe the administration will state that, at the end of the one hundred and twenty days, its position on the loan guarantees will, in no way, be related to the peace process?" Baker would not buy that. I proposed that we reach agreement now on guarantees for the first $2 billion worth of loans, postponing discussion of the rest until later, but Baker rejected that suggestion as well.

The next morning, having met with Feisal Husseini, Hanan Ashrawi, and Zakaria al-Agha in East Jerusalem on the previous afternoon, Baker was back with us. Reaching into his briefcase, he brought out a faxed copy of the *New York Times* editorial of the day before, headlined: "The President Is Right on Israel." Seeing that none of us seemed particularly impressed by it, Baker said, "I hope you can accept my six-point proposal. I know we have differences of opinion, but let's put them off until you have sat down with the Arabs; after all, that is what you have wanted all along, and here we are. We have just about arranged it. But you must understand that I cannot commit to unconditional support for the guarantees, and that we will not change our policy on the settlements, so let's find a way of saying jointly that this six-point proposal is satisfactory."

Shamir responded, "We are not imposing our views on settlements on you but we oppose your linking the settlements to the guarantees." Baker's reply was instant, and sharp. "If you want U.S. guarantees, you will have to accept our position on settlements." Trying to draw him out, I asked: "What are your terms on settlements? What are you asking for?" But Baker was too smart for that. "We will deal with that later. This is not the time for us to be explicit about our conditions. Accept the six points and, in the meantime, we will work on the terms of the guarantees. We can't just sign off on ten billion dollars."

Then Baker made his last offer: he would add to the six points the statement that the United States would support aid to Soviet immigrants to Israel under terms and conditions agreeable to it. "But that's not meaningful," I said. He didn't respond; instead, he went back to discussing settlements. "All we ask of you is that you stop settling in the territories. We are not going to fund settlement activity." To Shamir's protest that the money was not going to be used for settlements in the territories, Baker retorted: "We know that money is fungible and we are not going to avoid the fungibility question. It has been raised in the administration before, regarding other assistance given to Israel, and was bypassed. This time, we are not going to bypass it; we are not going to fund settlements in the territories." He went on to charge us with having expanded settlements in the territories by orders of magnitude: "You built forty thousand housing units in the territories over this past year," he said. We explained that forty thousand housing units had been built in all of Israel last year, but Baker wouldn't listen. He had his own information and was not satisfied with anything we had to say. Then, when Shamir suggested that discussions on the loan guarantees be continued in order to find a formulation agreeable to both sides, Baker repeated his last offer: the administration would agree to the guarantees after 120 days "on terms and conditions acceptable to it." We rejected the offer.

The evening before, Zvi Rafiah, who had served in the Israeli Embassy in Washington and had, over the years, maintained his many contacts among members of Congress, called to tell me that he had just returned from the United States and that he had found that AIPAC and our supporters in Congress were not eager "for a fight with the president." Senators Inouye and Kasten had obtained fifty-one signatures for a resolution backing the loan guarantees, but that was a long way from the two thirds needed to override a presidential veto. It didn't look good. Not only could we expect to lose the fight in Washington, but the issue was bound to boomerang, adversely affecting Shamir and the Likud at home.

After Baker left, I explained this to Shamir, pleading with him to "withdraw the request." He wanted to think about it; it would have to be coordinated with our friends in Washington since we might be pulling the rug out from under their feet. "Naturally, but I think they will welcome the news," I persisted. There the matter rested.

Shamir talked about the possibility of early elections. If the small right-wing parties were to make good their continuing threats to leave the government because of the negotiations with Baker, causing it to fall, there would be a Knesset majority for going to the polls. The negotiating process would then be suspended. The Likud would have the best of all possible worlds, having decided to go to the conference without becoming involved in the complications that were sure to arise with the beginning of the talks. I reminded Shamir that the time between a decision to go to early elections and the holding of these elections is usually no less than four months—and that a great many things could happen in the intervening period, making it difficult to base a rational strategy on the potential gains and losses of such a move.

Since both meetings with Baker had been overshadowed by the loan guarantees, not much time was left for the issues connected with the upcoming conference. Baker had brought with him a draft of the invitation; the text, he said, was not open to negotiation, but he was ready to consult with us on the subject. It did not spell out that the aim of the negotiations was to arrive at peace treaties, referring only generally to the establishment of "real peace" in the region. When I questioned Baker about this, he answered that the Arabs considered the term "peace treaty" as something of great symbolic value, and that they were not prepared to make that kind of concession to Israel. Shamir was not satisfied, but Baker—who had already shown it to the Palestinians—said he could not leave a copy of it with us. He proceeded to hold a brief press conference with Shamir—without overly emphasizing the differences of opinion that had arisen in his talks here—and was then off for Cairo. Once aboard his plane, however, he let fly, telling the accompanying reporters that he would not give "one inch of flexibility beyond the six points . . . which are damn forthcoming. . . . It is a case, frankly, of not being able to justify in our own minds, or to the other parties in the peace process, an unconditional ten billion dollar infusion. . . ."

On September 25, I reported to the government on Ivry's recent trip to Washington, where, on my instructions, he had negotiated Israel's adherence to the Missile Technology Control Regimes of January 1992, committing us to restrictions on export of missile technology. When he had concluded the agreement, Ivry asked that Israeli industries be permitted to participate in competitive bids for commercial satellite launchers in the United States. He was told by Assistant Secretary of State Reginald Bartholomew that it was U.S. policy not to help Israel in any way to develop its missile capability, and that permission would therefore be refused.

This came at a time when Iraqi missiles were again causing me considerable concern. As the UN teams inspecting Iraqi facilities were discovering just how close Iraq had come to acquiring nuclear capability, Saddam Hussein restricted their access to various installations. Bush, in return, threatened military action against Iraq unless the UN inspectors were allowed to see whatever they wanted to see, and U.S. aircraft had begun to move into the area. The Saudis informed Washington that unless Patriot batteries were deployed to Saudi Arabia, they would not permit the U.S. Air Force to use Saudi air bases in attacks against Iraq, and Patriot batteries, with their American crews, were promptly airlifted to Saudi Arabia. It was impossible for me to discount totally the possibility that if the United States were to launch military action against Iraq, Israel might again be subjected to Scud missile attacks.

There was also no question in my mind that in such an eventuality, we would respond at once—and we were determined not to be caught without the necessary photographic intelligence on the possible launching sites. But, as before, Washington had not bothered to update us on the results obtained by the UN inspection teams, or to keep us in the picture regarding their plans. I had instructed the air force to prepare a photo reconnaissance mission over western Iraq. The day after Baker departed, Shamir okayed the mission.

On October 4, I sat in the air force control center, breathing a sigh of relief when the plane touched down safely in Israel. The aerial photos obtained were of excellent quality, providing us with the information we needed. Washington was informed that same day. Within twenty-four hours, Bill Brown delivered a brutally phrased U.S. protest to Eli Rubinstein. "We expect an explanation for your action and that there will be no further actions of this sort," it concluded.

On October 8, the Iraqis submitted a protest to the United Nations which may enter history as a record in hypocrisy: the government that had, without provocation, launched missiles against Israel's cities, now protested that our aircraft had entered its airspace to take photographs. Iraq was joined by the United States in this protest. Our reply to Washington's protest was straightforward, contained no apologies, and made it clear that we would take whatever action we felt necessary for Israel's defense. I invited Weizman, Peres, and Rabin to the ministry to brief them on the mission, and to assure ourselves of Labor's support should there be a public confrontation with the United States, but the subject only came up again during Baker's visit to Israel on October 17.

Baker was apparently worn out by the shuttling. He hadn't looked forward to the trip and was weary of all the arguments. Nonetheless, he said, we were on the brink of direct bilateral negotiations "on your terms." It was a typical Baker approach, giving the impression that he had managed to secure what we had wanted all along so there was no reason for us to reject it. Essentially, he gave the Arabs the same message, that the negotiations would, in effect, produce what they had wanted all along, so there was no reason for them not to come to the negotiations or not to agree to the terms. Asked about the composition of the Palestinian delegation, he replied that he didn't yet know. He hoped to know more that evening after he and the Palestinians met. Once that issue was resolved, Bush wanted the conference to convene that month, which meant that the invitations would have to be sent within three or four days at the outside. What of the Syrians? They had decided not to participate in the regional meetings. Then he said that two weeks after the opening, there should be a meeting devoted to organizing the regional conference but not the beginning of negotiations, as had been previously agreed.

When I pointed this out, Baker replied, "If you don't want to go to this meeting, if you want that as an excuse and don't come, okay, I don't care." Shamir said, "If the Syrians don't come to the regional meetings, then we shouldn't join the bilateral negotiations with them." "You would be making a bad mistake if you hang your refusal on this issue," Baker answered. Then he turned to me in an aside. "Look, either you want to do it or you don't, but if you hang it on to Syria, you'll lose." I said that Syria's participation in the conference was a test of Syrian intentions. Baker replied, "You are better off without the Syrians in the negotiations. They will just be spoilers."

As we were about to break for lunch, I pulled Baker aside to remind him of how strained the U.S.-Israel relationship had been during the Gulf War, the Eagleburger and Wolfowitz mission, the tremendous risks we had undertaken, the damage inflicted on us by the Scuds, and how hurt most Israelis had been when the president afterward stated that U.S. servicemen had endangered their lives in Israel's defense. "And now," I said, "we have your very rude protest about our reconnaissance mission. But you know that in preparation for possible U.S. military action, you have deployed Patriots in Saudi Arabia in anticipation of an Iraqi response against that country. You also know that this would probably be accompanied by Iraqi missiles being launched against Israel as well. But you didn't consult us or even talk to us about any of this."

When we reassembled to discuss the assurances Baker was going to provide us together with the invitation to the conference, it was in the certain knowledge that we were on the threshold of a new chapter in Israel's long quest for peace. The venue of the conference had not been set yet, and certain details still needed to be worked out. But it was clear to all that a conference attended by Israel, the Palestinians, and Israel's Arab neighbors was going to take place, and that it would be followed by bilateral negotiations between Israel and them. In a pensive mood, taking a respite from the intensive negotiations, Shamir allowed himself for a moment a look into the future: "We must achieve a decent life for the Palestinians but not allow it to lead to independence. They can have their representatives in the Jordanian parliament, and their ministers in the Jordanian government—but not here." There was no reaction from Baker or anyone else in the room. I thought to myself that it was not realistic to deny permanently the Palestinians' participation in the political process in the area in which they lived, and to expect that participation-at-a-distance in Jordanian political institutions would serve as an adequate substitute. Nor was it consistent with the standards set by the democratic process in Israel itself, and would in due course be unacceptable to Israelis as well.

Next morning, following his meeting with the Palestinians, Baker arrived at the prime minister's office announcing that he had seven names which, "to the best of my knowledge," would be acceptable to us, and that he might get seven more—it having been agreed that the Palestinian delegation and the Jordanian delegation would each have fourteen members, although, at any one time, there were to be no more than fourteen delegates in the room. However, he had promised them not to give us the names. Baker was sure we had our own ways of finding out who the Palestinian delegates would be.

Then Baker turned to what he called the "bilats." Our position had been that they should take place in the region, alternately in Syria and Israel, alternately in Jordan and Israel, depending on whom we were talking to, but the Arabs had turned this down. They wanted the bilateral negotiations to be held in the same location as the conference. The secretary suggested that perhaps the first two sessions could be held at the conference site, and that later the United States would voice its opinion that they should be moved into the region. Shamir said he was ready to compromise: one session wherever the conference was held, and then into the Middle East. Since Baker did not agree, that was left open. But we were going to the conference; we knew it; the United States knew it; and the Palestinians knew it. So did the USSR. Having obviously received Baker's signal that the time was ripe for renewing diplomatic relations with Israel if the USSR wanted to be in at the conference, Foreign Minister Boris Pankin arrived in Jerusalem to sign the necessary documents while Baker was still around. At his brief meeting with Shamir, Pankin wanted to talk about the conference, but

Shamir cut him short. "Thank you for coming," he said. "We are renewing our relationship." They shook hands and that was that.

Afterward, Baker announced publicly, to everyone's surprise, that the conference would take place on October 30, in Madrid. The United States had not wanted Switzerland, not liking the arrangements there; the Syrians would not agree to The Hague. No one had objected to Madrid, so weeks of speculation at last came to an end.

In the cabinet meeting on October 20, Shamir reported on Baker's visit. Levy had nothing to add. I said that since our basic conditions had been met, we should go to the negotiations. It would have been better had we been able to begin the direct negotiations at once without the ceremonial opening, but that had been agreed to and gave us the opportunity to hold bilateral talks. The right-wingers among us who objected to Israel's participation in the conference evidently feared that we would not know how to negotiate properly or defend the positions that were important to us. But I thought, who could better stand up for Israel's rights than this government?

When it came to the vote, there were three against: Sharon (who had already called on the radio for Shamir's resignation, saying that he had failed in leading the State of Israel), Ne'eman, and Ze'evi. Three days later, Shamir, just returned from addressing the European Parliament in Strasbourg, called a meeting with Levy and myself in preparation for the conference. He had thought things over and it was now clearer to him than before how serious it would have been if we had opted not to attend. And he had decided that it was his duty to lead Israel's delegation himself.

Levy at once bristled; if no Arab head of state came to Madrid, Shamir should not be there either. They also disagreed about who should serve on the various negotiating teams, Levy arguing that Shamir's suggestions in effect "liquidated" the Foreign Ministry (Rubinstein was to head Israel's team for the Jordanian-Palestinian talks; Ben-Aharon to head the team for the Syrian talks; and, at my recommendation, Uri Lubrani to head the talks with the Lebanese, with only the multilateral talks being headed by a Foreign Ministry man).

Later in the day, faced by Shamir's insistence on heading the delegation, Levy charged that he had been discriminated against and announced that he would stay home—as, in the end, he did. He was, however, not entirely without support from the outside. Knesset members associated with him were already discussing his contesting the

Likud leadership; and Baker (and Pankin) issued a statement saying that the Madrid conference was being held at the foreign ministers' level, though not only had this never been brought up but both Bush and Gorbachev were going to be there.

Although we were on the eve of the formal launching of the peace process, what was going on around me felt much more like war. On October 28, a bus filled with settlers on their way to a Tel Aviv demonstration in support of the settlement activity and to encourage Shamir before Madrid was ambushed at the Tapuach intersection in Samaria. Two people were killed—the driver, Yitzhak Rofeh, and Rachel Druck, the mother of seven; and eleven were wounded, including five children. The next day, while I was with the army at the intersection, I was notified that three of our soldiers had been killed in Lebanon by an explosive charge, similar to one activated the week before, and that an action was still going on in the western part of South Lebanon against a group of Arab infiltrators trying to enter Israel in order to carry out terrorist acts. Two had been killed, one captured, and troops were searching for a possible fourth.

From Tapuach, I went to Shiloh, a settlement founded in 1977 halfway between Jerusalem and Nablus, to convey my condolences to David Druck, Rachel's husband. He had been up all night talking with his dead wife's parents. He wanted Rachel to be buried in Shiloh, but his in-laws were afraid that, in time, Israel might withdraw and that they might no longer be able to visit her grave. Druck wanted me to promise them that they would always be able to come to that grave. I said, "Tell them that I promise," but who knew what that promise would be worth in years to come?

There was no way of knowing the outcome of the conference that was finally launched at Madrid's Royal Palace on October 30, though no one could doubt its importance. We had succeeded in breaking through the barrier of the adamant Arab refusal to recognize and accept Israel's existence. Now the direct face-to-face bilateral peace talks between us and the Arabs—which each successive Israeli government had tried so hard to achieve—were about to begin. Whatever else was to happen, nothing would alter the fact that the Syrians, the Lebanese, the Jordanians, and the Palestinians were officially meeting with Israelis in Madrid to talk about peace. The talks would not be easy, but they might well lay the foundations for peace. The conference, which was limited to speeches by Bush, Gorbachev and the heads of the delegations, was to be followed by the initiation of direct negotiations between Israel and the Jordanian-Palestinian delegation, Israel and Syria, and Israel and Lebanon.

At the opening, Bush expressed himself in generalities, saying that "something must be developed . . . acceptable to Israel, the Palestinians and Jordan that gives the Palestinian people meaningful control over their own lives and fate and provides for the acceptance and security of Israel." Avoiding the words "territory for peace," the president talked instead of "territorial compromise," and of boundaries that reflected "the quality of both security and political arrangements." This angered the Syrians, who interpreted "territorial compromise" to mean that they would not get back the entire Golan and that we would not relinquish control over all of Judea and Samaria, though I was not at all sure that this was what Bush in fact meant.

Shamir opened by declaring that he spoke not only on behalf of the State of Israel but in the name of the Jewish people, who had "maintained an unbreakable bond with the Land of Israel for almost four thousand years"; he summed up the pain of the Jewish past, the destruction in the Holocaust of a third of the Jewish people, and the coming into being and development of the modern Jewish State against the background of continuous Arab aggression. That implacable Arab refusal to recognize the State of Israel's legitimacy was, he stated, the root cause of the conflict.

"We know that our partners to the negotiations will make territorial demands on Israel, but, as examination of the conflict's long history makes clear, its nature is not territorial. It raged well before Israel acquired Judea, Samaria, Gaza and the Golan in a defensive war. There was no hint of recognition of Israel before the war in 1967, when the territories in question were not under Israel control . . . . The issue is not territory but our existence. It will be regrettable if the talks focus primarily and exclusively on territory." Inviting "the partners to this process" to come to Israel for the first round of talks, Shamir announced that Israel was "ready to go to Jordan, Lebanon and Syria for the same purpose. There is no better way to make peace than to talk in each other's home."

Next came the Jordanian minister, Kamal Abu Jaber; the Palestinian representative, Haider Abd el-Shafi ("Palestinian Jerusalem, the capital of our homeland and future state [which] defines Palestinian existence —past, present, and future . . . has been excluded from this conference

257

and deprived of its calling. . . ."); and Syrian Foreign Minister Farouk al-Sharaa ("The claims invoked by Israel for the migration of world Jewry at the expense of the native Arab population are not sanctioned by any legal or humanitarian principle. . . . Israel alone resists the efforts for peace with all the influence it can muster. . . ."). They all spoke very belligerently. The issue of the location of the bilateral talks turned out to be a stumbling block, with the Arabs, especially the Syrians, demanding that these be held in Madrid and the Israelis insisting on the Middle East. However, we were willing to discuss logistics and venue in a first session to take place in Madrid.

On the whole, the Madrid Conference worked out well for us. Shamir had participated, despite everything that had been said and written about his wanting to derail it. He had given a good, comprehensive, and moving speech acclaimed by Israel's right and left and well received abroad, which had probably affected Israeli public opinion positively insofar as the Likud was concerned. At the same time, millions of people had seen who we had to deal with, and the extent of Arab intransigence—as characterized by the brandishing by al-Sharaa of a British police poster showing Shamir in his 1940 underground days as a "wanted" man, and saying that Israel's prime minister had been a terrorist then and remained one to this day.

In the final analysis, looking beyond ritual and platitudes, this was the first time since the establishment of the state that an Israeli prime minister had sat together with the foreign ministers of Syria, Lebanon, and Jordan, and, no less significantly, with a representative of the Palestinian population of Judea, Samaria, and Gaza, all committed to direct negotiations leading toward a peace settlement.

Important as the conference was, my own immediate anxieties centered on the unrest in the north, which had markedly increased. By the beginning of November, we had been pounding the exits and entrances to some of the Shiite villages along the border of the security zone in Lebanon for several days, trying to get the civilian population to force the Hezbollah out of the area or make it difficult for the terrorists to operate. Without our authorization, the South Lebanese Army, using loudspeakers, had demanded that some of these villages be evacuated, orders we at once rescinded.

In the afternoon of November 2, the day on which the ceremonial part of the Madrid Conference was concluded and discussion of the timing and venue of the bilateral talks had begun, Baker phoned me from Spain. They were getting disturbing reports on military activity in South Lebanon. "You don't have to worry about that," I said. Baker said they fully sympathized with our security concerns on the Lebanese frontier and knew that three soldiers had been killed, but "I have to ask you to refrain from that kind of activity. I am calling you," he said, "before I put through a call to the president so that he can call the prime minister." He hoped I could "temper the situation" because the Lebanese wanted to come to the negotiating table and "your activity might prevent them from coming."

I told him that he should tell the Lebanese to do their job. If they kept the Hezbollah from engaging in terrorist activity against us, there would be no reason for us to take military action. Okay, he said, "but again I ask you to please exercise restraint."

During the cabinet meeting next day, we received a report from Madrid that the Israeli meeting with the Palestinians and Jordanians had begun. The Syrians, wanting to emphasize that the bilateral talks were only a continuation of the conference, were adamant that the meetings should be held sequentially and in the same building—although the original plan had been for three parallel meetings (between the Jordanians and Palestinians and Israel; between Lebanon and Israel, and between Syria and Israel) in three different buildings. Shamir and I agreed not to make an issue of the switch, and it looked as though the meetings with the Syrians and the Lebanese would go forward.

That afternoon, I took off for Beijing on a secret trip, in a special plane, at the invitation of the Chinese government, to see what we could do to increase our defense sales to China. There could hardly have been a sharper shift of scene.

By the time I returned home on November 8, Shamir was preparing to leave for a ten-day trip to the United States. As usual, he had been kept waiting until one day prior to his departure for the announcement from the White House that the president would receive him. There was still no agreement on where the bilateral talks would be held; the Arabs continued to press for Madrid, the United States had suggested Washington, we were insisting on the Middle East. Shamir was to see Bush on November 22, but before that meeting was held, Baker had already sent out the invitations for the bilateral talks to open in Washington on December 4. It was a slap in Shamir's face. He had discussed the subject in Washington but had either not been told, or had not realized, that the invitations had been sent out; he had left Washington under the impression that this subject was still to be discussed. By the time he arrived back in Israel, the United States had succeeded in convincing the Arab delegations to accept that location, and that date, and Israel had been placed in the uncomfortable position of being odd man out. But, uncomfortable or not, the invitation had to be answered.

Meeting with Levy and myself, Shamir said that we should let the administration know that we wanted the meetings to be held in the region because that was where we felt they belonged, but that we had no objection in principle to Washington. He then reported that Bush had said to him: "Why are you so afraid of Washington, D.C.? After all, you have so much influence here in all spheres, and in the media." Shamir also proposed that we make clear that Israel did not favor simultaneous meetings with all of the Arab delegations, but wanted to hold talks with them one by one; and that we were ready to come to Washington for a session or two, but it must first be established that all subsequent talks would be held in the Middle East. And finally, he proposed that we suggest that the talks be held on December 9, December 4 being the Channukah holiday, which was a good reason for postponement.

Although Shamir and Levy had "made up," Levy seemed upset. "I see you have already talked to the Americans about this," he said to Shamir, "so why are you talking to us? This is not a real consultation." "No," Shamir replied, "I didn't tell the Americans what I am suggesting now." Levy said, "Do as you like." I told them that I thought it was important at this stage of the negotiations, when rules of play were being laid down, for us to make sure that all the subsequent negotiations would be carried out in a manner that we considered appropriate. The decision should be put to the government when it met the following Sunday, six days away, and the Americans should be informed of this. Shamir didn't agree; he thought the discussion should be held at the next inner cabinet meeting in two days' time.

So on November 27, after the intelligence reports and Sharon's criticism of the way the IDF was operating in southern Lebanon, we began to talk about the invitation to Washington for December 4. It turned out that the United States had included in its invitations what were, in effect, recommended agendas for substantive discussions. To the Syrians, it was suggested that they ask Israel whether we would be ready to give up the Golan Heights if Syria was ready to make peace with us—

with the complementary suggestion that Israel ask the Syrians if they would make peace with us, provided we conceded the Golan Heights. To the Lebanese, it was suggested that the Jezzin area be discussed first and that the Lebanese Army's control of it be established. And to Jordan, the suggestion was made that its territorial claims in the Arava Valley, south of the Dead Sea, should be brought up in the talks. It had been Israel's intention to discuss any and all substantive matters directly with the Arab delegations, and suggestions from Washington were neither anticipated nor welcomed. It all amounted to pretty heavy-handed U.S. intervention in the negotiations process.

Shamir's suggestion that our delegations begin negotiations in Washington on December 9 was accepted by the government, with only Sharon, Ne'eman, and Eitan voting against. But now we had two dates, the U.S. invitation for December 4, and the Israeli response for December 9. The U.S. administration stood fast: the doors would be open in the appropriate facilities at the stated time on December 4, and if the Israelis did not show up, well, too bad for them. At the government meeting on December 1, Shamir announced that we would abide by the inner cabinet decision taken the previous week. The Israeli delegation to the bilateral talks would present itself in Washington on December 9, and no one at the meeting disagreed.

On the night of December 6, the Israeli teams set off for Washington. Shamir had proposed that Israel drop its demand that the discussions with the various Arab delegations not take place simultaneously. Bibi Netanyahu was already in Washington explaining our position, and the American public—preoccupied by such events as the economic recession, the Smith-Kennedy rape trial, and John Sununu's resignation as White House chief of staff—paid little attention to the Arab display of outrage when the Israelis failed to appear at the designated U.S. government offices on December 4. We seemed not to have lost any significant PR points and we had certainly driven home the fact that we would not accept any arbitrary unilateral decision in these negotiations. On December 9, the Israelis were in place and the Arabs didn't show up.

The next day, however, the talks began. Our delegations met with the Syrians and, separately, with the Lebanese, and started a week of haggling in the corridors with the Jordanian-Palestinian delegation, the Palestinians proclaiming that they would participate only as a separate delegation from the Jordanians, which they had succeeded in doing to some extent in Madrid, despite the understandings reached prior to that.

The first round of the bilateral negotiations ended on December 19. There had been a number of meetings between us and the Syrians and Lebanese, devoted chiefly to rhetoric and formalities, not to any real business. With the Jordanian-Palestinian delegation, we were, literally, holding talks in the hallways about how the meetings should be held, the Palestinians still demanding recognition as a separate delegation. I thought we should not make too much of a fuss over this; after all, it was with the Palestinians, not the Jordanians, that we needed to talk directly. But if the Palestinians were now to be recognized as an independent delegation, they would probably appear as such also at the multilateral talks, thus assuming the trappings of a nation-state, something we were not interested in promoting. A way had to be found around that which would permit us to enter into substantive negotiations with them. Made up of disparate elements, on each single issue the members of the delegation looked right, then left, never arriving at a consensus on anything. It was a problem that would haunt us increasingly as the negotiations got underway.

Meanwhile, something of an upsurge in Arab violence was taking place in the territories, undoubtedly promoted by Palestinians opposing the peace process. A terrorist ambush on the heavily traveled road between Jerusalem and the settlements of Ophra, Beth El, and Shiloh, on December 1, had resulted in the death of Zvi Klein, a resident of Ophra. No trace was found of his assassin. Visiting the area the following morning, I decided to place it under curfew, to bring more troops into Judea and Samaria, and seize some buildings along the road. Gaza had quieted down, though there were still almost daily incidents there, but considering that a hostile population of 700,000 was holed up under terrible conditions, it was probably no more than one could expect. But the situation in Judea and Samaria was becoming a source of more acute concern. Obviously a concerted effort was being made by some of the terrorist gangs, including the Fatah, to murder Israelis on those vital roads.

On December 12, I called in Bill Brown to tell him that we were determined to stop the terror, and that one of the measures I intended to use was expulsion. "I must tell you," Brown said, "that the U.S. government is opposed to that." I said that if we did not control the situation, the results would be vigilante activities in the area by the settlers, Arabs killed, the peace process blown sky-high. It was not just a question of preventing murder—though that, in itself, was good enough reason to take whatever action we felt might be useful—it was a question of permitting the peace process to go on.

That night, at 1:00 A.M., Larry Eagleburger's call got me out of bed. The White House had instructed him, he said, to call me about our resorting to deportations. "We don't intend to deport anyone in the middle of the night," I said, "nor tomorrow morning either." He seemed embarrassed at having called at that hour, but he said that he wanted me to know that the U.S. government was opposed to expulsions and that if we did deport people, the Americans would stop trying to repeal the United Nation's Zionism-equals-racism resolution. Furthermore, if the question of deportations came before the Security Council, the United States would participate in condemning Israel. "Look," I told him, "people are being murdered on the roads. I think you would act no differently if you faced that kind of problem in the States. The peace process may be wrecked if we don't put an end to the terror." That was the end of the conversation, but I knew it was not the last we would hear on the subject. We would have to try to focus media attention on the severity of the problem we confronted.

Two days later, I showed a retinue of foreign media representatives just where Zvi Klein was killed, then drove toward Nablus past the Tapuach intersection where Rachel Druck had been murdered, and on to the settlement of Elon Moreh, where a car with three women and a man in it had been fired on four days before. I had made my point: we were dealing with cold-blooded murder on the roads that had to be stopped, and we would take whatever measures were required toward that end. I also went into some detail about the vigilante action by a small minority of settlers (in particular from Kiryat Arba outside Hebron) who, hoping to throw a monkey wrench into the Washington talks, were going on rampages through Arab villages, breaking windows of Arab cars, and uprooting trees in Arab olive groves.

Heading for Defeat

On December 24, 1991, Rafael Eitan, the crusty old former chief of staff–turned–politician, who had stayed at his command post on the Golan Heights when it was almost overrun by Syrian tanks during the Yom Kippur War, now the leader of the two-man Tsomet faction, announced that his party was leaving the government, thus reducing the coalition's Knesset majority to four. The previous week the Likud Central Committee, after a lengthy debate, had decided by a large majority to oppose Labor's parliamentary initiative to revise Israel's system of government so that the prime minister would be elected by direct popular vote, rather than being confirmed, together with his proposed government, by a vote of confidence in the Knesset—as had been the case throughout Israel's existence. Tsomet, which had adopted the direct election of the prime minister as one of its slogans, was withdrawing from the coalition in protest against the Likud's decision.

Since the last elections, the public had been given a dramatic demonstration of the system's inadequacies. Peres had attempted to inveigle Shas and Agudat Yisrael with promises of vast sums from the Israeli Treasury for their parties' foundations and institutions into abandoning the coalition and joining a new one without the Likud, to be led by himself in what Rabin, also a participant in these attempts, referred to as the "stinking maneuver." Breaking all the unwritten rules of Israeli politics, Peres had tried to bring down the Shamir government by promising Moda'i and his cohorts—all elected to the Knesset on the Likud ticket—positions in the new government he would form, as well as similar positions, following the coming elections, if Labor were to form the government then. Nor had the Likud been found wanting in its efforts to outbid Labor in the allocation of resources to the religious parties. It had even succeeded in enticing a Labor Knesset member— Efraim Gur, a new immigrant from Soviet Georgia—to cross party lines and join its Knesset faction.

All of these maneuverings, covered in minute detail by Israel's press, radio, and television, had brought forth public demands for a radical change in the system of government. The movement leading this drive, well funded by contributions from abroad, placed full-page advertisements in the newspapers and organized mass demonstrations, with some of their more fervent participants going on hunger strike, insisting that direct elections of the prime minister would be a cure-all for the defects of the present system.

The proposal was that on election day voters would cast two ballots: one for the party that they wanted to represent them in the Knesset, and one for their choice of prime minister. The prime minister would continue to be responsible to the Knesset and could be removed by its vote of no confidence. I was convinced that this proposal, far from improving on the existing system, was going to launch Israel's body politic into an experiment that was likely to make matters worse. The representation of the small parties would probably increase once voters had two ballots at their disposal, while coalition bargaining would now take place prior to the elections, the large parties vying for support for their candidate for prime minister from the leadership of the smaller ones. It was likely that the small, well-organized constituencies, such as the radical Arab parties or the ultra-Orthodox parties, would hold the balance in an election, and thereby be able to determine who the prime minister was going to be, after exacting the maximum price. Israel's Arab voters, already constituting over 10 percent of the electorate and their percentage still growing, might very well have the deciding voice in future elections.

Since negotiations with the Palestinians and Israel's Arab neighbors would probably continue to be among the major issues facing our leadership in the years to come, and since preparedness against possible Arab aggression would remain a requirement for Israel's survival in the Middle East, I had no doubt that the proposed reform was not in Israel's best interests. The primary cause for the difficulties of the existing system lay in the large number of small parties represented in the Knesset, a situation that could be at least partially remedied simply by increasing the minimum number of votes a party would have to achieve to be represented. Until now, 1 percent of the vote had sufficed, resulting in a fifteen-party Knesset. During the tenure of this Knesset, the threshold had been raised to 1.5 percent, and a threshold of 4 or 5 percent, reducing the number of parties in the Knesset to four or five, would make coalition forming a great deal more manageable.

But the public did not bother to analyze either the cause of the problem or the likelihood that the suggested reform might actually make matters worse. Disgusted by the unprincipled political behavior they had witnessed during the past few years, many Israelis concluded that any change would be for the better; many Knesset members were also swept away by the reformers' populist rhetoric at first. Rabin, and with him much of the Labor party, insisted that the proposed reform was the only sure way for Labor to return to power, and Labor's Central Committee decided that all its Knesset members had to support the measure when it came up for a vote. In the Likud, it was only after long, tiring debates that I succeeded in persuading a majority of the proposal's grave disadvantages. Its two most vociferous supporters were Rabin and Netanyahu, both confident of their ability to gain popular support in direct elections if such were held. Since Israel has no constitution, this major change in our political system would be decided by a majority of Knesset members, present and voting. The vote was going to be very close.

On the last day of 1991, and at the last minute of the fiscal year, the budget came to the Knesset for debate and vote. Obtaining Knesset approval for the annual budget is always a test of the government's strength, and now it served as an indicator of the difficulties Shamir's coalition faced. The ultra-Orthodox parties, utilizing the additional leverage they had gained with Tsomet's withdrawal from the coalition, pressed their demands, and negotiations with them dragged on to the very end. A defeat of the government's budget bill would have constituted a no-confidence vote and signaled the end of the Shamir government. Midnight passed and the new fiscal year began, and still there was no agreement.

Throughout the night, members of the religious parties and the Likud scurried back and forth while the rest of the Knesset members dozed in their seats or joylessly consumed the remnants of whatever food was still left in the Knesset cafeteria. In the meantime, heavy snow began to fall in Jerusalem; within a few hours the roads were blocked and the Knesset members were snowed in until army four-wheel-drive vehicles were mobilized to transport them to their hotels for breakfast. The negotiations continued through another night, with Shamir at one point threatening to resign. But finally after a third night of haggling, with the whole nation watching, an agreement for 1992's budget was passed by a narrow majority vote in the early hours of Thursday, January 2.

I had stayed in the Knesset building for two days in anticipation of the impending vote, carrying out my duties as defense minister from my small office in the building, the IDF generals making their way through the Jerusalem snow for meetings with me there. On the afternoon of January 1, I was informed that Doron Shorshan, a member of the Gaza Strip settlement Kfar Darom, had been shot and killed by a Palestinian at the Dir el-Balah road junction. The following day, the budget negotiations still unresolved, Israeli settlers in the vicinity began to assemble prefabricated housing at the site of the murder, announcing that they were putting up a new settlement in response. I ordered the army to remove the prefabs. Kfar Darom—then an isolated outpost in the desert —had been settled by Jewish pioneers during the days of the British Mandate over Palestine. In 1948 it had been overrun by the invading Egyptian Army, remaining under Egyptian control (as part of the Gaza Strip) until it was resettled after the Six-Day War. By then it was surrounded by Palestinian refugee camps. The Strip's population had more than doubled due to the influx of Palestinian refugees, and, given a record birth rate, the area was becoming one of the most densely populated in the world. I could sympathize with the desire to rebuild a settlement once destroyed by Arab aggression, as well as with the urge to respond to an act of terrorism by enlarging the existing settlement. But I had long ago concluded that the Strip's strategic value was minimal, and that it was in Israel's best interests to get out of there, without wasting resources we could not afford.

That was not the view of Sharon, or the Tehiyya Knesset members, or of the more extreme representatives of the National Religious party, and while others were still engrossed in the budget negotiations, a new drama unfolded in the Knesset. I became the object of the attentions of the extreme right wing, who begged, implored, and threatened me to revise my instructions. If I did not agree, they would ask Shamir to order me to do so. I replied that even if Shamir ordered me not to vacate the site, I would not change the instructions I had given to the army. This was my area of responsibility; I would take orders from no one. Sharon had gone straight to Shamir, who had simply referred him to me.

Immediately following the budget vote, the Knesset was scheduled to vote on the law providing for direct election of the prime minister. The promoters of the new settlement at Kfar Darom threatened that they would vote with the Labor party or abstain on this issue unless I relented. I did not change my instructions; the vote on direct elections of the prime minister was postponed; and the crisis passed. I did, however, give instructions for a list to be drawn up of Palestinians to be deported for inciting to terrorism in the areas in which the latest terrorist acts had occurred.

On the following Sunday, January 5, I went to the Gaza Strip, first to the road junction at Dir el-Balah where Doron Shorshan had been killed. He had evidently stopped his car at a stop sign when his killer approached and fired at point-blank range. I stood in the road, trying to visualize the murder: a life snuffed out, a family left without husband and father, the murderer escaped, and not much hope of our being able to prevent additional acts of terror in this overcrowded area where people were growing up in filth and poverty and where life seemed to have lost its value. From Dir el-Balah I proceeded to Kfar Darom to express my condolences to Shorshan's widow. Now facing the future alone with her small children, she insisted that she was going to stay on at Kfar Darom. The settlement numbered twenty families, most of whom had gathered in her home to share their grief and problems with me, while outside, a few hundred settlers from the other settlements in the Gaza Strip had assembled. I tried to talk to them, but they interrupted me with shouts: "This is war!," "Why don't you bomb the Palestinian villages like you do in Lebanon?," "Expel the Arabs!" They were far too angry to listen to explanations—that their presence in the Gaza Strip exposed them to danger; that even the utmost efforts of the IDF could not guarantee their safety from terrorist attacks; and that enlarging their tiny settlement could serve no useful purpose. I left with some sadness.

On January 6, the Knesset finally got around to debating and voting on the law calling for direct election of the prime minister. Again there were demonstrations in the streets and in front of the Knesset. All of the Labor Knesset members had accepted their party's decision and announced that they were going to vote for the law. Since the Likud's Central Committee had voted to oppose the law, Likud Knesset members were obliged to vote against it, but a few holdouts refused to abide by the Central Committee's decision. Netanyahu was among them, and no amount of argument would sway him. As the debate continued through the night, and it became clear that the outcome would hang on one or two votes, I demanded that Netanyahu vote with the Likud on this crucial issue, but he would not budge. At 2:00 A.M. the debate was adjourned until later in the morning. After endless appeals, Netanyahu finally agreed to vote with the Likud if it turned out that his would be the deciding vote.

When the vote was finally held on Wednesday at 3:00 A.M., it was indeed Netanyahu's vote that determined the result, but he had voted with Labor. The vote was 57 to 56. It seemed inconceivable to me that such a major change in the country's system of government was to be determined by a one-vote margin, without even an absolute majority of the Knesset's 120 members. But there it was. For lack of a constitution and simple common sense, an untried hybrid system was going to be foisted on Israel. The one saving grace was that its implementation was to be delayed until after the coming elections. I could only hope that the next Knesset would come to its senses and rescind the law.

Nothing halted the work of the terrorists. On January 14, shortly after sunset, a bus from Jerusalem to the Samaria settlement of Shiloh was ambushed near the Arab village of Ein Sinya. Seven people were injured, including the driver, an Arab from Jerusalem. A little over a year earlier, a similar ambush had taken place at almost the same place; then, as now, the tracks of the escaping terrorists had led east toward the Arab village of Silwad. That evening, even though I was not at home, a crowd of demonstrators screamed and chanted outside my home in Savyon, calling for my resignation, their protests directed not at the terrorists but at the man who was in charge of fighting terrorism.

The following morning, January 15, I went out to Ein Sinya, accompanied by Ehud Barak; Major General Danny Yatom, the commander of the Central Command; and Brigadier General Moshe "Boogy" Yaalon, in command of the troops in Judea and Samaria. At the headquarters of the Central Command I read the riot act to the assembled army brass: "We are facing a wave of terror aimed at killing Israelis and at interfering with the peace process. If we are not successful in stopping it, many people will lose their lives and the government will be hindered in pursuing its peace initiative. It is now the IDF's foremost mission to halt this wave of terror—nothing is more important. You must allocate the necessary resources, even to the detriment of other missions the IDF performs." I had the feeling that Barak was a little hesitant in cutting back on training exercises and transferring the additional units needed into the area, but I was determined to get him to do just that. My sense of urgency was reinforced when I was notified that an Israeli Druze, hunting in western Samaria, had just been killed by terrorists.

In the meantime, Israeli settlers in Samaria had begun to move prefab housing into unauthorized locations with the loudly announced intention of establishing new settlements. Some Israeli settlers had entered Arab villages in Samaria, vandalizing cars and shooting into the air. I ordered the army to remove the prefabs and stop the settlers' vigilante action. The voices of the demonstrators in front of my home were now augmented by Ariel Sharon's appearances on television. Openly on the warpath, although a member of the government himself, and thus sharing responsibility for its policies, Sharon accused the government of responsibility for the wave of terror. "Let him go home," he said, without naming names. "Anyone who is not successful, who can't handle this job, should leave, and give the job to those who know how to do it." There was no popular call for his return to the Defense Ministry.

In the evening of the 15th, the three-man Tehiyya faction announced that it too was leaving the government coalition, reducing the coalition's support in the Knesset to sixty-two. If the terrorists had intended to destabilize the Shamir government, they were succeeding, probably beyond their expectations. Within twenty-four hours, Ze'evi's two-man Moledet faction followed suit, leaving the government without a Knesset majority. The two right-wing parties explained that now that "progress" was being made in the negotiations with the Palestinians in Washington, they could no longer support the government. Actually, following lengthy sessions in the Washington corridors, the progress made so far was close to zero—the Palestinians had only just agreed to begin formal negotiations. But that was too much for Tehiyya and Moledet. Their leaderships, evidently convinced that the next election would again return a Likud-led coalition, were hoping to increase their support at the Likud's expense, by adopting positions more hawkish than those of the Shamir government. They seemed not to realize that they were paving the way to early elections that would bring Labor to power, eliminating them both as factors of any significance on the Israeli political scene.

That same night, there was another ambush, this time against the ambulance of the Itamar settlement near Nablus, as it passed the Askar Palestinian refugee camp. Fortunately no one was injured, but we had obviously reached a critical juncture. I called in the chief of staff and his senior generals to my office at the Defense Ministry, to read them the list of recent terrorist incidents and remind them that it was now the IDF's first priority to put an end to terror. Not only must the number of troops stationed in the territories be increased, but our elite units and special forces must also be deployed there. When Barak began to argue with me, I told him that if we were not successful in halting the wave of terror, the generals of his headquarters staff would have to move into Judea, Samaria, and Gaza to participate themselves in carrying out the task assigned to the IDF. There were no more arguments after that.

On Sunday, January 19, before the weekly government meeting, I met with Shamir, who had been holding consultations on how to deal with the coalition crisis now that we had become a minority government. "Take the initiative," I urged him. "The government's weakness will produce further demands by the religious parties, and giving in to them is bound to lead to a loss of public support for the Likud. Let's reach an agreement with the Labor party on a date for early elections. Once an early election bill has been passed in the Knesset, the government cannot be brought down by a Knesset vote and we can continue until the elections, which will probably be a few months away," I stressed. "This will give you a chance to replace Moda'i, who will be running against the Likud in the election at the head of his newly formed party, and to replace him with a finance minister who will bring new ideas to our economic policy, take steps to liberalize the economy and sell off government-owned companies, and thus be able to demonstrate that we are serious about revamping Israel's 'socialist' economy." Shamir listened to me, but as usual, made no comment.

On January 28, the first multilateral meeting to follow the Madrid Conference opened in Moscow, under the sponsorship of the United

States and USSR. The Syrians and the Lebanese boycotted the meeting; the Palestinians appeared, but when their demand to participate as an independent delegation was not accepted, they refused to take part. But Egypt, Jordan, Saudi Arabia, Oman, Morocco, and Tunisia were all represented. For the first time in Israel's history these countries, formally at war with Israel, met for formal discussions with us. The agenda of this first meeting was strictly organizational, dealing in separate sub-subcommittees with the procedural aspects of future meetings on subjects of regional interest, such as economic cooperation, environmental problems, refugees, and regional security and arms control. David Levy headed the Israeli delegation, and Baker came from Washington.

The peace initiative was slowly but surely becoming reality. Three years had passed since I had conceived the initiative, thirty-two months since it was adopted by Israel's government in May 1989. It had finally led to Madrid, to the bilateral negotiations in Washington, and now to the first multilateral meeting to deal with regional problems—an institutionalized process of negotiations with the declared objective of achieving peace.

With the support of the Likud, its coalition partners, and the Labor party, on February 4 the Knesset passed an early election law, setting June 23 as the date for the coming Knesset elections, more than five months ahead of the nominal election date in November. We had four and a half months in which to convince Israel's voters that the Likud should continue in power for another four years, and our candidate for prime minister would be a paramount consideration in their minds. Although on numerous occasions Shamir had confided to me that he would not continue as head of the party, and although in moments of internal crisis he had sometimes threatened to resign, he now let it be known that he intended to continue for another four years. Levy and Sharon were going to challenge him, but I was confident that the "Shamir-Arens" camp in the Likud could beat them.

However, from the electoral point of view, I thought it a mistake for Yitzhak Shamir to be the Likud's candidate again, running for a four-year term at the age of seventy-three, a man who, for much of the Israeli public, seemed to belong to the past, not the future. At a time when the country cried out for movement in economics and in foreign policy, he symbolized immobility, standing fast but not moving forward. Yet Levy and Sharon were far less able to lead Israel in the years to come, and aside from relatively small groups of ardent supporters, neither could claim much popularity among the general public.

I was committed to the Likud and considered the policies of Labor —especially the views expounded by the dovish wing, led by Peres— to be dangerous, but had never longed to be prime minister. I knew that I was widely regarded as Shamir's natural successor, and that on a number of occasions I had been close to becoming prime minister, but I had no wish to challenge him now. What was more, a four-way race, with all of the competitiveness that would inevitably ensue—only four months before the elections—was not going to further the cause of Likud.

When the more than three thousand members of the Likud Central Committee met on February 20 to elect the man who would head the Likud's list of Knesset candidates, and thus serve as its candidate for the post of prime minister, Shamir won, receiving 46 percent of the vote, to Levy's 31 percent and Sharon's 22 percent. Levy's announcement after the votes were counted, to the cheers of his followers, that he had scored a great victory, and that from now on his people must be allotted one third of the Likud's representation in all forums, served notice of what was to come.

Seven days later, the panel was chosen from which the party's future Knesset members were to be elected; neither Levy's "people" nor Levy himself did well.

On March 1, in rounds of seven at a time, internal elections were held to determine each newly elected MK's place on the slate, something that in turn determined the role, if any, that they would play in the new government. In that final polling, held at the Tel Aviv Fairgrounds in a carnival atmosphere of signs, billboards, and sound trucks promoting the candidates, the Shamir-Arens camp again came out on top. I beat Levy by 26 votes for the first slot on the slate, with Sharon coming in second, and Levy third. Levy took his disappointment badly, rushing to tell the press that a web of intrigue had been woven against him and his followers. There was some muttering about settling accounts, and even about leaving the Likud. What really mattered was the support for the prime minister and his senior colleagues, which had been publicly tested and strengthened, even if the public had been provided with the spectacle of dissension within the Likud.

Aside from their public images, it was the positions of the leaders of the two parties on the central issues that were going to determine the elections. For almost all Israelis, the immigration of Soviet Jewry and its successful absorption in Israel was one such issue, and for many it was the most significant. Uniting the Jews of the Soviet Union with their brethren in Israel was not only the realization of a seemingly impossible dream; it also represented a supremely important addition to the Jewish population, faced as it was by a growing Arab population in Israel itself, and an even faster-growing Arab population in the territories. In the final analysis, Israelis knew that it was the demographics that counted in terms of their nation's future.

Shamir had played a crucial role in directing the stream of Jews leaving the Soviet Union toward Israel. In meetings with the U.S. administration and U.S. Jewish leaders he had argued convincingly that Israel, and only Israel, should be the land of refuge for Soviet Jewry. When the immigrants began to arrive at a rate of a quarter of a million a year, Shamir's government had to deal with providing them with housing and employment opportunities, on an unprecedented scale. By Israeli law, the new immigrants became eligible to vote on the date of their arrival, and the Labor party was quick to appeal for their vote, claiming that the Likud government was not doing enough for the newcomers while it allocated vast resources to settlements in the territories.

Ever since September 6, 1991—when Zalman Shoval, on Shamir's instructions, had submitted Israel's request for $10 billion in loan guarantees to aid in the absorption of emigrants from the USSR—the tension between the Israeli government and Bush's administration had escalated weekly. Shamir continued to argue that the loan guarantees were indispensable for the absorption of the mass of immigrants arriving in Israel, and therefore for Israel's very future, while Bush and Baker insisted that they would only support the granting of those guarantees if Israel ceased all settlement activity in the "occupied territories" and East Jerusalem. Shamir, of course, adamantly refused to agree to Bush's condition, and believing that public support for the guarantees in the United States would be sufficient to change the president's position, persisted in pressing for them. I was convinced that the administration would not relent and pressed Shamir to withdraw the request. I warned him that his continued insistence on Israel's need for the loan guarantees would not only have no impact on Bush and Baker but would convince the Israeli public—as elections approached—that the one man in Israel who couldn't obtain them from the United States was Yitzhak Shamir. I was far from certain that these loan guarantees were really necessary, and I did not relish the idea of the government's pumping such vast sums of money into the economy. But Shamir would not listen, preferring the "good news" that was being passed on to him by his American informants that there was sufficient support in Congress to override Bush's objections.

In an appearance on February 25 before the House Appropriations Subcommittee on Foreign Operations, Baker stated: "This administration is ready to support loan guarantees of up to $2 billion a year for five years, provided though there is a halt or end to settlement activity. From our standpoint, it's up to Israel. She can determine whether she wants to take action which would permit the strong support of both the legislative and executive branches for these loan guarantees or not." And around the same time, the president reiterated that "It is a proper policy and has been the policy of the United States government for a long, long time." The argument between Jerusalem and Washington continued unabated in the months leading up to the Israeli elections.

The integration of new immigrants into Israeli society includes service in the IDF for men in accordance with their age, how long they have been in the country, and so forth. Even immigrants old enough upon arrival in Israel to be exempt from regular service may still be given a few weeks of elementary military training so that they can serve in the IDF reserve forces. A group of this kind was being trained in an IDF encampment not far from Hadera, between Haifa and Tel Aviv. On the night of February 15, three Arabs armed with knives and hatchets entered one of the tents, killed three Russian immigrants, wounded another three, and escaped. The guard, also a new Russian immigrant, had been slow to react.

Shortly afterward, the three Arab assailants were caught. They turned out, to my dismay, to be Israeli Arabs from a nearby village in Wadi Ara, members of the fundamentalist Islamic movement. It was rare for Israeli Arabs to engage in terrorist activity, but it was a sharp reminder of the dangers of the spread of Muslim fundamentalism among that population.

The following day, Barak, accompanied by Uri Saguy, the head of IDF Intelligence, asked to see me urgently. Within minutes, they were in my office seeking approval for an action that might have to be taken within hours. Information had just been received that on the anniversary of the death of a leading Hezbollah activist who had been killed a few years earlier, a memorial service would be held in the South Lebanese village of Jibsheet, a short distance beyond the Israeli security zone. It was likely that Abbas Musawi, the secretary general of the Shiite terrorist organization Hezbollah, would come from Beirut to attend the ceremonies. Musawi was responsible for a series of murderous actions that included the car bomb attacks on the U.S. embassy in Beirut and on the Marine compound; the kidnapping and murder of U.S. Marine Colonel William Higgins; and the kidnapping and murder of two Israeli soldiers. Now we had a chance to settle accounts with the man who had ordered these murders.

I had to make an instant decision, but it was an opportunity that might not come again. There was no margin for error. Musawi was identified. I authorized the air force to attack. There was no mistake: Musawi and about ten of his guards were killed. On Israeli television that night, explaining the attack, I said that "it must be clear to all terrorist organizations who open an account with Israel that sooner or later we will close that account."

The next day, Monday, February 17, a number of Katyusha rockets, launched from southern Lebanon, hit the Galilee panhandle. They caused no damage, but it was the first time in ten years—since the Lebanon War—that the civilian population in northern Israel had been subjected to this kind of attack. The following morning a rocket attack against the small town of Metulla again hurt nobody. So far we had been lucky, but I could not count on our luck holding. I flew to Metulla by helicopter to meet with the IDF commanders in the area. It was imperative that we make clear that we were not going to tolerate a continuation of these attacks. Unlike years past, there was now a central government in Beirut claiming to rule Lebanon, and the Syrian Army occupied a good part of Lebanon and wielded effective control of that country. There was no doubt in my mind that the Syrians could stop the Hezbollah from launching rockets against us—or order the Lebanese Army to do so. We decided to warn the inhabitants of the Lebanese villages from which the rockets were launched to leave their villages immediately, since they were about to be subjected to heavy shelling.

When the American ambassador, Bill Harrop, who had recently replaced Bill Brown, held a reception at his seaside residence in Herzliya on the evening of the 18th, I explained the situation and asked that the U.S. government convey to the Lebanese and Syrians that they must control the Hezbollah terrorists and that the attacks must cease. Harrop said he would pass on my message.

At the government meeting next morning, I reported on our attack against Musawi and the subsequent events on our northern border. I knew that the Syrians held the key to the situation, and I was convinced that nothing short of a mass exodus of the Shiite population of southern Lebanon toward Beirut, and the destabilizing effect that would have on the Syrian puppet government there, would get Assad to move in the right direction. It was important, therefore, to create the impression that we were determined to escalate the situation unless the shelling stopped.

Harrop called shortly to tell me that he had received a message from Baker that included the words: "Nobody will mourn the passing of a terrorist." I assumed that Baker's reaction reflected the closing of the long U.S. account with Musawi. But the Katyushas were still falling. At noon I was informed that rockets had landed in the northern town of Kiryat Shmona, this time causing some property damage, one falling into the local bus station but miraculously not injuring anybody. I was in the prime minister's office at the time and within minutes there was a call from the mayor of Kiryat Shmona, Prosper Azran, calling for action. Possibly the Syrians assumed that we were not prepared to go beyond shelling a few villages. I knew that if the rocket attacks did not stop, we would have to enlarge the security zone so that the northern part of Israel would be beyond the range of Katyushas fired from Lebanon.

Extending IDF control over additional areas of Lebanon was a distasteful prospect, but I thought it necessary to signal to the Syrians that we were prepared to clear the area of all civilians and then occupy it, if they did not cooperate. As part of this strategy, the IDF sent a company-sized unit of tanks and infantry into Kafra and Ya'atar, two neighboring villages outside the security zone from which Katyushas had been launched and whose population had fled, fearing our artillery. I told Harrop of this move, adding that we intended to withdraw our force within twenty-four hours. Harrop said he was disappointed that we had decided to make a military move before receiving responses to the messages delivered by the United States in Beirut and Damascus, but I explained that there was no time to lose in putting pressure on the Syrians and that I expected that our action and the United States diplomatic messages would be mutually reinforcing. As always, prices had to be paid: the IDF unit found Hezbollah fighters established in the abandoned villages, and in the ensuing combat two of our soldiers were killed. After expelling the Hezbollah from the two villages, the IDF unit withdrew.

By the time the twenty-four hours were up, on the morning of Friday, February 21, the Katyusha attacks had stopped. We received information that the Lebanese government as well as the Hezbollah leadership were concerned by the consequences of a further escalation. Just as I was about to leave my office at 3:00 P.M. for the Sabbath, convinced that we had coped well with a dangerous situation, I was notified that a single Katyusha had fallen into the western Galilee settlement of Granot, killing a five-year-old girl. It was no solace to learn that this rocket had been fired not by the Hezbollah, but by Palestinian terrorists.

The government, now reduced in number since Tsomet, Tehiyya, and Moledet had left it, met a number of times in February to hear Eli Rubinstein's report on the negotiations with the Palestinians in Washington, and to decide on the instructions to our delegates for the next round of meetings. The gap between us and the Palestinian representatives seemed insurmountable. Their position on Palestinian autonomy in Judea, Samaria, and Gaza was that it should have almost all the attributes of a Palestinian state. In our view, autonomy was considerably more limited. Were negotiations that had only just begun already on the point of breaking down? There was no question that the establishment of a self-governing authority for the Palestinian population would go a long way toward establishing a Palestinian state there.

Begin had insisted that the Camp David agreements in 1978 called for autonomy for the Palestinian population living in the area, but not autonomy over the geographic area itself. As long as there was no significant Jewish population in the territories in question, it could be argued that there was not much difference between the two concepts. But in the years since the Camp David agreements a hundred thousand Jews had settled in Judea and Samaria, and now constituted more than 10 percent of the population. At the time of the Camp David agreements, Sharon had been a member of Begin's government and had supported them. Now he was arguing fiercely that Palestinian autonomy was bound to lead to the establishment of a Palestinian state. If we could not change our basic position on this issue, he proposed that we grant autonomy only in prescribed areas densely populated by Palestinians. He had prepared a map showing a number of "islands" in which he suggested we agree to autonomy. He must of course have realized, as I did, that such a proposal, if put forward by the Israeli delegation at the next round of negotiations in Washington, would be interpreted as a departure from the Camp David agreements, as well as from the formulas that had served as the basis of the Madrid Conference, and would lead to a rupture of the negotiations.

At all these meetings, I insisted that it was vital for us to continue the negotiations with the Palestinians, making every attempt to arrive at an agreement, or at least to demonstrate our goodwill and our desire to reach an accommodation with them. "Our objectives," I argued, "must be realistic." There had been a time, before World War II, when Jabotinsky had insisted that a Jewish state be established on both sides of the Jordan River, in the entire area mandated to Britain for that purpose by the League of Nations. But with the destruction of European Jewry we had abandoned that claim, knowing that we lacked the resources to implement it. "So now too," I argued, "we must maintain a reasonable correlation between our objectives and our resources. As a nation dedicated to Western values and ideals, we must live by them not only in Israel itself, but also in dealing with the Palestinian population. We cannot continue to deny them participation in the political process that determines how they are governed. Autonomy will provide limited participation and is therefore a move in the right direction, but can serve as no more than a transition point to full participation, which must be granted them sooner or later."

Shamir summarized the discussion rather curtly, saying merely that we must continue the talks in Washington based on the principles of autonomy for the Palestinians as laid down at Camp David.

On my way to New York on March 12, I thought about a recent column by Ed Koch, the former mayor of New York City, published in the *New York Post* a few days earlier, which described a consultation on Republican campaign strategy held at the White House by the president and his advisers. One of the participants was reported as saying that if the administration continued with its negative approach toward Israel, refusing to approve the loan guarantees unless Israel ceased settlement activity, the Republicans would lose the Jewish vote. To which, according to Koch, Baker had responded with, "Fuck the Jews, they don't vote for us anyway." There was an immediate disclaimer from Margaret Tutweiler, Baker's spokesperson, denying that Baker had ever said anything like that. I had no way of knowing how true Koch's story was, but being aware how expletives are often used in the United States without implying real animosity, I did not take it as seriously as did many other Israelis. However, I thought, it was not a bad thing if the administration was beginning to concern itself with the effect its harsh policy toward Israel might have on Bush's election prospects. I hoped this might signal some kind of a change in the administration's attitude.

On March 16, I met with Dick Cheney at the Pentagon. Having shared many tense moments during the Gulf War, we had established a relationship of trust that had grown into friendship. But that morning I had the feeling that our relationship had undergone a change. As he informed me that no progress had yet been made in implementing the congressional resolution of last November to supply Israel with equipment from the stocks of the U.S. armed forces or for additional pre-positioning in Israel of U.S. military equipment, Cheney turned to the issue that had been hovering over us from the moment he met me on the steps of the Pentagon that morning.

Cheney said he had received reports of Israel passing on U.S. technology to foreign countries as part of its efforts to sell the Python 3 air-to-air missile, the Mapatz anti-tank missile, and the Popeye long-range air-to-ground missile. Then, looking me straight in the eye, he said, "But by far the most serious is the report we have received from intelligence sources, on which we place great reliance, that Israel has sold Patriot material and technology to China." Even though I should have been prepared for this, after seeing the stories that had been leaked to the media, I was astounded. As I began to refute the charges, I felt myself getting angry. "You have seen for yourself, during your recent visit to Israel, when we showed you our latest developments, that Israeli technology in this area is more advanced than U.S. technology," I protested. "What basis could there be to the charge that we are stealing U.S. technology in this field? The Popeye is an Israeli-developed missile that the U.S. Air Force decided to acquire from Israel; its technology, as you know, is Israeli, not American. There is no logic behind these allegations. I can only guess the motivation of the 'senior officials' leaking this stuff to the press." As for the accusation that we sold Patriot missiles or Patriot parts to China, I went on firmly, "there is not one grain of truth to it. What is its source?" Denying that the Pentagon had anything to do with leaking the story to the media, Cheney said that the source of the information had to be protected and that he could not disclose it to me.

I swallowed my pride and suggested that the secretary send an inspection team to Israel which would be given free access to our Patriot batteries and stores of spares so that it could verify that, in fact, nothing was missing. Cheney agreed to my proposal, but gave me no indication that he had changed his mind about the truth of the charges.

The rest of our conversation on U.S.-Israel cooperation in weapons development and the need to assist Israel in maintaining a quality edge over the weapons supplied to the Arab armies seemed pointless in light of the mood that had been created. The Bush administration had decided to put the screws to Israel: to deny us the military aid that had been legislated by Congress, and to accuse us of illegally selling U.S. technology, poison arrows fired at Israel and directed, first and foremost, against the Likud government to show the Israeli public that no improvement should be expected in the U.S.-Israel relationship as long as the Likud was in power. This, in addition to the repeated message that Shamir's government was not going to be granted the sought-after loan guarantees.

During my stay in Washington, Senators Kasten and Leahy tried to work out a compromise with Bush on the guarantees. When Patrick Leahy showed me the proposed language of the compromise, which he said was meeting Bush more than "halfway," I could see that it was unacceptable to us, but I made no comment. The proposed compromise drew a connection between the loan guarantees and settlement activity, and left the granting of guarantees to the president's discretion. As it turned out, even this watered-down version was rejected by the president.

In an address to the three thousand members of the Young Leadership Conference of the UJA that day, I talked about the inequalities involved in the administration's refusal to defer to Israel on an issue of such cardinal importance to us as Israeli settlements in Judea and Samaria—certainly of no great importance to the United States even though Israel had deferred to the United States in its hour of need when President Bush appealed to us not to retaliate for the Scud missiles falling on us. "The administration insists that these settlements are obstacles to peace," I said. But was it really the strengthening of the Israeli presence in those areas that constituted an obstacle, or was it rather Muslim fundamentalism, Syrian import of Scuds from North Korea, and Iraqi, Iranian and Libyan acquisition of nuclear technology? At all events, Israel would not renounce the right of Jews to live in Judea and Samaria, or abandon its defensive posture as a price for obtaining humanitarian assistance. Nor would we beg for this aid.

"We hope our friends in Washington will help us with the huge economic challenge we have accepted so that the Jews of Russia can come home to Israel at last. But if not," I ended, "then we shall have to do it ourselves. We in Israel and you here can do it together." The audience, representing Jewish communities throughout the United States, greeted my remarks with thunderous applause.

I had one more meeting in Washington. Dennis Ross, Baker's assistant, contacted Salai Meridor to suggest that I meet with Baker. I knew that Baker, still trying to promote his relationship with Levy, had let it be known in the past that meetings between us held at his initiative were actually in response to my request. Not eager for any further misunderstandings, I asked Salai to tell Ross that I would meet with the secretary if Baker requested the meeting; an invitation for me to come to the State Department followed immediately. It was a meeting unlike any other between us, unattended by any aides or notetakers.

Baker started by congratulating me on winning the Likud internal elections. Complimenting me on my abilities, he said jokingly that he would be ready to campaign for me or against me, whichever would do me the most good. He denied that he had ever used the expletive against the Jews, and said that the State Department was not behind the leaks accusing Israel of selling U.S. technology. When I told him that that same morning an Arab from Gaza had gone on a rampage in Jaffa, killing a nineteen-year-old girl and an Israeli Arab who tried to come to her assistance, he recalled the little girl killed by a Katyusha rocket in the Galilee a few weeks earlier. "You know," he said, "I have a little girl the same age. When I read the account of how that child was killed coming out of the house to greet her father, tears came to my eyes." We were sitting next to each other on the sofa in his office, and I could tell that he was deeply moved, an aspect of Baker I had never seen or even suspected.

We discussed the negotiations with the Palestinians, and I told him that I was concerned that the Palestinian delegation did not seem capable of agreeing to anything that might be interpreted as a compromise. "I told them to accept whatever Israel offers, and then go on to their other demands," Baker said. It was good advice for the Palestinians and for the process, but it looked as though they were not about to accept it.

When we turned to the U.S.-Israel relationship, he was very forthcoming. He urged me to agree to the conditions that Bush was placing on the loan guarantees, adding that there was no way of knowing who would be in the White House after the coming elections. He did not seem optimistic about Bush's prospects, predicting that by convention time he would be trailing the Democratic candidate by a significant margin. After an hour together, I left with the feeling that I had never really known him.

That day the Israeli Embassy in Buenos Aires was blown up by a car bomb that had been parked next to the building. There was no definite count of the victims, but I was informed that a number of Israelis and Argentinians had been killed. It was not known who the perpetrators were, but I suspected the Hezbollah seeking revenge for Musawi's death. In any case, it was a reminder of what the war against terrorism entailed. At the time of this writing, it is still a mystery, despite intensive efforts to identify the killers, who were to strike again on July 18, 1994, when 300 tons of explosives killed some 100 people in the offices of the Argentine Jewish Mutual Association.

On my way home, I visited Henry Kissinger in New York. I usually tried to meet with him when I was in the United States. We had become friends while I was ambassador in Washington, and since then I had solicited his opinion on problems I was dealing with. We discussed the Middle East peace process and Israel's proposal for Palestinian autonomy. Then I asked him who was behind the charges being leveled at us. Without responding directly, Kissinger said that he had attended a gathering in which the CIA Director Robert Gates had been present, and when asked by one of the participants if the story of Israel's transfer of Patriot technology to China was true, Gates replied, "No comment." "You know what that means?" Kissinger said. "It means that he is confirming the story."

Within a week the U.S. inspection team arrived in Israel, bringing with it a long list of written questions. We were asked to itemize the names of everyone who had visited the Patriot batteries deployed in Israel during the Gulf War. It was ridiculous; nothing can be learned about Patriot technology by viewing the missile on its launcher, besides which, numerous pictures of the missile had been published in the press. During the war, delegations of the United Jewish Appeal visiting Israel were usually taken to see the Patriot batteries operated by U.S. Army crews; could it be that it was suspected that these delegations included people spying for the Chinese? Nevertheless, I issued instructions for full cooperation with the American team and ordered that all questions be answered. The inspection team spent more than a week sifting through material that might be relevant to the quest and asking questions. The team's presence in Israel was no secret and was reported in the press, everyone eagerly awaiting the findings. Ambassador Harrop said that should it turn out that the allegations against Israel had been groundless, the United States would owe Israel an apology.

On April 2, Margaret Tutweiler announced at a State Department press briefing that the inspection team had returned, that Israeli cooperation with the team had been "superb," that Israel had been given a clean bill of health, and that there was no reason to suspect Israel of having transferred Patriot technology to anybody else. The people who leaked the accusations to the media owed an apology to Israel, she said. There was no official apology.

While I was in the United States, I had received almost daily telephone calls from Shamir. He complained that I had left him in the lurch, that other Likud ministers had also gone abroad, that he had not yet put together the election campaign committee. He told me that he had asked Ehud Olmert and Dan Meridor to try to negotiate a reconciliation with Levy, but that they had not yet succeeded. I had urged him to reshuffle his cabinet, to make some dynamic moves in the economic field that would dispel the image of immobility that had stuck to him; but I had not made much headway.

Shortly after my return to Israel, Levy had called a meeting of his supporters at the plush Daniel Hotel in Herzliya. His aides had let it be known that he was going to make a dramatic announcement that evening, and there was great anticipation throughout the country. In a long speech, Levy recounted his trials and tribulations within the party, claiming that he had suffered discrimination because he was a Moroccan Jew. This was the harshest, most damaging accusation that could be made against the Likud, which prided itself on the presence in its front ranks of immigrants from Arab-speaking countries and their sons, and had built a mass following in the immigrant townships of Israel. Now the charge came from a leading member of the party, a man who had risen to the position of foreign minister and deputy prime minister. It was sure to cause damage to the Likud in the elections. Levy closed his hour-and-a-half oration by announcing that he was resigning from the government, "for the good of the Likud, for the good of the country, and for the good of days still to come." There was no way of understanding this enigmatic statement, nor his decision to resign from the government while staying on in the Likud. What was easy to understand was that he had once again let his ego get the better of him, even if it meant striking a heavy blow against his own party.

The Labor party held countrywide primaries, in which over a hundred thousand party members participated without excessive rancor. Rabin defeated Peres for the top position, but immediately thereafter the two men and their followers closed ranks, underlining unity and their readiness to work as a team. The elected Labor slate was marked by a tilt to the left, candidates with the most dovish views attaining many of the top positions. But, significantly, leading the list was Yitzhak Rabin, a man known to the public as a hawk, a man capable of appealing to a great many Likud voters.

By Israeli law, resignations from the government must be submitted in writing at a government meeting, taking effect forty-eight hours later if the minister resigning has not changed his mind in the meantime. The government meeting at which Levy would presumably tender his resignation was to take place on Sunday, April 5, a week after his speech at the Daniel Hotel. Continuing in his quest for headlines, Levy told reporters that he wished there could have been a government meeting earlier so that he could have submitted his resignation without delay.

I had arranged to meet Shamir before the meeting to try to impress upon him again the need to reshuffle his government. On the way to Jerusalem, I heard Levy being interviewed on the radio; he announced that his letter of resignation was already written and he was just waiting for the government meeting to submit it. My message to Shamir was simple: We had less than three months to go until the elections and according to the opinion polls, the Likud was trailing Labor by a large margin; only a dramatic move on our part could better our situation. With Levy's resignation, Netanyahu should be appointed as acting foreign minister. "Bibi" had given an excellent account of himself as Israel's Ambassador to the United Nations, and again when he accompanied Shamir to Madrid. He was one of the most popular politicians in the country. Moda'i, who would be competing with us for support from Likud voters, should be fired, and Olmert or Meridor installed as acting finance minister. Either one could be trusted to begin moves to liberalize the economy and sell government-owned companies, things the Likud had talked about for years but done little to implement.

"This is literally the last moment to make these changes," I said. Shamir was at his desk, I sitting across from him. Glasses of tea and lemon had been served, and for the nth time I was pleading with him to help breathe life into the Likud before it was too late. Now, for the first time, I felt he was listening.

But there was disturbing background noise. As I had entered the prime minister's office, I had noticed Minister of Police Ronni Milo, one of Shamir's fair-haired boys, engaged in some kind of frenetic activity in the outer office where the prime minister's secretaries sat. Suddenly he burst into the room, interrupting our conversation, and handed Shamir some papers, saying, "Here's the agreement." From the few words they exchanged, I gathered that this was an agreement worked out with Levy. When I asked to see it, Milo let me look, but without letting go of the papers.

The first thing to meet my eye was a guarantee to Levy that he would be deputy prime minister and foreign minister in the next government and the right to appoint one other minister. There was no need for me to read any further. "This agreement should not be signed," I said to Shamir, and walked out of his office. As I left, climbing the stairs to the meeting room on the second floor, I saw tens of reporters and photographers whispering among themselves, already aware that instead of Levy's anticipated resignation from the government there would be something quite different to cover that morning.

When Shamir, followed by Milo, entered the cabinet room, the ministers were already seated around the long table in their assigned seats. Levy sat next to me, both of us facing Shamir. The prime minister motioned to the press corps to enter the room, an unusual move, and to the sound of popping flashbulbs, reporters and cameramen shoved and pushed their way in.

Shamir and then Levy announced that they had reached an agreement and that the crisis in the Likud had been resolved. The agreement that Shamir had signed that morning was a surrender to Levy's demands, arrived at in secret negotiations. Although Levy had lost in the Likud's internal elections, Shamir now crowned him as the number-two man in the Likud's hierarchy. In contravention of Israeli political tradition and the statutes of the Likud, he had agreed to delegate his authority to appoint a minister in his government to another minister. He had also agreed to Levy's appointing four additional members to the Likud Secretariat, of which I was the elected chairman, and had promised Levy's appointees representation on the Jewish Agency Executive.

The meeting was short. After the announcement of the Shamir-Levy agreement, the agenda was anticlimactic. Shamir let it be known that he wanted to meet with all the Likud ministers, except for Levy, in his

office. When we assembled there a few minutes later, he explained that
Milo had appeared in his office at eight-thirty that morning with the
text of an agreement with Levy that would put an end to the crisis in
the Likud. "This was very distasteful to me," he said, "but I had to do
it because this was the only way to put the crisis behind us." His
remarks were met with silence. Shamir looked around the room, evidently interpreting the silence as assent.

"Look," I said, "the damage to the Likud in the election campaign
has already been done. Levy has accused us of discrimination against
Israelis of Oriental background, the worst accusation that can be leveled
against a Jew or against any Israeli party. The agreement you have
signed with Levy, far from controlling the damage, will only cause
additional harm. Our movement has always believed in principles, but
you have behaved in an unprincipled manner in the mistaken belief that
you were improving our election prospects. On both counts, you have
failed. What's more, you had no authority to sign that agreement."

Shamir glared at me, then turned to the other ministers and said:
"Well, if you don't accept the agreement, then I will leave." I called out
to him, "You're beginning to behave like Levy," to which he replied,
"You too have threatened to resign on occasion." I couldn't imagine
what he was referring to, but I was sure that he had no intention of
resigning. Nobody spoke until the minister of transport, Moshe Katsav,
who had come to Israel as a small boy from Iran and grown up in the
immigrant township of Kiryat Malachi, said, "I don't want to take a
position one way or the other, but I must say that Levy's accusation is
not only damaging to the Likud but to Israel's entire society." Shamir
stood up. The meeting was over.

That evening I was scheduled to address a campaign kick-off rally of
Likud activists at our headquarters in Tel Aviv. I was in no mood to
appear there, but knowing that my absence would arouse speculation
harmful to the Likud, I decided to go. I had concluded that the time
had come for me to leave politics. I had stayed on in political life
through crisis after crisis, feeling that it was at such times that my
participation in the Likud leadership mattered, but the sham that had
just occurred was the last straw. I would make no announcements until
after the elections, but my mind was made up.

Three days later Moshe Nissim, as campaign chairman, called a meeting at the Likud's headquarters, attended by Shamir and Levy, to demonstrate to one and all that past quarrels in the Likud had now been

smoothed over. Levy threatened to spoil this show of unity and not attend the meeting unless he received a letter from Shamir appointing four of his cohorts to the Likud Secretariat; he had learned that his extortion tactics worked with Shamir, and again Shamir gave in. The meeting, well attended by the press, did not succeed in papering over the backbiting and bitterness that lay beneath the show of unity.

A few days later at my routine weekly meeting with Shamir, I told him that many Likud voters, including its Moroccan adherents, were sick and tired of Levy's shenanigans and didn't want him to head the party. Shamir, hunched over his desk, muttered something about maybe having been a little hasty. "But, Misha, you're making a tragedy of this. Don't take it so seriously. Everything will turn out okay." "No," I said. "As far as I'm concerned, it is not a tragedy. It is the end of the line. I've had enough, I'm going to leave politics right after the elections, regardless of the outcome." I felt that he did not take me seriously.

"I too intend to resign after the elections," he countered, yet once more.

I decided to devote much of my effort in the election campaign to Israel's minority population. In the past I had made the Muslim holiday of Id-el-Fitr, at the end of the month-long Ramadan fast, an occasion to visit Muslim communities. First, I went down to the Negev to visit the Bedouin reconnaissance unit recently set up by the IDF, composed of Bedouin youngsters from the Galilee and the Negev who had volunteered for three years of army service despite the fact that Israel's Arab citizens are exempt from serving in the IDF. I took great pride in the success thus far of my campaign to encourage Bedouin youngsters to enlist. Time and again I was told that this service in the IDF was the most successful bulwark against the spread of Muslim fundamentalism among the Bedouin.

In a large tent filled with Bedouin sheiks and other notables, the head of the Shoket Regional Council in the Negev announced that we were meeting to celebrate the unit's "adoption" by the regional council. Sitting cross-legged on a carpet, leaning on cushions, and having consumed lamb and many cups of coffee, I listened to speeches, in Arabic and Hebrew, lauding the State of Israel and the IDF, and greeting the reconnaissance unit and its commanding officer, a young Bedouin from Galilee. In my remarks, which were translated into Arabic, I commended the Bedouin elders for encouraging their sons to enlist in the IDF, and expressed the hope that the company-size unit would soon attain the size of a battalion and maybe someday a brigade. This was not just a figure of speech. Though the IDF had been unenthusiastic about my instructions to accept Bedouin youth in its ranks, two hundred young men had volunteered that year, and the indications were that the number would double in the following year.

Next on my itinerary were the Arab villages of Taibe and Baka el-Gharbiye, located in the "little triangle" on the western fringes of Samaria. Meeting with local councils and later with assembled residents of these villages, I spoke of their obligation to be loyal citizens of Israel, and of Israel's obligation to assure complete equality for its Arab citizens. I was impressed by the degree to which Israeli Arabs were becoming Israelized, adopting Israeli customs and dress, as well as Israeli values. But with this change had come also the realization that while equality prevailed in law, they were far from being treated equally in the allocation of government funds or employment opportunities. We had made considerable progress in this area since the state was created, but we still had a long way to go, and the younger generation was becoming impatient.

On the holiday of Nebi Shu'eib, when Druze make their annual pilgrimage to the grave of the man they believe to have been Jethro, Moses' father-in-law, I visited Druze villages in the Galilee, stopping off first to pay my respects to their spiritual leader, Sheik Amin Tarif, in the village of Julis. The frail nonagenarian, a hearing aid in his ear, greeted me at his residence, surrounded by priests and notables. When the traditional coffee was served, I reminded him of his visit to my office in the Defense Ministry almost ten years earlier, when he had come to intercede for the safety of the Druze community in Lebanon. He had not touched the coffee I offered him then, saying that he had sworn not to drink coffee as long as his brethren in Lebanon were in danger. I had promised him to do everything in my power to assure their safety and had subsequently made good on that promise. Now, the old white-bearded man smiled an angelic smile and patted my knee; for a moment, I felt like a child sitting next to him.

During the weeks leading up to the elections, there had been an escalation of activity against the IDF and the SLA in southern Lebanon by the Hezbollah and the Islamic Jihad. The chief of staff was abroad, so I asked his deputy, Amnon Shahak, to my office to discuss what actions we might have to take to deal with it. Thirty minutes after he left me, I was notified that a convoy of Israeli officers and soldiers visiting Shiite villages in the security zone had been ambushed. Two soldiers were killed and five wounded; one of the soldiers killed was a Druze medic who had rushed to the aid of the wounded.

I described the deteriorating situation to Ambassador Harrop, saying that we would have to do something about it, and asked that the United States pass this message on to Beirut and Damascus before the situation got out of control. Harrop was sympathetic. Four days later he reported that the U.S. ambassador in Beirut had spoken to Lebanese President Harawi, who had agreed to contact the "concerned parties," and that in Damascus, the U.S. ambassador had met with Syria's foreign minister, Farouk al-Sharaa, who gave him the usual rhetoric about Israeli aggression, insisting that Syria was opposed to any escalation in southern Lebanon. According to Harrop, the messages were stern, making it clear that the United States believed that these governments were able to tone things down, and that while the United States had asked Israel to practice restraint, it expected the Lebanese and Syrians to do their part.

That day in Metulla, Israel's northernmost town, I found IDF commander Major General Yitzhak Mordechai less than optimistic. There had been an additional encounter with the Hezbollah in which two terrorists had been killed. Everybody—on our side and in the SLA—seemed to be awaiting an Israeli response.

At the government meeting the following week, I reported on the situation in Lebanon, on my contact with Harrop, and the messages delivered through the United States ambassadors in Beirut and Damascus. I told the ministers that it was important to prevent further deterioration of the situation which might lead to a breakdown of the security zone. Since the Syrians were in control, we had to make it clear to them that we expected them to restrain the terrorist organizations operating against us. The Hezbollah bases and training grounds were located in the Bek'a Valley, close to the Syrian-Lebanese border, and were under the protection of Syrian-based surface-to-air missile batteries—an area Israel's air force had not flown over since the Lebanese War.

Now I proposed that we fly a reconnaissance mission over the valley to photograph the Hezbollah encampments in preparation for attacking them should the situation not quiet down. The flight would be monitored by the Syrians, and they would certainly understand that bombing the area would be our next step if terrorist activity continued. The flight entailed the danger of an escalation with the Syrians if they launched missiles against our aircraft, but that was a risk I felt we had to take. After some discussion, the reconnaissance flight was approved by the cabinet. It was carried out shortly without incident, in the hope that the Syrians would take the hint. But in the weeks that followed, it proved to have been a vain hope.

Toward the end of April, I visited a Golani infantry brigade unit stationed in Tulkarem. Everybody told me the Intifada was fading out, that the Palestinian population was tired and wanted to return to normal life. There were no more demonstrations or mass disturbances. In response, the extremist groups had stepped up their efforts to stage acts of terrorism against Israeli civilians. The introduction of IDF elite units and special forces into the area had proved to be an effective answer to the threat. Special teams, some disguised as Arabs, had been roaming the area during the past few weeks searching for terrorists, many of whom, on our "wanted" list, were apprehended or shot in encounters with the army. Most impressive of all was the growing number of known terrorists daily turning themselves in to the authorities, realizing that the noose was tightening around their necks.

One major indication of the ebbing of the Intifada in Judea, Samaria, and Gaza was the school system. When I took over the Defense Ministry from Rabin, I found all the schools, colleges, and universities in these territories closed. I had gradually reopened the educational system: first the elementary schools, then high schools and community colleges, and then one after another the universities: Bethlehem, Hebron, the Islamic University in Gaza, A-Najah in Nablus. Bir Zeit, located outside Ramallah, was the last to remain shut. In the heyday of the Intifada, it had been a hotbed of agitation, demonstrations, and violence, but the time had now come, I felt, to allow it too to open. The army and the security services responsible for the area strongly advised me against doing so, predicting that the faculty and student body would return to their old ways. I decided there could be no return to normal life in the area as long as the university remained closed.

I invited the Bir Zeit senior administrative and academic staff to the Defense Ministry. I could only imagine how they felt coming to Tel Aviv, through the gates of the Defense Ministry compound, and into the office of the man responsible for dealing with the Intifada. We began by discussing the current political situation and the outlook for the negotiations. I told them that opening Bir Zeit would be predicated on the assumption that it would be a center of learning, not of agitation to violence, and that I expected them to exert their influence toward that end. I received no promises that day, but the atmosphere of the meeting provided me with sufficient assurance that my decision was justified. Next day the announcement was made—and a big step toward returning life to normal in the area was completed.

Elections, 1992

On April 26, I began a two-day visit to Finland at the invitation of the Finnish defense minister, Elizabeth Rehn, who had recently been in Israel. From Finland, joined by my wife and two daughters, Aliza and Ruthie, I returned—after forty-four years—to Latvia and Lithuania, to the city of Kovno where I was born, and to Riga where I grew up. There, in Rumbuli Forest where some thirty thousand Jews were murdered in 1941 by the Nazis (among them children with whom I had gone to school), we joined a few hundred survivors in reciting the Jewish memorial prayers for the dead.

I returned to Israel on the week of Memorial Day, in time to address the bereaved families gathered at the Kiryat Shaul military cemetery in Tel Aviv, and to participate next day in the celebration of Israel's forty-fourth year of independence.

For a moment, many of the problems being heatedly debated in the ongoing election campaign seemed overshadowed by the great achievements of the past forty-four years. Nevertheless, the daily demands of the election campaign quickly returned my attention to everyday life and to the Likud's dim prospects.

An opening rally held in Jerusalem on May 3 brought thousands of supporters from all over the country to hear pep talks from the Likud leadership and to witness a somewhat forced display of unity as Shamir, Sharon, Levy, and I appeared on stage together. But nothing seemed to be going right. The advertising agency the Likud had hired for the campaign had come up with the idiotic slogan "The Likud Is Correct," which was now plastered on billboards all over the country. I pleaded with the campaign committee to drop the slogan, but to no avail. Meanwhile, our expectation that the recently arrived Russian immigrants with their memories of Socialist rule in the Soviet Union would naturally vote for the Likud proved unfounded; in meetings with groups of Russian immigrants, I learned that their overriding concerns were employment and housing, and that they fell easy prey to the Labor line claiming that the Likud had not done enough for them, and promising them improvement in their condition if Labor came to power.

The quarreling and backbiting among the Likud leadership continued, with accusations flying from Levy on one side and Sharon on the other. It was difficult to ask voters to have confidence in the Likud, when its leaders trumpeted their own lack of confidence in the party. As if that were not enough, just a few weeks before the elections, the state comptroller, Miriam Ben-Porat, a highly respected former Supreme Court judge, issued a report revealing a host of irregularities at Sharon's Housing Ministry, thus unintentionally providing ammunition for Labor's charges of corruption in the Likud government.

Furthermore, Shamir's request for the loan guarantees, and his insistence that they be provided unconditionally, came to haunt us now. It had become clear that the one man who would not receive these guarantees was Shamir, and his claim that the guarantees were all-important was working in Rabin's favor, since Rabin indicated that he was prepared to meet the conditions that Bush had set. Many voters believed Shamir's reelection would mean continuing confrontation with Washington. It was ironic that the negotiations with the Arab delegations in Washington—one of the great achievements of the Shamir government and the direct result of the May 1989 peace initiative—were now calling attention to the fact that Shamir's seemingly inflexible posture was liable to stalemate the peace process. His frequent reference to our right to "The Integral Land of Israel," applauded by traditional Likud supporters, was causing consternation to voters "floating" between Likud and Labor. Five years of Intifada had made it clear that the Palestinian problem in Judea, Samaria, and Gaza had to be addressed in some manner; although some advocated annexation of these areas to Israel, the majority of Israelis were too concerned with Jewish-Arab demographics to favor such annexation, or to see in the slogan "The Integral Land of Israel" an adequate response to the Palestinian problem.

The one area in which the Likud could have had a significant advantage over Labor was in the sphere of economics. Labor had been an orthodox Socialist party for most of its history. Only recently had it started to break away from Socialist doctrines, encumbered as it was by vast vested interests in the Histadrut Labor Federation, a mammoth organization which owned much of Israel's industry, its largest insurance company, its second-largest bank, and the medical and hospital organization that provided health care for more than two thirds of Israel's population. The Likud, and before it Jabotinsky's Revisionist movement, had been advocates of a liberal economy and privatization of government- and Histadrut-owned enterprises. But during its years in power the Likud had done almost nothing to implement these policies. Shamir, like Begin before him, had shown little interest in economics, leaving Moda'i to do more or less as he pleased. Although Moda'i was running on a rival ticket, he was still finance minister in the present government, so it was impossible to attack his policy of inaction, or to put forth a credible claim that the Likud seriously intended to reform Israel's anachronistic economic system.

Still, on the personal level, the Likud had a signal advantage over Labor in the form of its talented young leadership. Ehud Olmert, Dan Meridor, Moshe Katsav, Ronni Milo, Benny Begin, Bibi Netanyahu, Ovadia Eli, Uzi Landau, and Meir Shitrit were all generally considered capable followers of the present leadership. Labor's second tier of leadership seemed virtually nonexistent. But this handicap was cleverly handled by Labor strategists who directed the spotlight not on the collective leadership of the competing parties, but rather on their two leaders, making the campaign, in large measure, a contest between Yitzhak Rabin and Yitzhak Shamir. Rabin, though no youngster, was still a number of years younger than Shamir, and promised dynamic leadership, in contrast to what Labor called Shamir's bunker mentality. While Rabin flaunted his hawkish credentials, Peres and the rest of the Labor doves were kept hidden during the campaign, and the name of the Labor party's ticket changed from "The Labor Party" to "The Labor Party Led by Yitzhak Rabin."

It was no surprise when during the weeks leading up to the elections the polls showed Labor leading the Likud by about ten Knesset seats.

However, when it came to projecting the coalition that would be formed in the wake of the elections, it looked to be split right down the middle. Most polls showed sixty Knesset seats for the Likud, the parties to its right, and the religious parties, and sixty for Labor and the parties to its left, including the Communists. In dealing with this problem, Labor's potential coalition partners had acted far more intelligently than had the Likud's. Realizing that small parties might fail to reach the minimum threshold of votes (1.5 percent of the valid votes cast) required to obtain representation in the Knesset, three of the smaller parties to the left of Labor decided to run on a single ticket. To the right of the Likud, it was the very opposite—six small parties, each insisting on running independently. Since three of these parties did not attain the minimum threshold, the votes they received—which would have been crucial in determining the election results—were lost for a Likud-led coalition.

I hoped that the success we had been having in restoring a measure of tranquility to Judea and Samaria, and improving security for the Israeli settlers there, would work in our favor. In meetings with the mayors of Bethlehem and Jericho I was told that tourists, and with them prosperity, had recently returned to these towns. On visits to the settlements at Bet Arye in Samaria, and Efrat and Gush Etzion in Judea, I heard no complaints; on the contrary, an increased sense of security was attracting new settlers in growing numbers. Much of the change was the result of the effective operation of the IDF elite units I had ordered into the area.

However, on May 11, Bill Harrop came to see me and began reading from some "talking points" that had been transmitted from Washington. The State Department wanted to know if there was any truth to the allegations that we had changed the rules of engagement and now had IDF "death squads" operating in the area. I replied that these charges were groundless, the army's instructions to the troops had not changed, the men were allowed to fire only if lives were in danger or when suspects resisted arrest. In my opinion, the originators of these allegations were people who were disappointed to see us successfully dealing with the Intifada, including Israeli supporters of the Palestinian cause. But most Israelis seemed pleased that the army was showing itself effective in the fight against Palestinian terrorists.

Then, at 7:00 A.M. on May 24, tragedy struck. A fifteen-year-old girl, Helena Rapp, on her way to high school in the city of Bat Yam, south of Tel Aviv, was stabbed to death by a Palestinian from the Nusseirat refugee camp in the Gaza Strip. Shot and wounded by a passer-by, then arrested by the police, he claimed he had come to Bat Yam that morning looking for work, and frustrated by not finding it, had decided to kill the girl. The murder angered and alarmed Israelis; in Bat Yam, cries of "Death to the Arabs!" were heard at mass protest demonstrations which the police had difficulty controlling. It also gave birth to a new slogan in Labor's campaign: "The Likud Has Brought Gaza to Bat Yam." Asserting that the Likud had shown itself incapable of providing security for Israel's citizens on the streets of its cities, Labor spokesmen insisted that there had never been such occurrences when Rabin was defense minister and that he alone could restore safety to city streets. It seemed not to matter that there had been many similar incidents during Rabin's term of office; the message was believed by many, and, no doubt, strengthened the Labor campaign.

Months before, I had issued instructions that only Palestinians with steady work in Israel, as attested to by their employers, were to be given entry passes from the Gaza Strip into Israel. How was it then that the murderer had entered Israel "looking for work"? On questioning the army officer in charge, I learned that—without my approval—he had changed the instructions a few weeks earlier to allow unemployed Gazans to enter Israel so they could look for work. Beyond raging at the officer, who explained that he had only wanted to help ease the unemployment situation in Gaza and had not realized that the change in my instructions required my approval, there was nothing to be done.

I had no reason to assume that the opinion polls were not serving as reasonably good indicators of the defeat that lay in store for the Likud. We had made every mistake in the book; to the negative effect these mistakes had had on the voters had now been added the impact of Helena Rapp's murder in broad daylight. The only question remaining was the kind of coalition that could be put together—a single-seat margin could make all the difference. I devoted most of my time to electioneering among the Bedouin, in the Druze villages of the Galilee, and in Arab towns and villages. I appeared at election rallies in Nazareth, Israel's largest Arab city, and in the villages of Ilabun, Makr, Rama, Shfaram, Faradis, and Bir el-Maksur, everywhere encountering local Likud activists and enthusiastic audiences, the sole bright spot in our campaign.

When the results came in on the night of Tuesday, June 23, the full dimensions of our defeat became apparent. It was a disaster: our sup-

port had decreased everywhere except among the Arab voters (to everyone's surprise but my own, the number of votes for the Likud in
Bedouin encampments and Arab villages had more than doubled, but
this was not sufficient to offset the Labor landslide). Labor had come
up from thirty-nine Knesset seats to forty-four, while the Likud had
dropped from forty to thirty-two. Together with its potential coalition
partners, Labor had garnered sixty-one seats to the fifty-nine for potential members of a Likud-led coalition. As I thought of the many factors
that had contributed to our defeat—the disunity in our ranks, the
loan guarantee fiasco, the failure to implement our economic policies,
Shamir's inflexibility, the large number of small parties to our right that
had insisted on participating individually, the poor management of our
campaign—I realized that had we avoided even one of these mistakes,
the final outcome would have been radically different. That single-seat
advantage was going to make all the difference for Israel in the course
of the next crucial four years.

I spent that evening, together with most of the Likud leadership, at
Likud headquarters in Tel Aviv, watching the election update come in,
the coalition results wavering between sixty-sixty and sixty-one—fifty-
nine in Labor's favor. Seeing the televised celebrations at Labor headquarters and answering reporters' interminable questions, for the first
time I knew the smell of defeat.

At 2:00 A.M., Shamir arrived accompanied by Levy, to deliver a
speech for the benefit of the assembled party activists, the press, and
the TV cameras. It was all fire and brimstone. Going over the history of
the movement, its confrontations with the Labor party throughout the
years, he recalled the many crises our movement had overcome in the
past, insisting that this defeat would not break us. Listening to him, I
knew that he did not really understand what had happened.

On June 25, 1992, two days after the election, I announced my
retirement from politics. In the summer of 1973, at the urging of Haim
Landau, one of the leaders of the Herut party, I had agreed to appear
on the thirty-second slot of the Likud Knesset slate, intending to make
whatever contribution I could if elected to a four-year Knesset term.
But the four years had stretched into eighteen as I advanced from the
Knesset Finance Committee to key roles in the cabinet. I said that it
had been a privilege to serve my country as ambassador to Washington,
as minister in charge of minority affairs, as foreign minister, and as
defense minister, but that although I believed in service, I did not

believe in servitude. The time had come to close this chapter of my life. Shamir had tried to reach me earlier on the phone, but assuming that he would attempt to dissuade me, I did not return his call until after my resignation was announced.

For the next few days I was inundated by calls from people pleading with me to reconsider. Delegations from all over the country trekked to my home and office; I was particularly touched by the many Arab and Druze groups who insisted that, with my resignation, their communities would lose a friend on the Israeli political scene. One group of Bedouin from the Negev arrived at my home on Saturday and announced that they would remain, squatting on my lawn, until I changed my mind. Seeing that they were in earnest, I told them I would think over their arguments in the course of the next few days. But, of course, my decision had been made.

It took Rabin less than three weeks to put his coalition together. Able to block a Likud-led coalition by joining Labor and the far left Meretz faction, he succeeded in drawing Shas into his government. While assured of the support of the three-member Communist faction and the two-member Arab Democratic faction without taking either into the coalition, Rabin now had a sixty-two-member coalition and could count on the support of another five Knesset members. On Monday, July 13, he was scheduled to present his government to the Knesset for confirmation. That was the day of my farewell meeting with the IDF's general staff.

Accompanied by my military adjutants General "Yirmy" Olmert and Colonel Shimon Hefetz, I walked down the corridor to the chief of staff's conference room, where Ehud Barak and the IDF's major generals were waiting. I knew them all well; many had been appointed by me to their present positions. Some of them I had first encountered during my earlier tenure at the ministry: Amnon Shahak, now deputy chief of staff, I had met during my first visit to the army in Lebanon, when he commanded a division deployed outside Beirut; Emanuel Sakel, head of the Ground Forces Command, had commanded a division deployed in Lebanon's Bek'a Valley at the time; Uri Saguy, now chief of intelligence, had been assistant chief of operations then; Danny Yatom, now head of the Central Command, had been my trusted military adjutant; Herzl Bodinger, whose brilliant air force career was derailed because he had supported the Lavi project, was now air force commander; Nehemia Tamari, who had been slated to lead the Israeli action in western Iraq, was now assistant chief of operations. Looking at Ehud Barak, next to me, and at the other men around that table, I knew that the army was in good hands.

At 10:30 P.M., the Knesset voted confidence in the new government in which Rabin would serve as both prime minister and defense minister, and the awesome responsibility that had rested on my shoulders for the past two years was lifted. The following day Rabin came to the Defense Ministry and, for the second time in our careers, I turned it over to him. Raising my glass to wish him well, I said that we were all proud to belong to the only democracy in the Middle East—and that changes of administration were one of the hallmarks of democratic rule. "You win some, and you lose some," I said. "That is something I know the Likud will remember during the next four years, but that the Labor party should not forget either."

With that I went downstairs, accompanied by Rabin, Barak, and Ivry, to the courtyard, where the traditional IDF farewell parade stood ready for my review. While hundreds of Defense Ministry employees watched, some in the courtyard, others from the windows of their offices, I reviewed the guard, saluted the blue and white flag, and got into my car for the drive home to Savyon—a private citizen for the first time in eighteen years.

Epilogue

Just over four months later, George Bush was defeated in his attempt to obtain a second term. His administration's repeated attempts to interfere in Israel's internal politics had been without precedent in the history of the relations between the United States and Israel, and probably without precedent in the relationship between any two democratically elected governments. The traditional diplomatic dialogue between the president and the prime minister of Israel, and between the secretary of state and Israel's foreign minister, was often replaced or supplemented by backstage consultations and maneuvering between the White House and State Department and the leaders of Israel's Labor party.

Although in the months after the Likud defeat Bush gave Rabin everything he had withheld from Shamir, including the loan guarantees, he could not dispel the impression that his administration had been hostile to Israel. Bill Clinton had narrowly defeated Bush for the presidency of the United States. The vast majority of the Jewish community of America, as well as many non-Jews who were dedicated to the U.S.-Israel alliance, could not bring themselves to vote for George Bush. The Bush administration's confrontational style with Israel, especially the withholding of the loan guarantees, had contributed to the Likud's defeat and, considering Rabin's slim margin of victory, might well have been decisive. Now it seemed as if that same policy had contributed also to the Bush defeat, and that there too it might have been decisive.

By January 1993, Clinton was in the White House and U.S.-Israel relations resumed their normal course. The new president was clearly well disposed toward Israel. Rabin now had a free hand and could feel sure of Washington's support for virtually whatever policies he chose to follow. At that point, Rabin abandoned his previous position that Israel should not negotiate with the PLO but only with democratically elected representatives of the Palestinian population in Judea, Samaria, and Gaza. Without the knowledge of the Knesset or of most cabinet members, he negotiated and concluded the agreement signed by Yasser Arafat and himself on the White House lawn on September 13, 1993. This provided for gradual establishment of Palestinian autonomy under PLO tutelage in Judea, Samaria, and Gaza, with almost immediate withdrawal of the IDF from the Gaza Strip and the Jericho area. Along the lines of the Camp David Accords and Israel's peace initiative of May 1989, it also provided for negotiations to be held leading to a permanent settlement at the end of a five-year period.

However, the Rabin-Arafat agreement deviated in two major respects from the 1989 peace initiative: It had been concluded with the PLO; and Israel had agreed to include Jerusalem in the agenda of the final settlement negotiations, although all previous Israeli leaders, Labor and Likud alike, had declared that Jerusalem, Israel's capital, was non-negotiable. Nonetheless, both in Israel and abroad, many were impressed by the immediate fruits of Rabin's agreement with the PLO. The IDF was finally getting out of Gaza; the way was cleared for several Arab governments to begin initial contacts with Israel; the king of Morocco was prepared to enter some kind of relationship with us; and King Hussein openly signed a non-belligerency agreement with Rabin in Washington.

But in fact, as I write, the big problems are just around the corner. The extension of autonomy to the rest of Judea and Samaria, with Arafat's police force given responsibility for security in those areas, is likely to endanger the 120,000 Israelis who live there; Arafat still publicly insists that he intends to set up a Palestinian state with Jerusalem as its capital; and in the negotiations with Syria, Assad remains adamant that he will not settle for less than total Israeli evacuation of the Golan Heights—terms to which Rabin seems prepared to submit.

The progress made in Israel's forty-six-year-long quest for peace—

the 1979 Israeli-Egyptian treaty, the 1989 peace initiative, the Madrid Conference in 1991, and the latest agreements reached by the Rabin government—was based on one thing: the growing Arab perception that Israel could not be beaten on the battlefield. Change that perception, and everything changes; all of the agreements signed with Israel become valueless. Add to the existing Middle Eastern uncertainty the rising tide of Muslim fundamentalism, and the dangers involved in ceding to the Arabs territory essential for Israel's defense appear overwhelming.

For years, Israel's population kept up its guard in the face of threats and aggression from its Arab neighbors. This unflinching resolve, maintained at a heavy price, is what held those threats at bay—and kept Israel alive. Nor has that resolve ever weakened. And yet the Rabin government, reversing Israel's traditional policy of not surrendering to the demands of dictators, has created the impression that this determination is diminishing. What other explanation could there be for the abandonment of such key strategic positions as the Golan Heights? Since it is not likely that these concessions will put an end to Arab demands on Israel, what fills me with apprehension—greater by far than any I felt even during the difficult years I have described above— is the thought that when the day comes on which even the most dovish of Israelis will refuse to submit to further demands, Israel, weakened by territorial concessions, may then not be strong enough to defend itself.

Index

INDEX

Mubarak, Hosni (*cont.*)
initiative, 61–62, 78–79; and Israeli internal politics, 76, 77, 80, 82, 107, 115; and Jewish immigration, 136; and Madrid Conference, 238; and Palestinian delegation, 77–78, 238; and Palestinian elections, 61–62; peace plan of, 74–81, 83, 91; and PLO, 99; and settlement policies, 136; and Shamir, 49, 52, 62, 74, 80, 82–83, 104, 117, 221; speech of, 135–36
multilateral meetings (Moscow, 1992), 271–72
Musawi, Abbas, 275–76, 283
Muslim fundamentalism, 275, 281, 288–289, 303

National Unity government: and 1988 elections, 21; and Cairo talks, 116, 121–23; and coalitions, 24, 93, 114, 115, 119, 124, 127–28, 200; and confidence vote, 108, 112–13, 123–128; decline/downfall of, 113, 114, 116, 118, 121–28; divisiveness within, 78–79, 87–88, 94–95, 97, 98, 99–100, 105; and economic issues, 13; firing of Labor members of, 124, 126–27; formation of, 10–11, 15, 20–21, 24–25; and Israeli initiative, 125; Labor party's role in, 21, 24; and Palestinian delegation, 115, 119; and religious parties, 123, 124, 125, 127–28; swearing in of, 30; and terrorism, 112, 113; U.S. blamed for downfall of, 9; and Weizman firing, 105. *See also* cabinet (National Unity)
Ne'eman, Yuval, 184, 189, 219, 241, 255, 261
Netanyahu, Binyamin (Bibi): and Arens, 60, 285; and bilateral meetings, 261; and Cairo talks, 121; and elections of 1992, 285; and Israeli initiative, 61; and Likud party, 269, 295; as a member of Shamir inner circle, 53, 54; and political reform, 266, 269; and reshuffling of cabinet, 285; and Shevardnadze-Arens meeting, 50; U.S. trip of, 261; and U.S.-Israeli relations, 261
Nissim, Moshe, 121, 123–24, 125, 189–190, 235, 287

nuclear power, 135, 148–50, 192, 197, 215–16, 230, 251–52, 281
Nunn, Sam, 208, 234

Olmert, Ehud, 53, 54, 86–87, 90, 112, 284, 285, 295
Olson, Tom, 181, 182, 183, 186, 194
Operation Solomon, 231–32

Palestine Liberation Organization (PLO): and Cairo talks, 91, 92, 94, 96, 97–98, 99, 100–103, 104, 106, 109, 110, 122, 124–25; and Egypt, 97–98, 99, 100–103, 104, 109; and Gulf Crisis, 197, 219; and international conferences, 50–51, 101; and Iraq, 197; Israeli contacts with, 77, 99, 105, 115; and Israeli initiative, 61, 67, 73, 96, 120–21; and Jordan, 51; lack of Israeli recognition of, 88; and Madrid Conference, 236–37, 239, 241; and Mubarak plan, 75, 76, 77, 78, 79; and Mubarak-Arens meeting, 48–49; and Palestinian delegation, 85–86, 117, 236–37, 239, 241; and Palestinian elections, 61; as the Palestinian representative, 18, 49, 51, 83, 101, 120–21, 124–25; Palestinians' relations with, 74; and peace process, 37, 74; Rabin's agreement with, 302; and Shamir's U.S. visit, 59–60; and Shevardnadze-Arens meeting, 50–51; and Soviet Union, 40, 82; and Syria, 51; and terrorism, 38–39, 49, 56, 57, 136, 137, 161; and U.S., 38–39, 97, 117, 137; and U.S.-Israeli relations, 54–55, 56, 57–58
Palestine/Palestinians: and American Jewish community, 59; Arab population in, 17; and Arens' U.N. speech, 81; assimilation of, 17–18; and Baker's AIPAC speech, 69–70; Baker's meetings with, 221, 228, 236–37, 241; and bilateral meetings, 270; Bush administration's proposal about, 56–57; and democracy, 144, 254; deportation of, 224, 240, 262–263; and economic issues, 162–63, 219, 224, 225; and economic sanctions against Israel, 113, 114; and elections (Israel), 17, 294–95; French policy concerning, 43; and

INDEX

United Nations (*cont.*)
233, 235, 236, 237, 238, 239, 240;
observers in territories, 136; and
peace process, 240; and Peres'
international conference proposal,
31–32; Resolution 242 of, 67, 69,
218, 223; Resolution 338 of, 67, 218,
223; resolution about territories by,
162; and Syrian takeover of
Lebanon, 165; and terrorism, 136,
162, 165; and Zionism-equals-
racism resolution, 240, 263
United States: casualties in Gulf Crisis of,
211; sanctions against Israel by,
242–43. *See also* United States—aid
to Israel; United States—Arens trips
to; United States-Israeli relations;
specific person or issue
United States—aid to Israel: and
American Jewish community, 246–
247, 250; Arens' views about, 281–
282; and Arens' visits to U.S., 281;
and Bush administration policies, 58,
166, 281; and Camp David Accords,
26; and Congress, 160, 165, 246,
250, 274–75, 280, 281; and elections
of 1992 (Israel), 294, 298, 301; and
Gulf Crisis, 157–59, 164, 174–75,
205–7; and Israeli defense needs,
12, 150, 281; and Israeli-U.S.
agreements on Middle East conflict,
39; and Jewish immigration, 207,
234, 245, 246, 247, 248–50, 274–75,
281; and Likud party, 298, 301; and
the media/leaks, 205–7, 245, 246–
247, 249; and peace process, 245–50;
and Rabin government, 301; and
Saudi-U.S. arms sales, 160, 164; and
settlement policies, 234, 245, 248,
249–50, 274–75, 281–82; and
Shamir government, 281; and U.S.-
Israeli relations, 282–83
United States—Arens trips to: and
American Jewish community, 68;
and Cairo talks, 115, 116–17, 118,
119; and economic issues, 157–60;
and Egyptian-Israeli relations, 116,
117–18; and final status of
territories, 56, 57, 58; and Gulf
Crisis, 201–7; and Iraqi nuclear
program, 149–50; and Israeli

support in Congress, 234–35; and
Jewish immigration, 116, 117, 234;
and leaks, 55, 56–57; and Madrid
Conference, 234; and Mubarak
peace plan, 77, 78; and National
Unity government, 115, 116, 118;
and Palestinian elections, 118; and
peace initiative (Israel), 55, 56–57,
59, 68–70; and PLO, 54–55, 56,
57–58; and Quayle meeting, 234;
and settlement policies, 56, 117,
234; and U.N. visit, 79–83; and U.S.
aid to Israel, 58, 234; and U.S.-
Israeli relations, 53–59, 279–83
United States-Israeli relations: Arens'
speeches about, 281–82; and Baker-
Arens meetings, 282–83; and
Baker's AIPAC speech, 69, 70; and
Bush-Arens meeting, 206; and
Clinton administration, 302;
deterioration in, 117–18; and Israeli
internal politics, 9, 75, 78–79, 92,
301; and Israeli security, 26–27, 71,
222; and Mubarak peace plan, 76–
77; and rocket attacks on Israel, 277;
and U.S. domestic politics, 58–59;
and U.S. elections, 59, 279–80. *See
also* Bush administration; Camp
David Accords; Gulf Crisis; *specific
person or topic*

Van Den Broek, Hans, 45, 219, 229

Washington, D.C. *See* Palestinian
delegation: and bilateral meetings;
United States—Arens trips to;
specific person
Weizman, Ezer, 15, 16, 65, 73, 105, 252
West Bank, 17, 48–49, 54–55. *See also*
Gaza; Judea; Samaria
Wolfowitz, Paul, 149, 170, 174–75, 186–
188, 195, 204

Yatom, Danny, 193, 269–70, 299
Yosef, Ovadia, 123, 127–28

Ze'evi, Rechavam, 200, 207, 219, 226,
241, 255, 270
Zionism, 32–33
Zionism-equals-racism resolution, 240,
263

320